BOUND BY EXCLUSION AND VIOLENCE

A History of Belarusian Armed Struggle in the Twentieth Century

Aleksandra Pomiecko

Initially perceived as a peripheral region, Belarus has played a crucial role in shaping historical narratives. From the First World War to the Cold War, the activities of Belarusian nationalists were central to the country's involvement in broader geopolitical struggles. *Bound by Exclusion and Violence* uses the lives of these nationalists as a lens to explore their motivations and collaborations with various states and intelligence agencies, focusing on political activism, armed resistance, and covert espionage operations.

Drawing from archival research in seven countries that shed light on local, regional, and global dynamics, Aleksandra Pomiecko reveals Belarus's active role in key ideological, military, and political conflicts. The book offers a fresh perspective on the country's historical significance and its impact on major global events of the twentieth century. In today's era of heightened geopolitical awareness, *Bound by Exclusion and Violence* highlights Belarus's complex history and its continued relevance in contemporary discussions of political agency and international power dynamics.

ALEKSANDRA POMIECKO is a lecturer of modern history at King's College London.

Bound by Exclusion and Violence

A History of Belarusian Armed Struggle in the Twentieth Century

ALEKSANDRA POMIECKO

UNIVERSITY OF TORONTO PRESS
Toronto Buffalo London

Toronto Buffalo London
utppublishing.com

Printed in Canada

ISBN 978-1-4875-6265-6 (cloth) ISBN 978-1-4875-6268-7 (EPUB)
ISBN 978-1-4875-6266-3 (paper) ISBN 978-1-4875-6267-0 (PDF)

Library and Archives Canada Cataloguing in Publication

Title: Bound by exclusion and violence : a history of Belarusian armed struggle in the twentieth century / Aleksandra Pomiecko.
Names: Pomiecko, Aleksandra, author.
Description: Includes bibliographical references and index.
Identifiers: Canadiana (print) 20250132303 | Canadiana (ebook) 20250132311 | ISBN 9781487562656 (cloth) | ISBN 9781487562663 (paper) | ISBN 9781487562687 (EPUB) | ISBN 9781487562670 (PDF)
Subjects: LCSH: Belarusians—History—20th century. | LCSH: Violence—Belarus—History—20th century. | LCSH: War—History—20th century. | LCSH: Nationalism—Belarus—History—20th century. | LCSH: Belarus—History—20th century.
Classification: LCC DK507.23 .P66 2025 | DDC 947.8—dc23

Cover design: Val Cooke
Cover image: iStock.com/Saba Sabananthan; iStock.com/Aleksander

We wish to acknowledge the land on which the University of Toronto Press operates. This land is the traditional territory of the Wendat, the Anishnaabeg, the Haudenosaunee, the Métis, and the Mississaugas of the Credit First Nation.

University of Toronto Press acknowledges the financial support of the Government of Canada, the Canada Council for the Arts, and the Ontario Arts Council, an agency of the Government of Ontario, for its publishing activities.

Canada Council for the Arts Conseil des Arts du Canada

Funded by the Government of Canada Financé par le gouvernement du Canada Canada

Contents

List of Illustrations

A Note on Spelling, Language, and Terminology

In Belarusian, the word for "collaborate" is *supratsoŭnichats',* which translates more to "working together" rather than to "collaborate". The term *kalabaratsyianizm* was adopted to refer specifically to collaboration during the Second World War, as it was in other languages. In English, however, this term has both positive and negative connotations.[1] In this book, I use the term "collaboration" to refer to people or institutions that worked with others for a specific purpose.[2] The decision to use this rather general and, one may even say, oversimplified definition of this contentious term is intentional. As historian Leonid Rein notes, the term usually "includes a judgement" that obfuscates a sober historical examination, and it ignores any nuances in the context, modus operandi, and agency of collaborators.[3] Though there are numerous categories that have been developed by scholars to designate range within this term – passive, active, voluntary, and conditional to name a few – a satisfactory definition that captures such nuances does not exist. It is my hope that the complexities of the term, both in definition and in practice, will be reflected throughout various contexts and situations that these actors found themselves in.

Similar issues with definitions arise with another term used here to refer to these actors. I loosely define a "nationalist" as an individual who identifies with their nation, be it culturally, spiritually, historically, linguistically, politically, or in any other way.[4] This interpretation is particularly suited to this group of characters whose attachments to Belarus stemmed from different roots and developed over time. However, this broad definition also includes many other Belarusians outside of this particular network. For example, there were certainly Belarusian national activists who pursued the Soviet model of Belarusian statehood. There were also Belarusians serving in Soviet partisan units who were strongly against Belarusian forces collaborating with the Germans during the

Second World War. In this book, when using the term, I am referring to those involved in the nation-building project outside of and in opposition to the Soviet model, and I make note when mentioning any exceptions.

In spite of and perhaps for the very reason of these terminological issues, I choose to employ these terms consistently throughout this work. The individuals of this story have guided and shaped my decision to do so. Many of these Belarusians lived long enough to collaborate with multiple parties. Hence, I use the term collaboration when discussing their work with the Germans, Americans, and any other state or organization. I also use the term "nationalist" to refer to the early period, when the idea of a Belarusian nation was in its infancy, as well as when these individuals were living thousands of kilometres away from Belarus. This does not mean that the repercussions of collaboration or of being a nationalist are all equal. The actions perpetrated by the Belarusians of this study in the Second World War cannot be equated with their actions before and after.

Understandings of "Belarusian territory" and the people referred to as "Belarusian" are also multiple and complicated. Do we consider linguistic, ethno-national, religious, cultural, or historical factors when ascribing identity to a place or a person? Moreover, even if considering any of the latter, these earlier constructs were imagined and imposed by Belarus's historic neighbours to the east and west. In his work, cultural historian Simon Lewis carefully outlines different Polish and Russian literary imaginations of Belarus throughout time, noting how much these foreign constructs largely dominated popular understandings.[5] In her work on understandings of nationality in the late Russian Empire, Juliette Cadiot explores the various Tsarist political and ethnographic approaches to creating categories for censuses. Even when these categories were created from the top, they were understood differently among the Empire's inhabitants.[6] What constitutes Belarusian territory has also been contested through understandings of rurality and urban spaces, highlighting a socio-economic quality shared by Belarusians. Can we speak of a historic peasant quality shared by Belarusians? When it comes to urban spaces, one of the richest and most complex was the contemporary city of Vilnius, whose various spelling reiterations reflect the multiple national connections to it – Belarusian included.[7] Vilnius, however, falls just outside of territories with historically higher numbers of Belarusian speakers. Though shortcomings and insufficiencies can be easily pointed out in all of these approaches, it is much more difficult to come up with a satisfying solution for ascribing labels or establishing definitions. Here, when I refer to Belarusian territory, I have chosen to refer to the current, or post-1945, geopolitical demarcation, which includes the regions of Brėst, Hrodna, Minsk, Homel′, Mahilieŭ, and Vitsebsk. Though these regions were part of different empires and states throughout this period of study, their current location within contemporary Belarus hopefully offers a consistent point of reference.

~

The identification and spelling of names and locations is no easy task in this region. I have chosen to spell geographical locations based on what their official name was, depending on the state in which they were located at that time. When referring to present-day areas in Belarus prior to the First World War, I use the Russian spelling as they were part of the Russian Empire. Between the two world wars, names of regions and cities in the Second Polish Republic are written in the Polish spelling. For example, the former Russia Hrodno province became Grodno after the First World War, while Nesvizh became Nieśwież. During the Second World War, names in official documents often appear in Belarusian and in German and so I have chosen to use the Belarusian spelling. This format continues into the postwar period. The same formula applies in the footnotes. There are also many villages and towns whose names were completely erased due to war, violence, and displacement. When it comes to noting geographic location, the description refers to the present-day political map of Belarus

In terms of individual people, I have chosen to use the Belarusian spelling for purposes of consistency. Though they all felt a connection with their Belarusian Homeland, they may not, however, have gone by a Belarusian name or a Belarusianized version of their name. Some of these individuals were born with Polish or Russian names. However, in official documents, references made to them by other individuals are typically made in Belarusian, and alternative spellings usually appear in Polish or Soviet documents only. I have adopted the Library of Congress rules for the transliteration of Cyrillic text. The use of this standard for Belarusian text is, of course, controversial. Some scholars opt for the use of the "Instruction on Transliteration of Belarusian Geographical Names with Letters of the Latin Script," based on the traditional Łacinka alphabet, as they argue that the Library of Congress text reflects a Russified version of the Belarusian language and one pushed for during the Soviet period and more recently under the current regime. My decision to use the Library of Congress transliteration model is not a reflection of politics but rather a desire to remain consistent in terms of reference, particularly for an English-language audience.

I am responsible for all the translations from non-English text into English. Exceptions to this include published translated material, which are indicated in the footnotes.

Acknowledgments

My foray into this subject was a naive one, stemming more out of curiosity than out of an educated understanding of the topic at hand. In hindsight, I have been very lucky, most significantly due to the individuals I met – intentionally or not – who shaped and guided this project, and for whom I am incredibly thankful. In 2014, a trip to Minsk to study Belarusian led me to meet my teacher, Vol'ha Barysenka, who was patient enough to educate me about her culture and language. Her kindness and dedication have not gone unappreciated. Following this initial support, I have equally benefited from numerous librarians and archivists at the National Archive of Belarus, the National Library of Belarus, the Regional Archive of Hrodna, the Regional Archive of Brėst, the Local Archive of Maladzechna, the State Archive of the Minsk Region, and the Iakub Kolas Library. My longer stay in Minsk was possible due to my research time at the Republican Institute of Higher Education, where I was fortunate enough to regularly meet with Veranika Asachiova, Elena Dmitruk, and Siarheĭ Novikaŭ. The travels and trajectories between these numerous sites led to memorable conversations with individuals, either on local trains or on mashrutkas, that I will always think of fondly. During the longer research legs for this project, Vilnius served as a city of respite many times. Its proximity to Minsk and its vast array of experts and researchers drew me there often. The Lithuanian Extraordinary Archives were invaluable for filling in the archival pieces I hoped to find. There, I would like to thank Zbignev Urbanovič, as well as the archivists working at the Lithuanian Central State Archive whose knowledge was very helpful. Arūnas Bubnis was generous enough to impart his knowledge. Warsaw also became a home to explore the goings on of the characters of my story. The archivists at the Central Military Archive, the Archive of Modern Records, and Monika Harchut at the Archive of the East were invaluable during my time there.

My contribution to this topic is a small one and has relied significantly on others' work and specializations. Indeed, I am thankful for the opportunities I have had to present my research which have pushed this project further. On multiple occasions, the United States Holocaust Memorial Museum in Washington, DC, has been generous enough to allow me to work and present there as well as to support me through its many generous programmes abroad. I want to thank the helpful librarians, archivists, and staff at the Museum, including Vincent Slatt, Betsy Anthony, Elliott Wrenn, Liviu Carare, and Jan Lambertz, who all provided good suggestions and were important in the research process. The University College London and the Ostrogorski Centre serve as spaces where those interested in Belarus can gather and share ideas about their research. For these opportunities I would like to think Yarik Kryvoi and Andrew Wilson. I am also extremely fortunate to have been able to spend time at the Francis Skaryna Museum and Library in London, which has become a refuge for academic researchers, émigrés, and those simply interested in Belarusian studies. I am particularly grateful for my conversations with Karalina Matskevich, whose wealth of knowledge I absorbed as well as I could and whose conversations over tea I remember most fondly.

There were also numerous experts who significantly assisted in the research and conceptualization of the project and offered fantastic suggestions and feedback on various drafts of the manuscript. Some of these include Franziska Exeler, Iury Hryboŭski, Ivo Offenthaler, Adam Zítek, Vital Byl, Tomasz Kamusella, Timothy Sayle, Alison Smith, Mathew Light, Kate Brown, Andrew Kloes, Julia Elsky, Petru Negură, Simon Miles, and Bethany Mowry. I also must thank the many members of the University of Toronto kruzhok who offered great comments and support for significant parts of this project. To Oksana Dudko, Vojin Majstorović, and Nisrine Rahal – thank you for our long conversations that always come at a much-needed time. There are also many others who have hosted me during research trips and have become very much ingrained in this whole experience, whether they liked it or not. Thank you to Paulina and David in Warsaw, Trevor Wilson, Erin Graney, Nino Kiknadze-Siemens, Justin Temple, Monika Lutostanski, and Anya Melnyk. I would also like to thank Stephen Shapiro at the University of Toronto Press for his sharp, critical eye and astute suggestions, as well as for his patience. The anonymous reviewers also provided insightful feedback that I am thankful for.

I would be remiss not to mention my family including my parents, Marcela and Jan, as well as my brothers Kristofer and Marcelo. All of them maintain a level of work ethic and grounding that I often need to be reminded of. Aside from their unwavering support, however, it is their humour that I appreciate so much. It has offered comedic relief in especially challenging times.

I am indebted to many individuals who were generous enough with their time and whose research expertise far surpasses my own. Nevertheless, it is educators, professors, and advisors who have inspired me the most. Indeed, I have been extremely fortunate to have had many exceptional mentors in my life thus far. Piotr Wróbel, Lynne Viola, and Doris Bergen at the University of Toronto have been critical in the paths I have taken during and after the doctorate program. Needless to say, they all offered invaluable feedback on drafts of this book. More than that, however, each of them has imparted particular knowledge, a model of integrity, and a level of professionalism that I will always be very grateful for. During my MA studies at Uniwersytet Jagielloński, I took an unforgettable seminar with Jonathan Webber, by whose encyclopedic mind yet approachable character and fantastic dedication to teaching I was inspired. Ultimately, however, the opportunity and possibility for me to be able to even engage with the latter experts and pedagogues was primarily due to two individuals at the University of Pittsburgh – Volodia Padunov and Bill Chase. Our multiple conversations – which have continued since my time as an undergrad – have been some of the most memorable moments of my life. It is because of them that I could fathom pursuing a degree in History and even imagine that one day I could produce a book.

To the late Volodia, whose wild imagination, endless energy, and terrific personality I miss constantly. And to Bill, whose conversation with I cherish, more than he can imagine, every time.

I am forever thankful.

Abbreviations

AAN: Archive of Modern Records, in Warsaw (*Archiwum Akt Nowych*)
ABPS: Belarusian Union for the Developing Student Movement (*Ab'iadnan'ne belaruskaha pastupovaha studėnstva*)
AK: Polish Home Army (*Armia Krajowa*)
AW: Archive of the East, in Warsaw (*Archiwum Wschodnie*)
BA: German Federal Archive (*Bundesarchiv*)
BbiFS: Francis Skaryna Belarusian Library and Museum, in London (*Belaruskaia bibliiatėka i muzeĭ imia Frantsishka Skaryny*)
BKA: Belarusian Home Guard (*Belaruskaia kraiovaia abarona*)
BKS: Belarusian Self-Defense Corps (*Belaruski korpus samaakhovy*)
BNK: Belarusian National Committee (*Belaruski natsyianal'ny kamitėt*)
BNP: Belarusian Independence Party (*Belaruskaia nezalezhnitskaia partyia*)
BNR: Belarusian People's Republic (*Belaruskaia Narodnaia Rėspublika*)
BNS: Belarusian People's Self-Help (*Belaruskaia narodnaia samapomach*)
BNSP: Belarusian National Socialist Party (*Belaruskaia natsyianal-satsyialistychnaia partyia*)
BPSR: Belarusian Party of Socialist-Revolutionaries (*Belaruskaia partyia satsyialistaŭ-rėvaliutsyianeraŭ*)
BRP: Belarusian Revolutionary Party (*Belaruskaia rėvaliutsyĭnaia partyia*)
BSH: Belarusian Socialist Hramada (*Belaruskaia satsyialistychnaia hramada*)

BSP: Belarusian Self-Help Organization (*Belaruskaia samapomach'*)
BSRPK: Belarusian Peasant-Workers' Representative Club (*Belaruski sialianski-rabotnitski pasol'ski kliub*)
BSSR: Belarusian Soviet Socialist Republic (*Belaruskaia Savetskaia Satsyialistychnaia Rėspublika*)
BTDPV: Belarusian Assistance Society for War Victims (*Belaruskae tavarystva dapamohi patsiarpelym ad vaĭny*)
BTsR: Belarusian Central Rada (*Belaruskaia tsėntral'naia rada*)
BVK: Belarusian Military Commission (*Belaruskaia vaĭskovaia kamisiia*)
BWRH: Belarusian Peasant-Workers' Hramada (*Białoruska włościańsko-robotnicza hromada*)
BZV: Belarusian Youth Union (*Saiuz belaruskae moladzi*)
CAW: Central Military Archives, in Rembertów (*Centralne Archiwum Wojskowe*)
CIA: Central Intelligence Agency (United States)
DABV: State Archive of the Brėst Region (*Dziarzhaŭny arkhiŭ Brėstskaĭ voblastsi*)
DAHV: State Archive of the Hrodna Region (*Dziarzhaŭny arkhiŭ Hrodzenskaĭ voblastsi*)
DAMV: State Archive of the Minsk Region (*Dziarzhaŭny arkhiŭ Minskaĭ voblastsi*)
DP: Displaced Persons
IRO: International Refugee Organization
KDB: Committee of State Security of Belarus (*Kamitėt dziarzhaŭnaĭ biaspeki*). Alternatively referred to as KGB (*Komitet gosudarstvennoi bezopasnosti*).
KOP: Border Defense Corps (*Korpus Ochrony Pogranicza*)
KPP: Communist Party of Poland (*Komunistyczna Partia Polski*)
KPZB: Communist Party of Western Belarus (*Komunistyczna Partia Zachodniej Białorusi*)
KPB: Communist Party (Bolsheviks) of Belarus (*Kamunistychnaia partyia Belarusi*)
LCVA: Lithuanian Central State Archives (*Lietuvos centrinis valstybės archyvas*)
LLA: Lithuanian Liberation Army (*Lietuvos laisvės armija*)
LYA: Lithuanian Extraordinary Archives (*Lietuvos ypatingasis archyvas*)
MI6: foreign intelligence service of the United Kingdom
NARA: National Archives and Records Administration at College Park, Maryland

NAČR: National Archive of the Czech Republic (*Národni archiv České republiky*)
NARB: National Archive of the Republic of Belarus (*Natsyianal'ny arkhiŭ Rėspubliki Belarus'*)
NBP: Independent Belarusian Partisan Movement (*Nezalezhnaia belaruskaia partyzanka*)
NEP: New Economic Policy
NKVD: People's Commissariat of Internal Affairs (*Narodnyi komissariat vnutrennikh del*). Alternatively written in Belarusian as *Narodny kamisaryiat unutranykh spravaŭ* (NKUS)
NSC: National Security Council (United States)
OPC: Office of Policy Coordination (United States)
OSI: Office of Special Investigations (United States)
OUN: Organization of Ukrainian Nationalists (*Orhanizatsiia ukraïns'kykh natsionalistiv*)
RIS: Russian Intelligence Services
SBSO: Union of Belarusian Student Organizations in Prague (*Sjednocení běloruských studentských organisací*)
ZBK: Union of Belarusian Combatants (*Zuviaz' belaruskikh kambatantaŭ*)
UPA: Ukrainian Insurgent Army (*Ukraïns'ka povstans'ka armiia*)
USHMM: United States Holocaust Memorial Museum

BOUND BY EXCLUSION AND VIOLENCE

Introduction

This is a story about a multi-generational group of Belarusians who lived through some of the most important, dramatic, and violent events in the twentieth century. Some of them were born into a world of imperial breakdown, revolutions, and a world war that forever changed the European continent. Other individuals grew up during the political, territorial, and societal changes in Central and Eastern Europe that developed in the aftermath of those conflicts that shaped their lives. During the Second World War, many of these Belarusians fought in German-sponsored armed groups and participated in violence, including in the Holocaust in Belarus. Afterward, many of them avoided capture by the Red Army, escaped, and started new lives in western European states, in North America, South America, and in Australia. Far removed from Belarus, they worked with intelligence agencies, helping to coordinate anti-Soviet covert operations during the Cold War until the mid-1950s. Soviet security forces captured some and sent them to labour camps in the Soviet Union. Others simply lived out the rest of their lives peacefully as suburban dwellers in the United States and Canada. Still others lived in remote villages in South America. This book is an attempt to tell the story of this group of people and the period of history they lived that came to include the World Wars and the Cold War. It is a story about the long durée experience of personal and transnational struggle.

This book's cast of characters engaged in quite extraordinary acts but were not necessarily so extraordinary themselves. Frantsishak Kushal′ was a veteran of the First World War and subsequent civil wars that enveloped the European continent. Radaslaŭ Astroŭski was a schoolteacher in the town of Slutsk, south of Minsk, who was swept into local politics during the revolutionary years. Mykola Abramchyk was also interested in politics early on in his life and was well-connected with Belarusian émigrés across Europe. Their early lives paralleled that of so many in Europe at the turn of the century, yet their choices and activity would be, in many ways, quite different. The other Belarusians of this story, a younger generation, came of age during the interwar period, in the 1920s and 1930s. For them, their early formative years were marked with frustration. In the 1920s, Mikhal Vitushka and Dz'mitry Kasmovich struggled to find a Belarusian school in which to study and, like many minorities in Poland, traveled to other cities in Europe to receive a better education. Similarly in the 1930s, Barys Rahulia and Usevalad Rodz'ka hoped to attend medical school, also in Poland, but were denied the opportunity because they, too, were minorities. Other younger Belarusians living in Soviet Belarus in the 1920s and 1930s, saw their family members being exiled for real or alleged crimes and carried this resentment with them for years to come. Still a later group of young Belarusian teenagers would experience their earlier formative years much more violently – in the midst of the Second World War and early-postwar period, where they would participate in armed formations and covert espionage activity. Collectively, the individuals of all these generations were teachers, soldiers, students, and activists of all ages and of all political and ideological backgrounds. Throughout their period of operation from the First World War to the Cold War, they saw themselves as Belarusian patriots and repeatedly insisted that they were fighting for their *Bats'kaŭshchyna,* or Belarusian Homeland.[1]

Their attachment to the *Bats'kaŭshchyna* was subjective and derived from many, and sometimes overlapping, sources or inspirations, whether it be linguistic, familial, cultural, territorial, or spiritual. Notions of what exactly the Belarusian nation meant were never explicitly explained and their understanding of it varied among them, which is precisely reflected in the multiple understandings of uses of the term *Bats'kaŭshchyna.* There was no homogeneous religious basis for a Belarusian nation as they were Roman Catholic, Greek Catholic, or Orthodox Christian.[2] Linguistically, there was variation among these individuals as some did not even speak Belarusian but either Polish, Russian, or a combination of these. In political terms too, these Belarusians found themselves on different spectrums. Overall, they did not fit easily into the different European models of what constituted one's inclusion into a nation. What they did share was the belief that Belarusians were different from Poles, Russians, or anybody else. They advocated for Belarusian self-determination, independent of any influence or rule from other states. In the end, however, despite their various efforts, they were never able to achieve their visions or dreams for Belarus.

One might call their efforts a story of failure, or multiple failures, spanning several decades. One might also describe these people as nationalists without a nation.[3] Both are in many ways true. And yet precisely for this reason, one must ask how and why did these individuals continue to operate for such a long time, given their lack of clarity and unity on major issues. How were they able to work together and why did they do so? The failure of this network then highlights other aspects that drew and kept these Belarusians together. Though the motivation to join the Belarusian cause may have been a loosely defined love for the Homeland, this initial motivation does not satisfactorily explain what bound and kept these actors of differing ages, backgrounds, faiths, and beliefs together. Rather, two factors appear to have provided their relative cohesion throughout their decades of activity: shared experiences of being excluded in their personal and professional lives and their intimate relationship with violence and conflict. They were excluded at critical political and diplomatic junctures following wars when more powerful forces denied the legitimacy of their efforts to push for a Belarusian agenda. They were also excluded in their personal, professional, and educational pursuits. In many ways, they were excluded from Belarus itself and became personae non grata, as ultimately the majority of people living there, and the regime in power, did not embrace these individuals.

Violence also bounded them. They experienced it at the hands of various states, but they also participated in violent acts. Some served as formal soldiers in various national and imperial armies; others were insurrectionists who fought with partisan groups or other armed units. During the Second World War, they served as covert agents, fought partisans, organized and maintained ghettos, and perpetrated mass murder. After the war, some became recruiters for various foreign intelligence agencies, while others would be the ones recruited, trained, and dispatched as part of dangerous espionage operations during the Cold War. Through it all, the relationship between being Belarusian and the militant aspect of their struggle were very much connected. Indeed, examining these Belarusians and a history of Belarus through armed struggle allows for the inclusion of a diverse group of people, rather than focusing on followers of a particular party or ideology.[4] The sites where they met and operated stretched from the small cities in western Belarus of Niasvizh and Navahrudak, to large urban centres such as London and New York.

This book considers these individuals' ideological motivations to fight for their Belarusian homeland, but it especially explores factors unrelated to ideology. In examining the non-ideological motivations this work draws from a pool of literature that focuses on what encouraged soldiers and fighters to engage in violence, war and conflict.[5] Much of this scholarship has rightly noted that ideology was only one, sometimes minor, motivation for joining armed groups or perpetrating mass murder and violence. In the context of the Second World War, personal advancement or careerism drove individuals to serve in armed groups. At other times, it was previous shared fighting in the First World War or traumatic experiences that drew veterans together into paramilitary groups. Moreover having known people in the past, childhood friendships, or connections motivated some to join groups.[6] These studies have long shattered any myth concerning the homogeneity of soldiers or the assumption that fighters were motivated entirely by antisemitism or any other racially-driven ideology. Just because individuals were not ideologically-motivated to perpetrate mass murder and other forms of violence, however, does not diminish their crimes. In fact, they highlight, in a terrifying way, how everyday people perpetrated some of the most horrible acts.

The Belarusians who are the subjects of this study joined armed groups or engaged in covert operations for many of the same reasons as did other soldiers and fighters. Some did strongly fight and push for Belarusian self-determination, independent of Polish, Soviet or any other rule. However, other forces were also at play. Some Belarusian nationalists were enticed with the possibility of advancing in their careers or professions. Many times, Belarusians joined certain battalions because they had friends or neighbours who also did so. Others were attracted to power, be it in the form of working with more powerful states or in becoming leaders of their Belarusian émigré groups in certain parts of the world. Indeed, context and contingency, or being at the right place at the right time, determined some of these individuals' fates. Moreover, the reasons for joining this loose network of Belarusians were not necessarily the same as those for choosing to remain in it.

Examining these actors over the longer haul and over generations further underscores the importance of considering non-ideological factors. Indeed, throughout their lives, these individuals took a kaleidoscopic and sometimes contradictory ideological trajectory. The older Belarusians in question really began their political awakening around the time of the 1917 Russian Revolutions. By October of that year, on the territory of Belarus, there were approximately 22 political parties, nine of which were Belarusian national parties of mostly the socialist-revolutionary and social-democratic orientation.[7] The following year, the Belarusian Socialist-Revolutionary Party was formed, which would be a strong force within the political sphere in Belarus for a few years and would serve as the political foundation for older Belarusian activists. During the 1920s and 1930s, most of the characters of this story resided outside of Soviet Belarus, mainly in Poland, Lithuania, and Czechoslovakia, and created legal and illegal organizations there. Most notably these were the Communist Party of Western Belarus and the Belarusian Peasants-Workers'

Hramada, both of which were active until 1938 in Poland. Whereas some members of the earlier parties operating in 1918 in Belarus transitioned to these left-leaning ones, others went further west and formed the Belarusian National Socialist Party in 1933, whose party line was closely aligned with that of the German National Socialist Party. Younger Belarusians were mainly involved in student organizations in Vilnius, Kaunas, Warsaw, and Prague, where they focused their efforts on procuring funding for educational purposes and for the development of Belarusian language and cultural awareness.[8] During the Second World War, many of these Belarusians pivoted and collaborated with the Germans against the Soviet Union. After the war, some continued to stay connected within their respective émigré communities and joined various committees and organizations depending on where they were in the world. Thus, throughout this multi-generational network's experience, the labels anti-Soviet, anti-Fascist, nationalist, and communist would have been accurate at some points and misleading during others. Though the ideologies and political beliefs of these individuals may not have been consistent, the bonds and experiences shared were. Focusing on this group over this critical period in twentieth century history, allows us to see the complex motives of several generations of Belarusians.

In Belarus and among Belarusian circles, these actors have long been topics of research, speculation, and fascination.[9] They are sometimes elevated to the level of national heroes or freedom fighters, whereas other times they are described as collaborators who did more damage to Belarus than good. Soviet-era Belarusian officials and historians were the first to grapple with these individuals, but they did so in such a way as to dissuade any potential popular interest or dangerous admiration. They described Belarusians who collaborated with the Germans during the Second World War as insignificant and completely unrepresentative of the population in Belarus as a whole.[10] In fact, it was common for Soviet historians to describe dissident Belarusians and their anti-Soviet activity in the post 1921 era as only have been possible with the support of foreign aid.[11] In post-Soviet times, these Belarusians have received more attention, yet these discussions suffer from a lack of reliable sources and often depend on hearsay or interviews of members of this group.[12] Academic works discussing Belarusian anti-Soviet activity typically discuss it in the context of other parallel Lithuanian, Polish, and Ukrainian movements.[13]

The reasons behind the lacunae in the lives and activities of these actors are mostly obvious. Many of them tried to live clandestinely, especially in the postwar period, making it difficult to reconstruct their lives and frame them historically. There are also archival limitations still in place today that inhibit some of the research.[14] These shortcomings contribute to the proliferation of myths, legends, and speculation in popular historical writing surrounding many of these individuals. For example, one of the most notorious members of this group, Mikhal Vitushka, the so-called "Belarusian Bandera", has been the subject of much debate.[15] His culpability in certain operations comes into question and even his death arouses debate. Some give a date of death as early as 1945, others as late as 2006. Vitushka is not the only subject that has piqued popular interest. There has also been an increased interest in real or alleged anti-Soviet Belarusian resistance groups after the Second World War, but the lack of information beyond interviews and memoirs has made it difficult to determine the extent of such activity.[16] Even those whose lives we think we know more about still leave much to be desired. For example, after the Second World War, Barys Rahulia, lived most of his adult life in Ontario, Canada where he worked as a respected physician and even wrote a memoir. His recollections, however, do not necessarily match what appears in the archives.

There are certainly many known and notable actors of this story, but there are many silent ones who were instrumental in the operation of this group. Of one thing we can be certain, they were not all men. Combing through rosters and lists of those active in Belarusian organizations reveals a good number of women. However, little to no information exists beyond their name. Women served on Belarusian committees, including those that collaborated with the Germans during the Second World War. It was women who also educated Belarusian soldiers, teaching them songs and poetry so that they would become "conscious" of their identity. Some women parachuted out of aeroplanes, together with male agents, and participated in covert operations. Though most did not catch the attention of western intelligence services, in the postwar period women were critical in various espionage cells on the ground in Europe. They held meetings, served as couriers, and fed and hid partisans and spies.[17] Natallia Arsenneva, who was married to Frantsishak Kushal′, was a well-known poet. They experienced these years together. Born and initially home-schooled in Baku, she was displaced several times and ended up in Wilno, where she graduated from a Belarusian secondary school and began publishing her poetry in Russian. She met her future husband as he was moving up the ranks in the Polish Army. When he was captured in 1939 by the Soviet forces, she suffered the consequences as a wife of a Polish officer and was deported to Kazakhstan with her two sons. Because of her fame in Belarus as a poet, the Union of Soviet Belarusian Writers appealed on her behalf to allow her to return to Belarus. She also used her position to negotiate the release of her husband from the Lubianka prison in Moscow. During the German occupation of Belarus, she lived in Minsk, writing for the city paper, translating literature, and publishing her work in Belarusian. In 1944, she escaped with her husband and ended up moving to the United States where she lived until her passing.[18] While their numbers may be fewer, the role of women among this group is important and, especially in the context of Belarus, challenges the traditional narrative of women during the war either joining the Soviet partisans and becoming the lovers of partisan leaders, or of women fiercely resisting and fighting the Germans.[19]

The other major actor in this story is the state.[20] It is the state and relations between states that shaped and framed the activity of these Belarusians. The dissolution of various empires during and after the First World War ushered in a new European order and led to the creation or resurrection of some states. Newly created countries laid claim to Belarusian territory and effectively divided the land, resulting in starkly different experiences for those living on the ground. These new postwar states had to deal with minorities, and Belarusians were always a minority regardless of where they lived. Restrictions and limitations on Belarusians elicited resentment and prompted them to move to different countries or somehow deal with the opportunities available to them. Some resisted the state passively, others more actively by joining illegal parties or even engaging in violent anti-state activity on all sides of the border. In the 1930s, the Abwehr, or German military intelligence service, recruited various Belarusians to engage in anti-Soviet activity. These individuals then continued to work and collaborate with the Germans more intimately in 1941, when the occupation of Belarus began. During this time, they still had agency. They were able to use their positions as collaborators to get more provisions and concessions from the Germans. They also had a degree of agency when it came to the treatment of Jews and other locals. In exchange for their collaboration, they continued to demand more things from the Third Reich, such as the creation of Belarusian organizations and armed groups. After 1944, this group of Belarusians were recruited once again, this time by western states, for their knowledge of the region and for their anti-Soviet attitudes. They participated in anti-Soviet activity in many countries such as England, Belgium, and in the Soviet Union. They learned how to negotiate better and how to be more persistent in their demands, knowing that these foreign institutions needed their help as much as they needed these states.

Belarus is also critical to this story. The territory itself was conquered, destroyed, and overrun by armies, and suffered devastating violence. Far from being merely a borderland region or a buffer, it marked a centre of ideological clashes and was also at the heart of the struggle between great powers. This quality has been rightly analyzed in the context of recent events by scholars such as Paul Hansbury, but Belarus's strategic location and importance far predates the current situation.[21] Located on the western periphery of the Soviet state, the Belarusian Soviet Socialist Republic was extremely important to the state's security. Even across the Atlantic Ocean, US intelligence services saw Belarus as one of the most important arenas for the battle over intelligence and espionage. Ironically, despite its geopolitical importance, it was a region that western states new very little about. The territory never lost its strategic importance and remained extremely important throughout the twentieth century.

While this study focuses on a specific group of Belarusian actors, their life trajectories very much paralleled those of others in Eastern Europe. These similarities are especially visible when examining the activity of similar individuals that operated to the north and south of Belarus. Many of these people experienced or were born into a series of revolutionary waves and conflicts. They came of age in the aftermath of the First World War, where competing visions of the state – whether it be Wilsonian or Soviet – impacted their lives and earlier foundational years. They were also no strangers to war, and especially to violence, if not already in the First World War then certainly later during the Second World War through their collaboration with Germany and other forces. Like others, they needed to re-situate themselves in the postwar period. Many attempted to evade Soviet rule and escaped westward. Some changed their identities and background stories in order to evade the legal and criminal ramifications for their wartime actions. Others were recruited by western intelligence services early on in the Cold War and engaged in espionage activity targeted against the Soviet Union and communist governments. Because they knew the languages and the regions, intelligence services of western countries needed them.

Motivations, as this book argues, varied and depended on the individuals themselves. And yet, even though this study examines many non-ideological factors, the question of ideology – as it relates to the nation and race – is ever present. Radical nationalism has been used as a term to identify beliefs that express extremist views regarding the nation – namely that one's nation is superior to others and that its very survival is dependent on excluding others who do not belong by whatever means possible. Other radical means of preserving one's nation include redesigning existing world orders in order to preserve or develop the community. These more radicalized visions of the nation appeared more prominently during and after the First World War, however their roots emerged in the nineteenth century and some would say even during the French Revolution.[22] But to begin to understand the provocations of radical nationalism, particularly in Europe, the context and use of the term "nationalist" deserves explanation. In Western popular and academic discourse, soldiers fighting in the First World War from Central and Eastern Europe are referred to as nationalists, whereas their equivalents serving in the French or British Armies, for example, are referred to as patriots or just soldiers. In practice and in this specific historical moment, most of them were fighting for a state, whether in the national or imperial context, and yet from this point on a negative connotation is associated with the term "nationalist." In the central and eastern European space, the label "radical nationalist" has been used, in part, due the necessity of differentiating individuals who were "patriotic", or nationalists, from those who subscribed to radicalized views regarding the nation and race. In this context, radical nationalism advocated for exclusion based on race, by propagating the elimination of certain groups of people from one's nation, notably Jews, but also other ethnic, national, or religious communities that were seen as a threat to the very survival of the nation or as inhibitors to the latter's irridentist ambitions. For radical nationalists, the use of violence, whether physical, political, or other, was justified for the creation and preservation of their nation. Some radical nationalists made their ideas known through direct action, whereas others did so from their pens and papers. However, individuals' participation in violence was not necessarily an indication that they were radical themselves. People who were entangled in fighting during the world wars, for example, may not have necessarily believed in radicalized visions of their nation.

Here it may be useful to reflect on some parallels and differences between Belarusian combatants with that of other national groups in the region. In particular, the neighbouring cases of Ukraine, Poland, and Lithuania serve as the most important context and frame for understanding where Belarusian nationalists and radical nationalists fit. Their concepts of nationalism were, in part, strongly tied to territoriality, and historically these areas were all seen as integral parts of each other. All these regions also had significant Jewish populations whose relationships with non-Jews had varied over time; at the end of the Second World War, the absence of a once vibrant Jewish community was one thing these regions shared. Finally, one collective enemy all these respective national movements shared was the Soviet state.[23]

Of the four cases in question, it was Belarus and Ukraine that did not exist as non-Soviet entities following the First World War. Recent scholarship, especially on Ukraine, has deepened and nuanced understandings of the Ukrainian national and radical national movements in the twentieth century through studies on the Organization of Ukrainian Nationalists (OUN) and the Ukrainian Insurgent Army (UPA). According to scholars, several reasons contributed to the radicalization of members of the OUN. The failure to establish an independent Ukrainian state following the First World War and numerous conflicts that followed in Ukraine left many frustrated. Further contributing to radicalization was the belief that this failure was in part due to the lack of unity and organization among Ukrainian nationalists, who were too fragmented in their political orientations. Hitler's rise to power, his anti-Soviet beliefs, and his desire to redraw the map of Europe appealed to some radical members of the OUN.[24] For the future prominent leader of the organization, Stepan Bandera, all of these factors made a deep impact on his radicalization process during the interwar period, which for him was intimately connected with religion and antisemitism.[25] During the interwar period, Ukrainian nationalists operated outside of Soviet Ukraine and formed organizations in other western European cities. Later during the Second World War, members of the OUN murdered Jews, whether as part of the auxiliary police under German command or as part of the UPA units.[26] The other component of UPA's national determination was a desire de-Polonize certain Ukrainian regions. This it did through the ethnic cleansing of Poles in Volhynia; whether by expulsion or murder.[27]

Differing from the interwar Belarusian and Ukrainian trajectories, Poland and Lithuania did not become Soviet republics after the First World War but independent states, albeit with territorial contentions. After 1926, both states turned to the political right under the respective leaders of Józef Piłsudski and Antanas Smetona. Rule under both leaders involved promoting the state's national identities in both peaceful and repressive ways. Later during the Second World War, various national armed irregulars were created to defend their countries and restore their independent status. The Polish Home Army, or Armia Krajowa (AK), fought both the Germans and later Soviet partisans. In recent works on the Polish Home Army, the question of this group's attitudes toward Jews has been explored more. Using Jewish postwar testimonies has revealed that many Jews both in and outside of the Home Army concealed their identity. Other survivors recalled that some AK units also murdered Jews. And yet, both documentary and Jewish testimonies also recall AK members who were not antisemitic.[28] In other cases antisemitism was reflected in the comments of several of the Home Army members who noted that Jews were supporting and joining Soviet partisans. In joining Soviet partisans, they were viewed as anti-Polish and therefore a threat to Polish survival; a sentiment that reflected longer-existing views of judeo-bolshevism.[29] Historian Joshua Zimmerman has worked on the complexity of this AK-Jewish relationship noting that the AK's behaviour toward Jews "reveals both profoundly disturbing acts of violence as well as extraordinary acts of aid and compassion."[30]

To the north of Belarus, the complicity of Lithuanian armed units in the murder of Jews in Lithuania has long been studied, as has various combatants' anti-Polish attitudes and intentions. Aside from Lithuanian auxiliary police forces, the Lithuanian Territorial Defense Force (LTDF) was established towards the very end of the German-occupied period in Lithuania, which included some former auxiliary policemen. Organized by the Germans in the spring of 1944, this organization came to include around 20,000 Lithuanian men and was intended to be a more national armed formation than the largely German-controlled units. The LTDF's primary responsibilities included fighting against Soviet partisans, but it also found itself in skirmishes with the Polish Home Army. In her work, historian Justina Smalkyte argues that, though motivations varied, many of these Lithuanian fighters were particularly encouraged by "ethnicised gendered images of masculine honour and national belonging".[31] Past shame, or humiliation, was one of the driving forces for members of the Defense Force to engage in bitter anti-Polish fighting in the Vilnius region – a contested territory ceded to Poland twenty-four years prior. In the same year as the LTDF was created, so too was the Lithuanian Freedom Army whose members fought against the Germans and Soviet partisans. Members of the postwar anti-Soviet resistance included former members of the prewar Lithuanian Army, members of the auxiliary police, and other insurgents whose motivations varied. The question of these individuals' views on Jews is difficult to determine, as by this point in time, many Jewish communities had been completely destroyed.[32]

Where did these Belarusians fit among their neighbouring national equivalents? As historian Franziska Exeler notes, there were fewer Belarusian radical nationalists, compared to those in neighbouring national groups.[33] Nevertheless, the roots of the more radicalized aspects of the Belarusian national movement, similarly to the Ukrainian one, really began in the interwar period, in large part due to frustration at the lack of an independent Belarusian state. During the Second World War, similarly to the Ukrainian and Lithuanian cases, Belarusian nationalists were spread among different armed organizations, sometimes working together but other times not. During the war, various Belarusian armed groups participated in the same kinds of activities as their national counterparts. Some fought Soviet partisans, others were complicit in the repression and murder of Jews. In certain areas of western Belarus, tensions between Belarusian armed groups and the Polish Home Army were especially high leading to many armed confrontations. If we later compare the strength of postwar, anti-Soviet resistance in the western regions of the Soviet Union, the numbers of Belarusian insurgents were significantly lower than those of Lithuanians or Ukrainians. Historian Alexander Statiev cautiously offers some figures for numbers of national resistance fighters of the Estonian, Latvian, Lithuanian, Ukrainian, and Belarusian Soviet republics actively battling Soviet security forces. He notes that between 1944 and 1950, the Ukrainian resistance was the largest at an estimated 400,000 people, and it was the most centralized movement. For the same time frame, there were around 100,000 Lithuanian insurgents. When it comes to Belarusians, using Soviet documents, his research reveals that there were only handful of anti-Soviet Belarusian insurgents arrested in the spring of 1945.[34] In terms of surviving sources – both produced by the actors themselves and those offered by various states – fewer exist on Belarus. For example, documentation pertaining to postwar collaboration between the CIA and Ukrainian nationalists amounts to over two dozen volumes at the National Archives in College Park, whereas that with Belarusians includes a mere four. Moreover, archival restrictions in Belarus, and especially restricted access to the KDB, or KGB, Archive in Minsk, limits the ability to procure potentially insightful information. The former KGB Archives in Lithuania and Ukraine are largely open for research purposes. Similarly, documents on the Polish Home Army are available through various archival institutions in Poland.

Thus, when viewed in comparison with its neighbours, the Belarusian national armed movement appears to be one of the weaker, if not weakest, of them all. And yet I would argue that despite its appearance, there is still much value in studying this network of people. For many years, and still today, many have argued that Belarusian self-awareness and nationalism, were weak and that Belarusian nationalists were merely used by stronger states.[35] However, having a strong sense of national awareness did not mean individuals had more agency or were somehow more successful in their goals. Equally, having a weaker, or perceived to be weaker, sense of nationalism did not mean such people were merely pawns of more powerful states. In fact, the longevity of this multi-generational group of Belarusians was in part due to their perceived lack of strong national awareness, precisely because stronger states did not see them as a threat and therefore never felt the need to completely eliminate them. In using this group of Belarusians as a case study, this work examines the ways in which multi-generational groups of people operated in these periods of peace and crises, how they navigated their relationships with powerful states and organizations, and how they adapted to changing circumstances over time. Examining both their ideological and non-ideological motivations moves the discussion away from what

Belarusian nationalism was, to what motivated some Belarusians to operate as they did and how they were able to do so. It is also an opportunity to see how shared experiences may have shaped any ideological and non-ideological motivations.[36]

In thinking about these entangled individuals across the region and their activity – real, alleged, or unknown – the question of sources becomes challenging. Existing memoirs reveal very sentimental references to Belarus and the authors define their activity as patriotic or as having been done to serve the Homeland. Not surprisingly, nothing is mentioned regarding the murder of Jews, POWs, and other victims of the Holocaust in Belarus. Similarly, any mention of postwar intelligence work and anti-Soviet operations is also omitted from their recollections. For this and many other reasons, the use of these particular memoirs, personal letters, postwar testimonies, and other documents produced by these Belarusians is done so very critically. I examine these sources to better understand the individuals who wrote them. Indeed, a personal source that proves to be rather inaccurate says much about the writer. The scapegoating of individuals in various memoirs reveals a lot about their personalities, and it sheds light on internal struggles within the group. CIA officers were also quite candid about these individuals' personalities – something they perhaps captured more accurately than they did any actual information about Belarus itself.

State or official documents are equally difficult to parse through. This research includes previously used as well as new, declassified material from the United States, in addition to untapped primary source material in Belarus, Canada, the Czech Republic, Germany, Lithuania, Poland, and the United Kingdom. Despite my attempts to search for, track, and trace these actors, many times their whereabouts are only visible because the state saw these actors. Others who seem to be "missing" may simply have not been that interesting or known to various officials. Some Belarusians also changed their names and hid their identities, precisely because they did not want to be found. At the risk of producing a hagiographic account based solely on murky traces from some of these individuals, the inclusion of these actors and their activity rests largely on the archival and personal footprint they left and on whether existing information can be corroborated with other sources. Indeed, there are many actors who were part of this broad network but who receive little to no attention here.

This is not a story about a group of patriotic Belarusians in pursuit of their goals, but rather a story about individuals with complex and compromising stories that I hope offer some analytical benefit. In using this prosopographic approach, I explore the lives and connections of these people and use them to try to understand the world they lived in and the contexts in which they found themselves. This book presents a history of this long durée struggle that extends beyond isolated periods or conflicts to show how they are very much connected. It is organized chronologically, beginning with the earlier generation of Belarusians who experienced the First World War, revolutions, and emerged from a world of imperial rule and ethno-national diversity, to one that was fixated on homogeneity. They began to think of themselves in these ways as well and carried over their activism into the postwar period where they continued to build up their connections in various countries. Other younger Belarusians were merely teenagers trying to learn the Belarusian language or attend school and university as minorities in new states. By the German occupation of Belarus in June 1941, many had travelled to Belarus with the intention of setting up institutions and taking up administrative roles. They collaborated with the Germans, hoping they would procure moderate positions of power, especially over other national groups. These opportunities, however, came at a very violent cost. The later years of the war only saw an increase in violence and destruction on Belarusian lands, which made many of these actors unpopular in the eyes of locals. After their evacuation from Belarus in the summer of 1944, some changed their names and vanished, avoiding any repercussions for the crimes they committed. Others returned to Soviet Belarus to engage in anti-Soviet partisan activity, whereas some worked with western intelligence services for the same goal. By the mid-1950s, however, this network of Belarusians had splintered off into different émigré groups all over the world and sometimes competed with each other. The shifting geopolitical order and mood of the developing Cold War also thawed their armed and covert activity.

Ultimately, the acts these Belarusians committed and activities in which they engaged were extraordinary but the means by which they got there were not. It was a network of individuals who needed each other to survive, who used whomever and whatever they could to do so, and who were dependent on time and space. By the end, they had exhausted their available resources and connections and had failed to produce the kind of Belarusian state they envisioned. Their involvement in extreme violence in the Holocaust, and toward the very people they considered their own, is the darkest part of this story.

1
The Crumbs of a Nation in the Ruins of War

In his recollections from the 1990s, eighty-year-old Vitaŭt Tumash paid his respects to a man he saw as being critical to Belarusian independence efforts in the twentieth century. He was talking about Frantsishak Kushal′ whom he met for the first time in Wilno prior to the Second World War. Tumash recalled that, "Already then my eyes were fixated on his disciplined officer posture, which he maintained until the eightieth year of his life, until his death [...] General Kushal′ was one of the most active participants in the most important aspects of the Belarusian military and its beginning. [His] first and last name are tied to all the most important events in the realm of the Belarusian military during the twentieth century."[1] Kushal′ was born in 1895 in the town of Pershai, about seventy kilometres west of Minsk. For the next few decades, Kushal′ dedicated himself to the development of Belarusian affairs, mainly in his capacity as a military man. This journey took him from the Russian Empire, to Poland, Ukraine, the Lubianka prison in Moscow, German-occupied Belarus, various Displaced Persons' camps in Europe, and eventually to the United States. Tumash's life would equally be shaped by war and his position as a Belarusian nationalist, beginning in Belarus and ending in the United States.

As with Tumash, Kushal′ similarly inspired many other younger Belarusians who would dedicate themselves to the Belarusian cause, especially militarily through their participation in armed groups and operations. For this and other reasons, Kushal′ would become one of the most prominent figures in this multi-generational network of Belarusian nationalists in the twentieth century. But before he could become this important figure, Kushal′, like other Belarusians of his generation, was born and raised in a tumultuous world and experienced his earlier formative years during some of the most violent events in the early twentieth century. The story of this cast of characters begins with Kushal′'s generation – born around the turn of the twentieth century when Belarus was part of the Russian Empire and who experienced the devastating effects of the 1905 and 1917 Revolutions, the First World War, the subsequent civil wars, displacement, and postwar chaos.

In addition to being born and raised during these important events, this generation of Belarusian actors came in contact with the slowly developing idea of a Belarusian nation. Unlike neighbouring national movements such as the Polish and Ukrainian ones, the development of Belarusian nationalism came much later. In the early part of the twentieth century, Belarusian nationalism developed in reaction to and in the context of three important elements: revolutionary processes arising in 1905 and 1917, the movement and occupation of militaries, and the series of wars that enveloped Central and Eastern Europe.[2] These factors were far from mutually exclusive and created the context in which Belarusian nationalists, including Kushal′, were born and raised. Moreover, much of these actors' earlier formative experiences influenced their later activity and dictated the ways in which they interacted with and trained younger generations of Belarusians.

Revolutionary Processes and the Foundation for Belarusian Nationalists

The turn of the twentieth century saw the rise of national movements in the western regions of the Russian Empire. They were resurrected after having been violently quashed under Tsarist rule during a series of revolutions in the nineteenth century, particularly in 1830, 1848, and 1863. For Belarusians, the most important figure from the nineteenth century was Kastus′ Kalinoŭski, seen as a hero of the 1863 revolt in the Russian Empire. In the nineteenth century, however, ideas of regarding a Belarusian nation were largely tied to the Polish and Lithuanian national movements. The romanticized Polish national movement envisioned a recreation of the former Polish-Lithuanian Commonwealth and saw Poles as leading this multi-religious and multi-linguistic entity. Lithuanian thinkers largely rebuked any romantic Polish notions of being at the helm of such a re-created state and rather harkened back to the nostalgic memory of the Grand Duchy of Lithuania. In both romanticized versions of state re-creation, Belarusians were envisioned as the natural subjects of both entities yet having no significant political power. Belarusian elites and thinkers only really began conceptualizing their own visions for Belarus in the early 20th century – decades after the Ukrainians, Poles, and Lithuanians. There are some practical reasons for this significant chronological latency. All of the former Belarusian parts of the Commonwealth had been absorbed into the Russian Empire, whereas western parts of Ukraine and various parts of Poland existed under the Habsburg and German ones. It was primarily in these non-Russian parts that these Ukrainian and Polish national movements developed in the 19th century. Furthermore, until 1905, the Russian Empire banned printing in Belarusian which precluded the writing of books that could subsequently be disseminated more broadly and promote the language. Moreover, anyone who wanted to move up professionally, educationally or socially, would have to either speak Polish or Russian – seen as the more privileged languages. Belarusian was seen as a simple, peasant way of communication.[3]

Like other developing national movements in Eastern Europe, the small pockets of active Belarusian nationalists looked to western Europe for a model of what a nation-state should look like. Some of them were more interested in the cultural promotion of Belarusian affairs through literature and language. Others were, indeed, interested in resurrecting some form of federation with neighbouring Poland and Lithuania, reminiscent of the Grand Duchy nearly a century prior. At this point in time, very few Belarusian elites saw their nation as distinct within the Slavic world and imagined complete independence. Many locals living on Belarusian territory, moreover, had no interest in ethno-national labels and saw themselves tied to their local towns and regions, not to a particular national identity. Indeed, early Belarusian nationalists advocating for any type of autonomy, or even later independence, were only a small niche of the larger Belarusian-speaking population.

The majority of Belarusian speakers who were politically oriented in some way at turn of the twentieth century leaned toward socialism.[4] The most important topic discussed among Belarusians was not independence or even autonomy but the distribution of land. The 1905 Revolution on Belarusian territory prompted serious discussions by activists on the issue of peasants and the agrarian question.[5] During a meeting in March 1905, the Socialist Revolutionaries and members of the Belarusian Socialist Hramada (*Belaruskaia satsyialistychnaia hramada,* BSH) agreed that land had to be taken by force and distributed to peasants.[6] Eventually in the summer of 1905, peasants took matters into their own hands by doing exactly that and striking. The Hrodna region, for example, experienced particularly high strike rates and peasant unrest, some of which were led by Belarusian activists themselves who mobilized peasant support.[7] As in other parts of the Russian Empire, the 1905 revolution also affected soldiers in Belarus, many of whom deserted the Tsarist Army because of poor provisions and military breakdown. Many of these soldiers came from peasant backgrounds and contributed to the continued instability in the countryside. Soldiers who returned to their hometowns and villages participated in strikes and protests against the state.[8]

These reactions resulting from the 1905 Revolution ushered in a thaw period in the western regions of the Russian Empire, which witnessed an easing of educational and cultural restrictions placed by the Tsarist regime.[9] In 1924, a group of Belarusians representing all political spectrums noted in hindsight that it was only after 1905 that real Belarusian poetry and literature began to be produced.[10] Belarusian newspapers – including *Nasha niva* (Our field) in 1905 and later *Nasha dolia* (Our fate) in the fall of 1906 – emerged in this important moment.[11] Belarusian literature and poetry made its debut in the post-1905 period, pioneered by famous literary figures such as Ianka Kupala and Iakub Kolas. In 1910, Vatslaŭ Lastoŭski wrote the first history of Belarus in Belarusian, titled *Karotkaia historyia Belarusi* (A Short History of Belarus).[12] Furthermore, the revolution prompted the Socialist Hramada to finally create a programme that advocated for a nationally and culturally autonomous Belarus, engaged in class warfare and with land concessions for peasants.[13]

Years later, the 1917 Russian Revolution further triggered the ongoing development of Belarusian affairs. As was true for many national groups, Belarusian activists saw 1917 as a form of liberation; whether it be ethno-national or socio-economic. Twenty-six political parties, of which 14 labeled themselves as "Belarusian", became active in the region during this period, albeit not all explicitly supported the Belarusian nation-building goal.[14] In 1917, various meetings of Belarusian organizations took place in order to discuss the nature and future of the Belarusian movement, a matter interpreted by the participants in a wide range of ways. Belarusian Socialist Revolutionaries were at the helm of these meetings, two of which took place in March and July 1917. In 1917, there were around 30,000 members of the Socialist Revolutionary organization on Belarusian territory, primarily peasants but also soldiers and officers, who tended to care less for the issue of the Belarusian national movement.[15] The influence of Bolsheviks on Belarusian territory, including those of Belarusian background, also intensified at this time and contributed to the focus on socio-economic issues as well as on the effects of the devastating war.[16] Finally in August of that year, the first session of the Central Rada of Belarusian Organizations was put together for the explicit purpose of centralizing these various Belarusian parties. This Rada would organize free elections and was to coordinate all the existing Belarusian groups and parties operating in the region. The Rada also tried to negotiate with the Provisional Government in Petrograd, created in the aftermath of the February 1917 Revolution, and asked that it recognize Belarusian autonomy. The

Provisional Government stalled its decision by saying that autonomy could only be granted by the Constitutional Assembly, which was yet to be organized in the territories of the former Russian Empire. After October 1917 relations with the Provisional Government ceased to exist when the Bolsheviks took over power. Though Bolshevik official proclamations recognized non-Russian nations and their right to self-determination, on the ground things looked different. Bolsheviks in Minsk established their own Soviet committee, whose members were not open to Belarusian national aspirations outside of the Soviet project.[17]

During this tumultuous year, the Belarusian national movement suffered from a lack of financial resources, lack of unity regarding a programme moving forward, and from competition with other political influences and parties. Even so, 1917 was not a completely lost cause for the Belarusian national movement. The most important meeting of that year involving Belarusians who wanted some sort of national self-determination was the All-Belarusian Congress, organized on 14 December 1917. In attendance were 1782 delegates, from various political and cultural organizations and of different socio-economic backgrounds.[18] Some representatives called for the creation of a separate Belarusian region, whereas others advocated for some form of autonomous status for Belarus within a larger federation. Still at this moment in time, the members of the Congress did not call for complete independence.[19]

Though there was no clearly-defined platform or vision during the gathering, its importance came through in the space it created for important Belarusian figures to meet. One participant of the Congress later recalled that:

> Since the moment of the 1917 Revolution, the Belarusian issue increasingly spread, not in a matter of years, but with every week. [...] After this Revolution, this movement became freer, and this Belarusian work developed not in one way, but spread in different directions and almost all over Belarus.[20]

Another individual, Todar Daniliuk, remarked that "from the first days of the Revolution, national self-awareness amongst Belarusians widened with the speed of an electric spark."[21] Todar Daniliuk would work closely with Kushal′ and be best known for his role as a soldier and spokesperson for Belarusian affairs. Also among the attendees of the congress was Radaslaŭ Astroŭski, the future president of the Belarusian collaborationist government during the Second World War. Though it was not known at the time, this gathering of Belarusian delegates served as the nucleus of future meetings and permanently enmeshed individuals who would continue to work together for decades to come.

Belarusian organizations during and in the aftermath of the revolutions were the initial points where this story's older individuals met and worked together. Other notable Belarusians also met through the military. Many of these groups and formations were initially created by the Tsarist state and later Provisional Government in Petrograd, which lacked the military resources to operate in its western provinces. Because the state lacked sufficient resources to send extra soldiers to the western peripheries of the Empire, it sought to secure the area by allowing for the creation of national and local armed formations.[22] One such Belarusian unit appeared under the leadership of Iazėp Mamon'ka in May 1917 in Riga. Later in mid-October 1917, Mamon'ka and his men continued their efforts of building a Belarusian army by organizing the Central Belarusian Military Rada. Here the participants all agreed that it was crucial to create a Belarusian Army, and they also supported the All-Belarusian Congress.[23] This Military Rada brought notable Belarusian actors together with Mamon'ka, including Symon Rak-Mikhaĭloŭski and Kanstantyn Ezavitaŭ.[24] Rak-Mikhaĭloŭski and Ezavitaŭ would remain close, and both would collaborate with the Germans during the Second World War. In these critical sites, meetings, congresses, literary groups, and armed formations, Belarusians managed to forge connections with each other that would serve as the foundation for their future activity.

Experience of War, Displacement, and Violence

Ongoing along with the revolutionary processes were the First World War and military occupations on Belarusian territory. Belarusian territory was strategically important for two warring empires, the German and Russian, as it straddled their borders. In 1914, the Russian Imperial Army began mobilizing male residents, confiscating horses, cattle, and other livestock, and requisitioning grain. By the Spring and Summer of 1915 when the Russian Army began its retreat eastward and the German Army followed, Belarusian lands became some of the main arenas of fighting. The Russian and German armies significantly shaped the demographic and physical landscape of Belarusian territory. With the movement of armies came the physical destruction of land, resulting from scorched earth policies intending to leave nothing for the approaching enemy.[25]

These devasting circumstances forced individuals to make the difficult decision to either remain where they were or to flee with the departing army. Tsarist authorities spread rumours and propaganda about German barbarities, including that the latter cut off women's breasts and the noses and ears of children. The Orthodox Church perpetuated these stories as well, at times motivating entire parishes to relocate.[26] Ultimately, the Russian Army's "great retreat", during which it evacuated about three hundred thousand square miles of territory, led to the departure of not only soldiers but also individuals whose fears were fueled by such rumours and realities.[27] By 1917, estimates place the number of refugees from the western imperial peripheries deported to present-day Russia at around 7 million.[28] The number of individuals escaping eastward from contemporary Belarusian territory specifically, ranges between 1.4 and 2.3 million.[29]

Many times, the decision to leave was not voluntary.[30] Tsarist authorities deported people whom they perceived to be dangerous or those they thought could become spies for the enemy. These forced deportations occurred in several waves: first in the fall of 1914 and then again in the first half of 1915.[31] There was an ethno-national component to forced deportations as the Tsarist state in particular targeted locals of Jewish and German descent, despite the fact that they had lived in the Russian Empire for generations. Ethnic Germans had begun traveling to Eastern European already in the thirteenth century, where they were active in trade and in the urban construction of cities ever since. Jews had historically also long lived in these lands. During Catherine the Great's rule over Imperial Russia, Jews were constrained to living in the Pale of Settlement and remained in this area spanning from the Baltic region to the Black Sea. During the First World War, Tsarist authorities believed that Jews and Germans were sympathetic to the enemy, could become possible spies or saboteurs, and thus undermine the Russian war effort.[32] These beliefs justified the state's forced evacuations of Jews and ethnic Germans, as well as members of the intelligentsia of different national and ethnic backgrounds.[33] Though ethnic Germans never historically inhabited Belarusian territory, individuals with German-sounding surnames could become targets for deportation.[34]

Jews, however, did historically live on Belarusian territory to a significant extent and thus the population was very much affected. In addition to forced deportations, the summer and fall of 1915 witnessed anti-Jewish pogroms, which devastated many towns and villages.[35] Jews became victims of abuse, murder, and rape.[36] Many of the places where pogroms occurred were also where the Belarusians in question lived and came from.[37] Another wave of anti-Jewish violence came between 1919 and 1921, this time perpetrated by local partisan groups. General Stanisław Bułak-Bałachowicz, a self-proclaimed leader of a Belarusian Army in the Palesse region of today's Belarus, repeatedly threatened Jews with death if they showed any sympathy to Bolshevik forces. His men often robbed Jews of food and other valuables which often involved torturing them as well. In some cases, such as in the town of Turaŭ, pogroms involved cases of sexual violence. During this time period, Polish army soldiers and those of the Red Army also participated in pogroms in other towns and cities in the region.[38]

Commenting in hindsight, one Belarusian noted that during this period, "Belarusian territories [...] were arenas of global acts, which ruined this country just as economically as it did culturally. [...] Almost all cultural groups, as well as peasants were mobilized to the army, or repeatedly evacuated under the pressure of forceful armies."[39] Already in the fall of 1915, only around 2.9 million inhabitants remained in the area, compared to the pre-war population of 4.2 million. Towns and villages that had been the home to a multicultural, diverse population for generations ceased to exist.[40] In the words of historian Stanislaŭ Rudovich, "between the summer and fall of 1915 Belarus was converted into a literal refugee camp."[41]

Belarusian Encounters with Germans, Poles, and Lithuanians

During the turbulent years of the revolution, the First World War, and subsequent border wars between newly (re)emerging states, the territory of present-day Belarus and its inhabitants encountered different national armies and military occupations. They were affected by armed conflict, regime mandates, and diplomatic agreements. Prominent Belarusian elites attempted to negotiate with these different parties and participate in ongoing conversations to create Belarusian organizations and armed formations. Moreover, this period set the tone for the development of a more concerted Belarusian national movement. This effort was heavily affected by the activities of other national movements, other states, and other border conflicts and peace treaties, which used, sidelined, and dismissed Belarusian national aspirations.

The first of these encounters was with the Germans, when the latter established the military occupation zone known as *Ober Ost* that included territory which is now part of the Baltics, Belarus, and Poland.[42] As the Russian Army retreated eastward in 1915, the Germans entered and occupied this area that was already significantly affected by the war merely a year into the conflict. This German military occupation lasted from 1915 to 1918. It was the Supreme Military Commander of the East (*Oberbefehlshaber Ost*) that ruled over the area, first under Paul von Hindenburg until 1916 and later under Prince Leopold of Bavaria. The individual primarily in charge of the occupied region's administration was Hindenburg's chief of staff, Erich Ludendorff. Unlike German rule in other parts of occupied Europe, where locally-elected individuals were placed in charge, German military officials had direct control over the administration of *Ober Ost*.[43] Only in cases when there was a shortage of candidates from the ranks of the German Army would locals work as administrators.[44] Ludendorff believed that German victory could only be possible by extracting all local economic resources for military success.[45] With no civilian oversight to balance the German military administration, this policy was not challenged.

As a result of this military rule on Belarusian territory, the experience under *Ober Ost* was one of colonization. The Germans saw the inhabitants of this occupied region as resources to be used for the benefit of their army and nothing more.[46] Because the region was largely agrarian, occupation policies mainly sought to exploit the territory's agriculture and forests. Equally important for the war effort was efficient transportation and infrastructure, leading to the deployment of thousands of locals for railroad construction in the region. German authorities used such official terms as "unemployed" and "unwilling to work" to simply round up poverty-stricken and desperate people who were passing by and send them away as forced labourers. German officials also rounded up some individuals into "Civil Workers' Batallions" (*Zivil-Arbeiter-Bataillone*), which meant longer deployment and forced labour on bigger projects around the *Ober Ost* region.[47] Indeed, historian Christian Westerhoff refers to these German-occupied regions as "a kind of Siberia" due to parallels in forms of forced labour practices.[48]

In addition to forced labour, German authorities strictly enforced security precautions and surveillance measures in the occupied territory. They required inhabitants to have permits to move between areas. These mobility limitations were implemented for several reasons. They ensured that farms, especially ones abandoned during the war, would be staffed with labourers and would continue to produce food and other vital goods. The Germans also restricted the movement of people to limit the spread of diseases. Those seeking permission to travel or relocate had to have their state of health approved by two physicians. Furthermore, German policies in mobility restriction also allowed them to surveil suspicious, or potentially dangerous, individuals, such as enemy deserters or soldiers who had been left behind by their units.[49]

The period of *Ober Ost* on Belarusian territory was certainly one that colonized and exploited the territory's human and natural resources, but it was also one of experimentation. German authorities knew little about the territory and the region's inhabitants. Unlike other neighbouring parts of Eastern Europe, Germans historically had not travelled to or settled in Belarus. For example, to the north and west, German communities had lived in the Baltic region and in Poland for centuries. In southern Ukrainian territory, the German Mennonite community, too, had resided for a long time. When the Germans occupied these regions, they treated these minorities and the areas they inhabited better and expected that these German communities would support their authority. German minorities were even employed in administrative positions in *Ober Ost*, over other ethno-national groups.[50] Because Belarusian territory did not have a historically ethnic German community, they had to think of another approach towards the occupied inhabitants.

Ultimately, the Germans approached the population on Belarusian territory through a policy of equalization, meaning that each ethno-national group would receive the same rights and could exert its ethno-national identity on an even level. Part of this approach also meant that the Germans adopted a policy of "limited autonomy" in *Ober Ost*, allowing small concessions for particularly weak national groups, or perceived to be weak nations.[51] This approach was in some ways done to garner support from certain parts of the population living in *Ober Ost*, yet it was also meant to prevent any national group from overpowering others and especially the occupiers.[52] Weaker national groups were allowed to develop culturally, linguistically, and educationally in order to offset the stronger ones. Because the Germans perceived ethnic Belarusians to be the weakest national group in the occupied territory, especially compared to Poles and Russians, they allowed them to pursue their national development.

Not surprisingly, Belarusian activists welcomed this policy. Belarusians opened schools and published literary works and newspapers in Belarusian. In October 1916, for example, there were eight Belarusian language schools in the region, whereas by December 1917 there were fifteen.[53] A Belarusian Club was also opened with a goal of promoting Belarusian culture and identity through organized gatherings and social activities. It was responsible for publishing the paper *Homan* (Clamour), considered the successor to the earlier paper, *Nasha niva*. The Germans also incorporated a multilingual passport system, where Belarusian appeared for the first time. Although some Belarusians may have welcomed linguistic and cultural concessions, others did not share this sentiment. Some individuals complained that the nature of promoting Belarusian identity was forced upon them. For example, parents whose children did not attend Belarusian schools were fined. Among the peasants, this policy was particularly unpopular as children were expected to work on the land to help their families.[54]

Equalizing the resident national groups living in *Ober Ost* meant the Germans not only bolstered weaker groups, but they also repressed those that were, or seemed, stronger. In 1917 Ludendorff declared an outright war against "Polish imperialism", because he failed to see the progression of this equalization policy in curbing strong Polish national sentiment.[55] In addition to Poles, German authorities also saw ethnic Russians as a group whose nationalist fervour had to be repressed. In the Vil′na region, for example, a German proclamation banned the use of Russian by officials and then more broadly in the whole region on 22 December 1916.[56] Ludendorff described these measures against Poles and Russians as ways of liberating weaker national groups from the yoke of Polish and Russian rule. Far from wanting to be benevolent to what it saw as "weaker" national projects, however, this entire equalization process was part of a broader occupation plan, that prioritized German conquest.

The movement of the German Army further into Belarusian territory and the eventual signing of the Treaty of Brėst-Litovsk on 3 March 1918 ushered in diplomatic peace between the Germans and Bolsheviks. Several Belarusian elites travelled there in the hopes of being at least somewhat part of the ongoing negotiations, but they were denied entry to the talks, marking the first of many such failed diplomatic efforts to promote their cause. Back in now German-occupied Minsk, the participants of the All-Belarusian Congress, who had met in December 1917, organized the first of three meetings in 1918. The first meeting took place on 21 February 1918, when they organized an Executive Committee to tackle the Belarusian situation and potential future given the conditions at the time. After this first meeting in February, they issued a statement to the public:

> Our homeland is experiencing a new critical moment. The former power left without a trace. Now we stand facing the possibility of the German army taking over. You must take your destiny in your own hands. The Belarusian people must exercise their inalienable rights for complete self-determination, and national minorities – to their personal autonomy.[57]

During their second meeting, which took place on 9 March 1918, the Belarusian representatives in attendance sharpened their ideas pertaining to their "destiny". This time, they went beyond a general appeal to the public and outlined their vision for Belarus:

> In the times of the World War, which strengthens some strong states and weakens others, Belarus has awoken to its existence as a sovereign state. After three and a half centuries of subjugation, the Belarusian nation, once again, tells the world that it is alive and will continue to be alive.[58]

Following this proclamation, the delegates listed numerous tenets to be adopted by a future Belarusian entity. Geopolitically, they envisioned a Belarusian autonomous region within a larger Federation.[59] They also advocated for free, equal, and proportional representation in a future parliament. The new Belarusian entity would also grant freedom of speech in addition to the right to assemble and strike. It concluded by guaranteeing land for those who worked on it and established an eight-hour workday.[60]

The third and most important gathering occurred on 25 March 1918 when the Belarusian delegates in session voted on the official creation of the Belarusian People's Republic (*Belaruskaia Narodnaia Rėspublika,* BNR).[61] This time, the declaration for a Belarusian state situated the Belarusian struggle for self-determination within the context of revolution, war, and violence:

> A year ago, the Belarusian peoples together with the Russian peoples overturned the Russian tsarist yoke, with the Belarusians pressuring the hardest, and our land was plunged into the fires of war, which completely demolished Belarusian towns and villages. Now we, the Rada of the Belarusian People's Republic, rid ourselves of the last yoke of dependence, which the Russian tsars took through force… From this point forward, the Belarusian People's Republic declares itself an independent and free nation.[62]

Not everyone in attendance, however, voted in favour of the declaration. Those who supported the BNR included members of the previous 1917 First-All Belarusian Congress as well as Belarusian nationalists based in Vil'na. However, Belarusian Socialist Revolutionaries abstained from the vote. The BNR positioned itself against both the former Tsarist and current Bolshevik regime, yet refrained from vilifying the Germans. Aside from the internal debate among the meeting's attendees, the official announcement of the BNR ruffled relations between Belarusians and the occupying German authorities. While the Germans allowed for the development of Belarusian education, language, and literature, they forbid any form of political activity. As a result, the Germans dissolved the BNR Rada. After some time and after negotiations between Belarusian leaders and the Germans, the BNR was allowed to operate again strictly in an organizational, educational, cultural, and welfare capacity.[63] After the war, when the Germans retreated, the BNR headquarters and its members retreated westward and re-settled themselves in Kaunas. The BNR would continue to represent a strong symbol for Belarusian nationalists during the interwar period and afterward, operating in exile in numerous cities worldwide. Furthermore, it would serve as a point of convergence for those outside of Belarus and would mobilize individuals for the struggle of Belarusian nationalism and self-determination.

What are the legacies of these interactions between Germans and Belarusians? Certainly, the fact that Belarusians were given some concessions during the German occupation during the First World War left them with a less negative impression of the Germans compared to other national groups. Though the Germans would eventually lose the First World War and forcibly give up all the occupied territory of *Ober Ost* to new emerging states, interactions between Belarusian nationalists and German authorities continued in the postwar period.

Continuing to Secure Allies

Though the Germans lost the war in 1918, the geopolitical fate of Belarus would not be completely decided until almost three years later. The series of border wars that ensued after the First World War between competing Polish, Lithuanian, Ukrainian, and Bolshevik states meant that Belarusian territory would be contested. Moreover, as historian Lizaveta Kasmach carefully notes, 1918 proved to be a critical year for the idea of Belarusian statehood, which became associated with two projects: the Belarusian People's Republic and the Socialist Soviet Republic of Belarus.[64] Belarusian activists of the non-Soviet flavour saw the chaotic years after 1918 as critical to the salvation of their national project and thus pursued relationships with other states and national armies in the hopes of procuring some external, much needed support.

Many Belarusian nationalists fled from Bolshevik-controlled areas of Belarus and sought refuge in Poland and Lithuania where authorities allowed them to live and create their organizations, at least for the time being.[65] Belarusians fleeing westward to Poland tended to operate out of Wilno and Grodno, both of which, following the Polish-Lithuanian War (September – October 1920), would become part of the official Second Polish Republic (1918–1939). Those fleeing to Lithuania, mostly operated out of Kaunas, which became Lithuania's capital after 1920. Aside from safety reasons, Belarusian activists operated out of these areas because they were open to the idea of creating some form of future Belarusian-Lithuanian-Polish federation, though many iterations of this pseudo federation would be conceptualized and pushed for until 1921.

Initially, Belarusians were optimistic about getting support from Poland in large part due to Marshall Józef Piłsudski, who would be both the legitimate and de-facto leader of Poland until 1935. During Poland's high point of the Polish-Bolshevik War (1919–1921), the Polish Army occupied Minsk. Indeed, the tides of this war and of its peace would shape the activities of Belarusian national activists. Piłsudski traveled to Minsk in mid-September 1919 where the local population welcomed him. His arrival was met with a celebration, including the presence of village and town leaders and members of the Orthodox Christian community.[66] The festivities included a few cultural presentations and a concert by a Belarusian choir.[67] Testimonies of Belarusian activists present in Minsk during Piłsudski's visit noted that Poland's leader promised to help liberate Belarus from the Bolsheviks, feed the hungry, and let locals decide their own future. Piłsudski also asserted that he would support free elections. Belarusians were especially pleasantly surprised that Piłsudski addressed the public in Belarusian.

> Having a small piece of paper in his hand he gave a long political speech in proper Belarusian. He spoke in his natural, strong, and firm tone. He promised wide autonomy, and he asked for trust and loyalty for the republic.[68]

Faith in Piłsudski was fortified when he allowed Belarusians to organize their own national armed formations under his army in 1919 and supported the creation of the Belarusian Military Commission (*Belaruskaia vaĭskovaia kamisiia,* BVK), in October of that year.[69] Its two centres of operation were Kaunas and Grodno, totaling 200 and 1027 soldiers respectively.[70] Piłsudski's support and the creation of the military commission was a major source of reassurance for Belarusians who believed they could work with the Poles, while still retain some power and agency in their operations.[71] The Poles gave the military commission structural support to organize Belarusian fighting units on a volunteer basis. These volunteers were to be trained in Warsaw, and furthermore, Belarusians who became officers would receive equal status as officers in Polish units.[72] The commission's responsibilities included educating its soldiers on Belarusian nationalism and the national question, organizing support for the soldiers, and assembling uniforms.[73] The additional stipulation was that Belarusian troops were to be dispatched only on Belarusian soil. Two notable individuals, Kushal' and Mikalaĭ Dziamidaŭ were on the commission's committee.[74]

Despite the initial promising plan, the Poles delayed the organization of these training schools for Belarusian soldiers and only began in the spring of 1920, more than a year after the Military Commission was created. The leaders in charge reported difficulties in recruiting locals into their ranks. One recruiter noted that when he approached peasants, they were convinced he was a Polish spy and had not even heard of a Belarusian Military Commission: "The volunteers do not believe they are actually fighting for their Belarusian homeland, and instead, believe they are being taken to fight for the Polish Army."[75] There were various reasons for why faith in cooperating with Poland was ultimately lost. One was that, despite repeated insistence by Belarusian leaders, Polish authorities refused to recognize the Belarusian People's Republic that had been proclaimed in March of 1918.[76] Moreover, the changing tides of the Polish-Bolshevik War also affected Poland's attitude and behaviour toward Belarusians. Under the provisional agreements of the Treaty of Riga that began in October 1920, a border was agreed upon between Polish and Bolshevik delegates. As per the border agreement, the Polish Army was to retreat westward, evacuating its forces and in theory abandoning any support for Belarusian armed groups. Some Belarusian soldiers subsequently joined other fighting units in the region. However, the majority moved westward into Poland, where authorities disarmed them and interned them in camps as late as the spring of 1921. The signing of the Treaty of Riga in March 1921 saw the official conclusion of the Polish-Bolshevik War and, just as with the Treaty of Brėst-Litovsk, Belarusian national activists were denied entry to the negotiating table.[77] This peace was a huge blow to the Belarusian national movement and affected many prominent Belarusian activists. Kushal′ lost his position in the Military Commission when it was dissolved. Dziamidaŭ attempted to join other armed groups and was subsequently arrested by Polish authorities and interned until the May of 1921. Despite their failed efforts in 1921, it would not be the last time the latter two would work together. Twenty years later, Dziamidaŭ and Kushal′ would collaborate once again to organize Belarusian armed groups, albeit in a very different context.

Aside from Poland, Belarusian nationalists also looked to Lithuania for assistance and potential aid. With the Lithuanians, Belarusians pushed for a sort of re-incarnation of the Grand Duchy of Lithuania, but Lithuanian leaders were uninterested in resurrecting any type of Belarusian-Lithuanian federation. What they did offer was limited Belarusian representation in the *taryba,* or governing council, in exchange for a possibility of ethnic Belarusian lands being part of a postwar Lithuanian state.[78] In the fall of 1920, Belarusians agreed to mobilize their constituents to vote in favour of Lithuania during a plebiscite that was to decide whether contested territory would be part of Poland or Lithuania. In exchange for the Belarusian vote, Lithuanian authorities would increase their support for Belarusian armed units in Kaunas.[79] A Belarusian unit had already been operating under the Lithuanian Army and was to be built up further.[80] Lithuanian authorities also agreed to offer monetary concessions to the Belarusian People's Republic, in exchange for Belarusian electoral support during the plebiscite.[81]

Ultimately, however, Belarusian-Lithuanian relations concluded far away in Brussels, when Polish and Lithuanian delegates agreed on a diplomatic border. One disgruntled Belarusian noted that, "Now the

Lithuanians are no longer in a union with us – they have to save their own skin… During the negotiations in Brussels, they are going to divide our lands with the Poles."[82] The Lithuanians also did not push for the inclusion of Belarusian lands into their postwar new state. After a series of border wars, Lithuania was not in a position to compromise its embryonic state by insisting that ethnic Belarusian lands – now occupied by the Poles and Bolsheviks – be theirs.

Thus concluded any significant prospect for Belarusian autonomy within the Polish and Lithuanian context. Furthermore, the fact that nation states, such as Poland and Lithuania, were able to establish themselves following a series of wars, further frustrated Belarusian nationalists. Though they did not support the Soviet model for a Belarusian state, it would be the only one that would emerge in the postwar period.

The Slutsk Insurrection

For Belarusian nationalists, one more event would mark the end of this bellicose and turbulent period. This event was the Slutsk armed insurrection, which took place in the Slutsk district, south of Minsk.[83] This insurrection was sparked by diplomatic agreements underway in Riga in October 1920 between the Poles and Bolsheviks that would solidify the border between these two parties and divide Belarusian territory for the next nineteen years. The negotiations in October, situated the Polish-Bolshevik border just west of the Slutsk district, which meant that the area would fall under Bolshevik control. When the Slutsk region was delegated to the Bolshevik side of the border, it sparked a reaction by both locals there and Belarusians scattered in different areas. This reaction in Slutsk was not random, as the city and surrounding region had experienced heightened political activity ever since the 1917 revolutions. More Belarusian activists were concentrated here than in other parts of Belarusian territory, especially after they had escaped Minsk from the incoming Red Army.[84] Moreover Belarusian nationalists were frustrated as they had hoped Polish authorities would push for the area to be included in Poland, avoiding its absorption into Bolshevik territory.[85]

The events in Slutsk offer important insights into the mindsets of some notable Belarusian figures and also highlight key aspects of the "postwar" period at the local level. A report from a Polish inspector surveying the Slutsk region in 1920 noted several complaints by the local population. They worried over the lack of stability, rule of law, and of the shortage of necessary supplies to survive, such as medical assistance and food. Diseases, including typhus and syphilis, spread among locals, soldiers, and among refugees who all co-habited the area.[86] According to a July 1920 report, ten people died daily in the Slutsk county, partly due to a lack of medical care and supplies.[87] Many individuals subsequently joined armies or armed groups to garner at least some benefits. Some of those who would fight in the insurrection in November and December 1920 were people with a lack of job prospects and former soldiers or deserters of various armies.[88] These individuals were largely unaffected by ideas of Belarusian national self-awareness but were more desperately concerned about their economic situation, as well as with acquiring food through available rations for soldiers and dealing with devastation and displacement.[89]

Thus, it was local participation as well as involvement by Belarusian elites that fomented resistance in Slutsk. Regardless of their visions, united by an anti-Bolshevik sentiment, when Belarusians became aware of the agreements made in Riga in October 1920, activists from other parts of the borderland region travelled to Slutsk. They organized a Slutsk Rada, composed of members from various political parties and people of different personal and professional backgrounds.[90] In addition to political organization, Belarusian leaders began putting together two Slutsk Brigades with the intention of training and preparing soldiers to fight the Red Army and resist Bolshevik rule.[91]

To bolster their chances against the Red Army, Belarusian representatives of the Rada secretly reached out to the Polish 4th Army that was stationed nearby Slutsk and asked for help.[92] The Polish 4th Army offered supplies and instructors to train Belarusian soldiers. Furthermore, the mere presence of the Polish Army in the area stalled the arrival of the Red Army and gave Belarusians much needed time to organize themselves.[93] When the Polish Army did finally retreat in late November 1920 and the Red Army entered the Slutsk area, fighting broke out and would continue for about a month. The Slutsk Brigades did have some initial successes against the Bolsheviks, largely due to Polish assistance, yet ultimately the Red Army defeated the Slutsk fighters by mid-December.[94] Some Slutsk soldiers crossed into Poland where they were subsequently disarmed and held in a prisoner-of-war camp in Dorohusk as late as May 1921.[95] Others continued operating in partisan groups around the borderland region, well into the mid-1920s.

Despite this failed insurrection, Slutsk was a site and a moment in Belarusian history that brought many key actors together. Radaslaŭ Astroŭski, a local of Slutsk who worked as a teacher, was active in Belarusian circles in the city. Todar Daniliuk traveled from Grodno, where he was stationed as a lieutenant in the Lithuanian Army, to Slutsk. He too participated in the insurrection, lived to tell the tale, and later gave motivational speeches to Belarusian soldiers during the Second World War.[96] Anton Sokal-Kutyloŭski, another key participant of the insurrection, would later be responsible for organizing Belarusian armed formations, also during the Second World War.

When slightly untangling the events in Slutsk from the intentions and visions of Belarusian nationalists, this case also offers insight into the legacies of war and conflict in the region. Despite its distance from centres of power, Slutsk was significantly affected by ideas, politics, and agendas from the top. Political instability and socio-economic insecurity would continue to affect Slutsk and other Belarusian areas for years to come, even with their official inclusion into different states. Slutsk serves as a case study of broader occurrences on Belarusian territory and reveals that this region was at the centre of competing visions for nation-state building projects and, with that, war and atrocity. For locals, it represented destruction and a struggle to survive. In the hearts and minds of Belarusian nationalists, however, Slutsk became a critical event in the history of the Belarusian armed struggle – a narrative that would be recycled in nationalist discourse for years to come.[97]

Belarusian Partisan Activity in the 1920s

The last form of armed Belarusian activity during this time period came through partisan fighting. Because this territory was located far from centres of power in newly developing states, it would take time for the respective state to access, secure, and control these areas. Thus, for several years after the official signing of peace treaties, warlords, partisans, and bandits roamed these lands. Some of these individuals were ideologically motivated and were sometimes supported by certain states to engage in outlaw activity. Others, however, participated in banditry as a means of survival. The lack of job prospects, need for basic necessities, and lack of support by developing states pushed people to engage in illicit activity in order to survive.

One of the most notable Belarusian partisan groups that emerged at this time in the immediate aftermath of the First World War was the *Zialony dub,* or the Green Oak, group. This group was led by Viachaslaŭ Adamovich (junior), more colloquially known as Ataman Dziarhach. The *Zialony dub* group came to include as many as five thousand partisans operating primarily in the former Polesie region of Poland, today in southwest Belarus and small portions of Ukraine.[98] Adamovich was born in present-day Lithuania in 1890. He studied both in Kaunas and in St. Petersburg, after which he was mobilized to fight in the First World War. During this time and after, he was increasingly active in Belarusian cultural circles, primarily in Minsk, where he served as a correspondent for Belarusian magazines. Together with Kushal′ and Dziamidaŭ, he worked in the Belarusian Military Commission in 1920 and organized training courses for soldiers. Later that year he traveled to Slutsk and Babruĭsk to organize volunteer groups for what would be the future *Zialony dub,* around the same time that the Slutsk insurrection was taking place.[99]

Those fighting in *Zialony dub* consisted of locals, former Red Army deserters, and even White Russians. It also came to include some four hundred former Slutsk insurgents, who joined the group after the insurrection fizzled out.[100] Similar to the Slutsk fighters, this partisan group repeatedly sought out help from the Poles, usually asking for weapons and medical supplies.[101] From the Polish perspective, supporting an anti-Bolshevik force had its strategic and security benefits. Polish authorities believed that bolstering up *Zialony dub* would distract and occupy Bolshevik forces as they focused their attention on defeating the fighters. A sort of buffer of local instability would occupy Bolshevik authorities and curb their revolutionary struggle westward. However, the partisans operating in *Zialony dub* were not necessarily pro-Polish. In a secret correspondence between Adamovich and another insurgent, the former notes that many under his command were even sympathetic toward the Bolshevik cause. Moreover, *Zialony dub* was also not so transparent in its activities as Polish authorities were led to believe. In April 1921, the Polish Army discovered that there were only 450 soldiers still part of the partisan group, all the while the Poles had been providing supplies for a group of allegedly three thousand. *Zialony dub* was selling the excess provisions on the black market to make a profit.[102]

The Poles eventually disarmed and disbanded *Zialony dub* for its indiscretions but also because of the general tide of the postwar period. After the signing of the Treaty of Riga, the Polish government no longer wanted to jeopardize the delicate diplomatic settlement by continuing to sponsor a partisan group fighting the Bolsheviks. Following *Zialony dub*'s dissolution and after spending some time in a prisoner of war camp, Adamovich continued his advocacy for the Belarusian cause albeit in murky ways. Speculations of his alleged espionage for multiple parties arose throughout his life, all of which are yet to be fully confirmed. Other *Zialony dub* partisans that decided to return to their homes, later in Soviet territory, were accused of participating in anti-Bolshevik activity for allegedly murdering state officials and for participating in pogroms. In the 1920s, Soviet authorities apprehended former fighters and exiled them to remote parts of the Soviet Union for forced labour work.[103]

Poland's eventual refusal to assist partisan groups was received very negatively by Belarusian partisan leaders. After the Slutsk insurrection and dissolution of *Zialony dub,* another group emerged in 1921, this time led by Viachaslaŭ Razumovich, or Ataman Khmara as he was known more commonly. This group was more resistant to Polish appeals and orders.[104]

For example, one notable member of Razumovich's group was a woman by the name of Vera Masloŭska. She was a Belarusian teacher who was instrumental in organizing this partisan group, despite warnings by Polish authorities. For her activity she was eventually arrested by the Polish police.[105] Razumovich was also not shy about his grievances against Polish authorities. In a piece he wrote, he noted that

> The Revolution of 1917 brought freedom to many nations and only we, Belarusians, as a result of the lies and fraud of the Polish gendarme suffer captivity, we rot in prison... they shoot us... and they heavily abuse us. They loot our rich land, rob our forests, sell them abroad, and with that money they pay their gendarmes, clerks, and agitators... Piłsudski himself promised the Belarusian people protection from the Russian Bolsheviks, freedom and independence... What a vile untruth Piłsudski told.[106]

He continued his thoughts with:

> We Belarusians cannot wait anymore. Enough. The end has come. Our famous Belarusian partisans are fighting for our freedom. [...] Do not waste time: incite uprisings against the occupiers, beat up the gendarmes [and] clerks, rip apart the bridges, the iron railroads, and more importantly, drive out those Polish spiders from their fortified estates in Belarus. It is time for us to speak with the smoke, fire, and echoes of shots. Perhaps then, the Entente will hear our voice.[107]

Razumovich's comments make clear that he was vehemently resentful of Polish authorities. His commitment to Belarusian independence, however, is less convincing especially when considering his later writings during the interwar period. In his diary written in the 1930s, he referred to Belarusians as a people that ultimately belonged under the larger Russian spirit. Whatever his beliefs actually were, Razumovich never committed to any formal political organization and continued to welcome aid from many states. At one point Polish authorities suspected his group of receiving financial support from Lithuanians, and these suspicions were confirmed.[108] Razumovich also sought seeking financial support and weapons supply from the Germans.[109]

Razumovich's group, consisting of five to six thousand fighters, did commit some serious crimes such as attacking a forest ranger's family in Witów and murdering his wife and two children.[110] The insurgents also burned forests between towns and coordinated attacks against a local police post in Kleszczele, stealing guns and ammunition and killing a police officer.[111] Eventually, Polish authorities managed to find and arrest many of the partisans by the summer of 1922. As with the failure of previous partisan groups, the ultimate blow came when foreign support ceased to come through. In this case, when Lithuanian authorities decided to stop supporting Razumovich's group in favour of better diplomatic relations with Poland, these partisans were quickly disbanded or absorbed into national armies.[112] The activity of Adamovich and Razumovich's partisan groups are the last examples of armed activity linked to some form of Belarusian activism in the 1920s, however nominal or marginal. Though there would be smaller cases of armed activity throughout the interwar period, these were sporadic and less coordinated. Both partisan leaders would carry out their Belarusian activism during into the 1920s and 1930s in northern Poland, attempting procure foreign support from different Baltic states.[113]

This period marked the point when some of the most important individuals of this story met for the first time and bonded during extreme moments of violence and turmoil. Whether it was through committees, insurrections, partisan groups, or correspondence, many key Belarusians became linked during these earlier experiences. In addition to being bound by these earlier encounters, 1921 would be forever imbedded in the memories of Belarusian activists who saw the year as a painful halt to the progression of the Belarusian cause. In his memoir, Dz′mitry Kasmovich, passionately recalled that:

> These were tragic times for the Belarusian people. With bloody hands, the Poles and Moscow cut the living body of Belarus and divided it between themselves. This brutal act was consolidated with the so-called Riga Treaty of March 18, 1921. Millions of Belarusians were inhumanely separated.[114]

Belarusian intellectuals and activists also expressed much disappointment and frustration during meetings and saw themselves as having been betrayed, whereas other national groups experienced liberation and state formation. In a speech delivered in Prague in the 1930s to a group of individuals from various nationalities, Vasil′ Rusak – a Belarusian student at the time and former Slutsk participant with ties to the BNR – passionately scorned neighbouring nations for having abandoned Belarusians in their self-determination aspirations.[115]

For the time being, these Belarusians would have to operate and work creatively and many times clandestinely, depending on where they were living in Europe. Belarusian émigré hubs located in Vilnius, Kaunas, Warsaw, Prague, and Berlin became important meeting sites.[116] Moreover, this older generation of Belarusians would continue using their organizational, coordination, and networking skills to enlist the support and interest of younger generations.

2
A Belarusian "Interwar" Period

After the dissolution of Belarusian armed formations and partisan groups, many actors of this story fled to different parts of Europe. Some of them organized Belarusian groups in their new homes, whereas others tried to assimilate to their new professions and lives. Frantsishak Kushal′ served in the Polish Army, whereas Radaslaŭ Astroŭski was active among Belarusian circles in Wilno. Other Belarusians of this generation sought to push for the Belarusian cause through lobbying, either in the countries they were living in or at more international, diplomatic settings. At the same time, while these more seasoned individuals brought their experiences with them into the interwar period, a younger generation of future Belarusian activists was being born and raised in this new post-war world. Many of them grew up in small towns and villages in eastern Poland, would travel for education purposes to other countries and were conditioned and encouraged to embrace their Belarusian identity. Whether it be the older generation or the younger one, these individuals knew each other, or of each other, and would develop their relationships during this period.

The interwar sites of bonding and shared experiences included clubs, political parties, the military as well as schools and family homes. These spaces were shaped depending on the country they were in, including Poland, Soviet Belarus, Czechoslovakia, or Germany.[1] Older Belarusians were keen on continuing to promote their language and literature, keeping in touch with Belarusian soldiers in the Polish Army and working with foreign states for their cause. Younger Belarusians sought to learn the language and pursue their academic and professional aspirations. Both generations faced personal and professional barriers stemming from limitations imposed on them by various states. Far from being a stagnant period merely bookended by two world wars, this interwar period witnessed significant Belarusian activism and mobilization.

Examining this particular period through the experiences of these Belarusians also offers an interesting chronological perspective. Though for many people 1939 marked the beginning of the Second World War and served as a watershed moment in Central and Eastern Europe, for these particular individuals 1941 was that year. Though Belarusian speaking territories that had been part of Poland were united – albeit forcefully – into the Soviet Union in 1939, it was not until 1941 that, according to Belarusian nationalists, these unified territories were "liberated from Polish and Soviet rule upon the German invasion. This 1921 to 1941 "interwar" period witnessed an escalating attempt by Belarusian activists to develop their connections with foreign states and between themselves, in anticipation and preparation for the outbreak of a new future war. More importantly, the relationships and bonds forged over this period were extremely important for the future activity of these individuals during their collaboration with the Germans in the Second World War.

Between Poland and Soviet Belarus

The city of Niasvizh, located today just southwest of Belarus's capital, has a long history of being absorbed into multiple states since its founding in the 13th century. The city's most prominent structure is the Niasvizh castle and the history of the building itself reflects these changes in occupation and power. For centuries, the castle was part of the royal estate belonging to the prominent dynastic Radziwiłł family of the Grand Duchy of Lithuania. After the partitions of Poland, the Russian Empire took over the castle in 1793 but permitted members of the Radziwiłł family to reside on the estate. Following the revolutions and wars in the early twentieth century, the castle then became part of Poland. Later during the Soviet invasion of Poland in September 1939, the Red Army expelled the Radziwiłł family, who would never again return to their estate after centuries of running it. Upon arrival in Niasvizh, Soviet authorities emptied the castle of its extensive library and archival collections, transferring most of it to the Academy of Sciences in Minsk or simply distributing it to locals. In June 1941, Germany invaded the Soviet Union and the castle once again changed owners and was used as a hospital for wounded German soldiers and officers. After the German evacuation of Belarus in July 1944, the castle once again fell to the Red Army and for the next few decades operated as a sanatarium, until finally becoming a museum and recognized as a UNESCO world heritage site.

Much like the Niasvizh castle, the local residents living in the town during the twentieth century witnessed and experienced these occupations. Until the castle was taken over by Poland in 1921, a Belarusian school operated on the premises. Nine-year old Dz'mitry Kasmovich began his second year of studies at the school in the fall of 1920. To pay for his education, Kasmovich's father rented out half of the family home to Polish tenants. Kasmovich managed to attend school only inconsistently, however, because his family could not afford it financially and because he had to help his father with the field work, a reality that was not unique to him.[2]

When the Niasvizh castle became part of Poland, the Belarusian school that operated on the estate was replaced with a Polish school. In order to continue providing some form of Belarusian education, the mother of one of the students agreed to host the school in the family home. Kasmovich soon began attending this home school, along with other boys who would later become notable Belarusian actors, including Mikhal Vitushka, Ėmanuil Iasiuk, Aliaksandar Kalosha, Aliaksandar Kryt, and Vitushka's cousin, Aliaksandar. Girls also attended this school. A few years later in 1926, Polish authorities shut down the Belarusian school in the town.[3] By this point, only three Belarusian schools remained in Poland: in Nowogródek, Radoszkowice, and Wilno. Kasmovich, Vitushka, and several others subsequently continued their education in Radoszkowicze.[4] Kasmovich noted that "the gimnazjum's students were Belarusian, as well as local Jews, who also felt Belarusian. Both endured suffering at the hands of the Polish state, which limited the possibility for Belarusians and Jews to study in institutions of higher education."[5] Eventually, when Polish authorities shut down all the Belarusian schools, many of these students continued their education in different cities. Vitushka and his cousin moved to Prague, Iasiuk travelled to Liège, and others moved to Warsaw and Berlin.

Another Belarusian student by the name of Barys Rahulia also recalled his frustration with the education system in Poland. Rahulia and another one of his Belarusian peers, Usevalad Rodz'ka, had been accepted into the prestigious medical programme at the Stefan Batory University in Wilno. Out of the 1,600 applicants to the programme, only 100 were accepted per year, of which only five spots were reserved for minorities, including Belarusians, Jews, Ukrainians, and Lithuanians. Though both students had been accepted into the programme and should have been officially except from military service, they were informed that they had to report for their reserve armed training. Ultimately, both young men were forced to decline their acceptance to the Batory medical school and complete their military training instead. In his memoir, Rahulia expresses frustration stemming from his situation:

> Several influential Polish nationalists had intervened when they learned that three Belarusians had won coveted places at the university… A few weeks later, the university notified me that another candidate would be

> taking my place. Later I came to realize that we could turn this predicament to our advantage – we could use our military training to further the cause of Belarusian political and cultural autonomy.[6]

The degree to which Rahulia actually saw it as an opportunity to push for the Belarusian cause is uncertain if not doubtful. In any case, it is almost certain he felt slighted at the opportunity to pursue his medical degree.

The experiences of lost opportunity and professional repression were not limited to only these young Belarusians. Non-ethnic Poles living in Poland during the 1920s and 1930s faced limitations enacted by Polish law and authorities. This repression was especially jarring considering that a significant portion of the population in Poland at the time consisted of non-ethnic Poles. A 1931 census indicates that there were approximately 31,916,000 inhabitants in Poland, out of which Belarusians, Ukrainians, and Jews made up about 25 percent.[7] Approximately 3 million Belarusians resided in Poland, primarily in the northeastern regions of the republic.[8] Most resided in the countryside.[9] Though the Polish Republic's March 1921 constitution guaranteed the sanctity of property, freedom, and life to all residents, regardless of religion, nationality, ethnicity, or sex, the reality was that the government's policies toward its minorities treated them as colonial subjects, and it was especially the case after the mid-1920s. The government implemented a policy of *sanacja,* intended to "heal" the Polish political body and to eliminate any perceived to be threat to the developing state. This policy targeted far left and far right organizations, in addition to various ethno-national minority parties. Poland was also concerned about any foreign influence affecting its domestic affairs, particularly any Soviet propaganda or mobilization of non-Polish groups against the state. These concerns also reveal how little the Polish state thought of its minorities, and especially Belarusians, whom they saw as passive, poorly educated peasants and, therefore, easily manipulated.

Another aspect of this *sanacja* programme was to assimilate minorities through *polonization.*[10] To *polonize* its non-ethnic citizens, the state disbanded non-Polish schools and pedagogical, cultural, and publishing centres.[11] In the voivodship of Wilno, locals issued a series of complaints to authorities about the "reforming" – in reality closing – of Belarusian-language schools, which were then converted into Polish ones. In other cases, locals opened their own private schools and operated in secret.[12] If the state found out that students had stopped attending the Polish schools in favour of the clandestine ones, it fined the parents for their children's absence.[13] A 1925 report indicates that out of the 400 Belarusian schools in existence during the First World War, Polish authorities dissolved 382 of them.[14] Belarusian high schools and teaching schools met similar fates.[15]

The Polish state saw Belarusian organizations, schools, newspapers, and churches as sites where anti-Polish propaganda and activity could flourish.[16] In one case, suspicion arose about a Belarusian Club, resulting in the closing of the organization's canteen, where many individuals gathered for social activities.[17] The state also halted the distribution of papers that could spread propaganda. In 1927 alone, just in the Brześć region, Polish authorities shut down the publication of *Malanka, Nasha volia,* and *Narodny zvon* and arrested some of the writers and editors, most of whom were young adults and teenagers.[18] Belarusian organizations with real or alleged communist sympathizers, made these places more susceptible to Polish crackdown as well.[19]

Other elements of repression involved land reform, which was disproportionately distributed in favour of ethnic Poles.[20] In the northeastern provinces of Poland, for example, Poles consisted of anywhere between 14 and 60 percent of the population, yet owned 85 percent of the land there.[21] Sometimes this land had been previously owned by locals displaced by earlier wars, and they returned only to find that their plots had been confiscated and given to somebody else.[22] Minorities also experienced shortages of basic resources, which were not only legacies of the wars but also were further exacerbated by economic reforms enacted by Władysław Grabski, the Prime Minister of Poland in the early to mid-1920s.[23] In the eastern provinces of Poland, a socio-economic hierarchy quickly appeared. Minorities, Belarusians included, worked under landowning Poles, digging up potatoes, cutting wood, or performing other menial tasks. Their conditions, even according to Polish testimonies, were much worse than those of ethnic Poles. One individual by the name of Stanisław Piętka recalled this:

> Before the war that started in 1939 Belarusians often came to work on our farm. They dug potatoes, mowed the meadows, cut down trees – they were simply workers on the farm. They happily came to work for us because they got paid and received meals throughout the day. Belarusians fared far worse than Poles.[24]

All of these issues, economic and structural, positioned Poles at the top of the socio-economic ladder.

Politically, Belarusians were also excluded either because they were members of Belarusian organizations or other parties that were banned by the Polish state. Throughout the existence of the Second Polish Republic, there were many Belarusian organizations and parties with varying ideologies and goals.[25] Based on popular support and influence through legal and illegal channels, the two most significant Belarusian parties were the Belarusian Peasant-Workers' Hramada (*Białoruska włościańsko-robotnicza hromada*, BWRH) and the Communist Party of Western Belarus (*Komunistyczna Partia Zachodniej Białorusi*, KPZB). This Hramada, founded in 1925 in Wilno, was created as a means to use legal channels to express the desires of many Belarusians residing in interwar Poland. At its peak, the party had a membership of around 120,000 people and included individuals of a variety of political orientations. The leaders of the party drafted a programme which included demands to give land to the peasants, to separate the church and state, and to release political prisoners. The KPZB was created in October 1923, was directly connected to Moscow, and throughout its existence in Poland operated clandestinely.

In practice, both parties often worked together in both legal and clandestine ways. They shared visions for similar land reforms for peasants, and both appealed to peasants and workers of Belarusian and of Polish background. The issue regarding the unification of Belarusian territories was a popular one amongst many people, albeit through different visions. Some Belarusians saw unification as including the territories from Dvinsk to Pinsk, from Belastok to Minsk as a separate, independent entity. Others, especially members of the Communist party and some in the Hramada, wanted to unify the eastern Belarusian-dominated provinces of Poland with the existing Belarusian Soviet Socialist Republic.[26] Only two years after its creation, Polish authorities banned the Hramada in 1927.[27] The state arrested and incarcerated many of its activists, sometimes multiple times, whereas other individuals were heavily surveilled. Nevertheless, many individuals continued to operate clandestinely and sometimes in armed resistance cells, especially along the Polish – Soviet border, until 1938.[28] Polish authorities never ceased to worry about a potential anti-Polish insurrection that would threaten the security of the state.[29]

It was in these political spaces where some key Belarusians spent the interwar period. In Wilno, a Belarusian National Committee operated, whose members included Rahulia, Astroŭski, and many others.[30] These organizations, both legal and illegal, saw the interaction of different generations of Belarusian activists. The acceptance of Belarusians from different political and ideological beliefs meant that these organizations drew more people. The younger members of these Belarusian circles, in particular, went through different waves of ideological predilections. Iulian Sakovich was a Belarusian student in the town of Radoszkowice where, similarly to Nieśwież, was one of the few places where a Belarusian school operated. Dz'mitry Kasmovich began to attend school in

Radoszkowice after the Nieśwież Belarusian school was forced to shut and met Iulian Sakovich. Unlike his peers, Sakovich was very active in the Communist Party of Western Belarus. Kasmovich recalled that Polish authorities arrested Sakovich on numerous occasions.[31] According to his criminal record, he illegally transported communist literature and maintained close ties with other Belarusian organizations, such as the Hramada. The authorities arrested and imprisoned Sakovich once in 1926 for two years and again in 1930, 1931, and in 1932.[32] In 1936, he was once again arrested but this time sent to Bereza Kartuska, one of the most notorious camps for political prisoners in Poland, where he remained until April 1937.[33] Later during the Second World War, Sakovich played an important role in organizing and commanding Belarusian armed units, along with his Belarusian school mates he met in Radoszkowice.[34]

Some Belarusians, however, experienced professional and career advancement during these years in Poland. The life of Frantsishak Kushal′ is one example. After the conclusion of the Polish-Bolshevik War, Kushal′ joined the Polish Army.[35] While in the Polish Army, he completed an officers' training programme, specialized in the use of heavy machine weaponry in Toruń, and became commander of the regiment's officer school in Warsaw.[36] Reports from his personnel file between 1921 and 1937 reveal nothing but "good" or "very good" marks regarding his performance and skills.[37] Another military report from Chełmno indicates that Kushal′ had

> a very big ability for leadership. [He is a] very good educator and commander of the company. [...] for a long time, he has developed his work, knowledge and conscientiousness with outstanding results. Especially as a company commander [...] thanks to his knowledge of the subject, he has positioned his company on a very high training level.[38]

His leadership abilities were also recognized in diplomatic situations.[39] It is unclear if Kushal′ was ever a member of a Belarusian political party during this time. If he was not, it could partially explain his professional success. His connections and work also trickled down to contacts with numerous Belarusian soldiers, who composed approximately 10 percent of the Polish Army.[40] It was during this time and setting that younger Belarusians in the military, such as Usevalad Rodz′ka, Barys Rahulia, and another young man by the name of Uladzimir Kachan, potentially met each other and Kushal′.

The Polish Army, indeed, would prove to be one of the most important sites where Belarusians met and connected. The majority of Belarusians serving in the Polish armed forces were of peasant background. Many

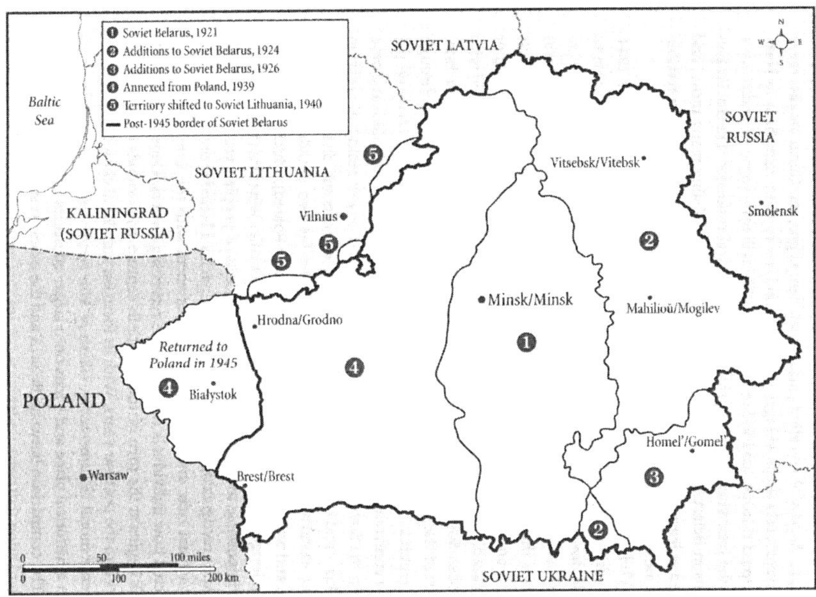

Figure 1: Shifts in territorial boundaries of Soviet Belarus from 1921–41.

Source: Map by Mike Bechthold. By permission of Cornell University Press. From *Ghosts of War: Nazi Occupation and Its Aftermath in Soviet Belarus,* by Franziska Exeler, published by Cornell University Press. Copyright © 2022 by Cornell University. Reprinted by permission of the publisher.

were illiterate, did not speak Polish, and were not Polish patriots. As an institution, the military was conceptualized as a space to assimilate non-ethnic Poles. To bolster the "Polish" constitution of the military, all Belarusians who identified as Roman Catholic were immediately recognized as Polish, whereas those who were Orthodox Christian were believed to be sympathetic to communism and needed to be assimilated.[41] Despite attempts by the military to create a Polish Army and assimilate soldiers of other backgrounds, this process was not easy. Many soldiers deserted or refused to show up for training.[42] Rahulia, himself, even managed to run away from his unit and return home to Nowogródek.[43]

For some living in Poland, frustrations arose especially when comparing their situation in the 1920s with that of the neighbouring Belarusian Soviet Socialist Republic (BSSR).[44] The BSSR was, at least initially, seen as a more welcoming haven for different ethnic and national groups as well as for peasants.[45] Unlike Poland's crackdown on its minorities, the 1920s in the BSSR witnessed a push for the development of

Belarusian identity and culture, especially through the policy of *korenizatsiia* or "indigenization."[46] The plan for what historian Terry Martin calls the "Affirmative Action Empire" sought to support national territories, languages, elites, and cultures.[47] The idea was that controlling national development within Soviet parameters would prevent these movements from becoming counter-revolutionary.[48] This policy of guided Belarusian national development operated through a process of *belarusization,* under the umbrella of *korenizatsiia.*[49] The BSSR used *belarusization* as a vehicle for creating the new Soviet Belarusian citizen: "national in form, socialist in content."[50] Creating a Belarusian identity involved appropriating historical events and commemorating important dates such as the publication of Soviet Belarusian newspapers and founding of universities. It also involved territorial, linguistic, and cultural considerations, which were published in textbooks disseminated in schools and the workplace, albeit with different rates of success.[51] The contrast between the BSSR and Poland in terms of policies toward education and schools was especially marked in the 1920s. Rather than cracking down on schools, the Soviet Belarusian leadership pushed for the opening of schools in Belarusian, which included training Belarusian instructors, providing necessary support for education and spreading Belarusian literature among peasants.[52] Education became free and students had to take mandatory Belarusian-language courses. The state also encouraged people to pursue Belarusian higher education, opened a Belarusian theatre, and, finally in 1928, opened the Belarusian Academy of Sciences.[53] These policies were also paired with fairer distributions of land to Belarusian peasants, starkly contrasting those in Poland. For Belarusian nationalists, the conditions for national development in Soviet Belarus in the 1920s were more favourable than in Poland.[54]

Although these Soviet official measures were quite different than the policies enacted to the West of the BSSR's border, they were by no means always uniform nor consistent. Historian Alena Marková has carefully examined the processes of *belarusization* that took hold in varied ways depending on the region and resources available, noting differences when it came to, for example, education and pedagogy.[55] It was the Soviet state, and the Soviet state only, that could guide the development of *belarusization.* One case exhibits the constraints and control over the *belarusization* process. In the city of Slutsk, there lived a man by the name of Iurka Listapad. He had been one of the critical organizers and participants of the Slutsk armed insurrection in 1920 and knew many of the former participants who now lived in Poland. Unlike many other insurgents, he had decided to return to his home that became part of the BSSR following the failed insurrection. For the next six years, he was encouraged by the Soviet state's promotion of Belarusian culture and language and taught classes on these topics. However, in 1926, he was arrested and tried for his participation in the insurrection as well as for his alleged subversive teaching. Along with five other teachers and students, he was charged and sentenced to prison for allegedly recruiting young Belarusians, trying to brainwash them, and for fomenting anti-Soviet activity.[56] Listapad's followers, mainly students, were called the *listapadaŭtsy,* and the term became a label continually used by the Soviet regime to accuse individuals of being involved in Belarusian bourgeois, anti-Soviet activity.[57] In Poland, Listapad's story was published and distributed among Belarusian circles and among individuals who personally knew him during the insurrection.[58]

Listapad was not the only one who was arrested by Soviet authorities for allegedly deviating from or abusing the *belarusization* process. By the late 1920s, Soviet Belarusian authorities began repressing individuals with real or perceived ties to non-Soviet groups or for promoting counter-revolutionary and anti-Soviet ideology. This number included the repression, arrest, or expulsion of around ten thousand people.[59] As in other parts of the Soviet Union, *korenizatsiia* came to an end in the 1930s. State attacks on wealthier peasants or "kulaks" continued into the late 1920s and early 1930s, whereas any "ideological foreign elements" were also quashed.[60] The state also repressed institutions that were allegedly subversive organizations, involving the work of "[nationally] conscious Belarusians" (*sviadomykh belarusaŭ*). This term took on a dangerous connotation, as it was used to label counter-revolutionary Belarusians who sought to infiltrate state and public institutions. For example, at one point authorities warned that a Belarusian bourgeois-nationalist organization, known as the "Union for the Independence of Belarus", was seriously threatening the state. The alleged discovery of the "Union" led to the arrest of 108 people, including Socialist Revolutionaries, yet this attack also affected Belarusian members of the Communist Party. The actual existence of this group has not been verified to this day.[61]

Other victims of Soviet repression and violence included individuals associated with Belarusian nationalists living outside of the Soviet Union. Such individuals, the state argued, could be nationalist proxies who could carry out foreign agendas on Soviet territory and spread propaganda.[62] Ultimately, as in other parts of the Soviet Union, the massive terror campaign repressed individuals based on ethnicity, nationality, and class, through arrests, mass operations, forced deportations, and executions.[63] There are various figures posited to account for the number of victims in Soviet Belarus during the period. Some historians note that between 1935 and 1940 in the BSSR, approximately eighty thousand people were arrested out of which twenty-eight thousand were executed.[64] When considering a longer durée figure for victimhood between 1917 and 1939, some scholars note that approximately 331,000 inhabitants of Belarus were targeted by Soviet authorities as either part of de-kulakization waves or specific orders focusing on special groups.[65]

One of the most important symbols of the terror and violence in Belarus is Kurapaty, located ten kilometres northeast of Minsk's city centre. Today it is a forested area, tucked away just next to a highway, with large crosses marking the site of mass killings during the Stalinist period.[66] The mass graves of Kurapaty did not become public knowledge until an article came out in 1988, offering testimonies of individuals who claimed that it was an execution site from 1937 to 1941. Witness accounts attested that Soviet security forces organized shootings three times a day and later more frequently.[67] Soviet authorities, however, claimed these were victims of German mass killings that occurred upon their invasion of Soviet Belarus in June 1941. One state investigatory report even suggested that the Germans and their collaborators used Soviet pistols and ammunition, found in local towns, which is why Soviet equipment had been discovered at the site. Soviet authorities also claimed that the Germans killed Soviet prisoners and other individuals brought in from Germany, Austria, and Czechoslovakia.[68] Estimates for the numbers of victims vary between 100,000 and 500,000.[69] The number and composition of these victims remains unknown.

For some individuals, the repression experienced in the BSSR would fuel their anti-Soviet activity during and after the Second World War. It would also inform their decision to join Belarusian nationalists active abroad or underground. Though many actors of this story lived outside the BSSR, they hoped to fuel any anti-Soviet sentiments among locals in support of their agenda and, later, in support of the future German occupying regime. Exclusion and repression, on both sides of the border, alienated Belarusian nationalists, while also giving them a shared experience, regardless of their ideology or political inclinations.

Searching for Opportunities Elsewhere

As prospects in Poland and Soviet Belarus became slimmer, many Belarusians looked to other places to live and study. Countries such as Latvia, Czechoslovakia, and Germany offered refuge, in addition to political and financial support for many Belarusians.[70] Belarusian émigrés, with the help of state funding, put together organizations and educational opportunities to promote their culture and language. These opportunities also allowed individuals to foster relations with other Belarusian activists across the continent and to develop connections with authorities and institutions in different countries.

In the 1920s and 1930s, Czechoslovakia was one of the main anti-Soviet émigré hubs in Europe, particularly for national groups from the former Russian Empire. Belarusian-Czechoslovak connections, however, began already in 1905 with the creation of a Belarusian youth group at Charles University in Prague.[71] After 1921, Czechoslovakia became even more important for Belarusian émigrés for both political and educational purposes.[72] A short-lived Belarusian Hramada existed until 1924 and included some well-known Belarusian Socialist-Revolutionaries.[73] In 1923 the headquarters of the Belarusian People's Republic moved out of Kaunas and officially reopened in Prague the following year.[74] Many Belarusian elites and activists, especially more well-known individuals who had been a part of the Slutsk insurrection or part of diplomatic missions, relocated to Czechoslovakia after 1921. One of these Belarusians was Vasil' Zakharka, who had been part of a Belarusian delegation sent to the League of Nations to appeal for independence. Zakharka served as president of the Belarusian People's Republic until his death in 1943 in Prague.[75] His successor, Mykola Abramchyk, also spent a lot of time there and studied philosophy at Charles University.[76]

Zakharka, Abramchyk, and others were responsible for creating organizations and for appealing to the state for financial aid that could support Belarusian students in Czechoslovakia. Some organizations were cultural and educational, whereas others had political agendas. One was the Belarusian Peasant Union (*Belaruski sialianski saiuz,* BSS), which opened in the fall of 1922, whose members included Christian Democrats. From the left political camp, there was the Belarusian Union for the Developing Student Movement (*Ab'iadnan'ne belaruskaha pastupovaha studėnstva,* ABPS).[77] Belarusian students were particularly attracted to Czechoslovakia due to available scholarships and grants for them for the pursuit of higher education degrees.[78] The approximate number of Belarusians who went to study in Czechoslovakia in the interwar period reached as many as 600. Out of this number, 150 received scholarships from the Czech-Ukrainian Committee, whereas 400 received grants directly from the Czechoslovak state.[79] Scholarships were given to students who previously studied at Imperial Russian schools and universities but fled westward during and after the revolutions. Grants were also provided to Belarusians, Ukrainians and others who were unable to study in their current states.[80] For example, with the crackdown on Belarusian schools in Poland, Mikhal Vitushka and his cousin, Aliaksandar Vitushka, moved to Prague to continue their education. Aliaksandar attended medical school in Prague and organized the Union of Belarusian Student

Organizations (*Sjednocení běloruských studentských organisací,* SBSO) in April 1936.[81] Mikhal, financially supported with a scholarship, was able to complete a technical degree.[82] It was in Prague and through organizations that both quickly found Belarusian company and developed relationships that would last well into the Second World War.

Not all activity among Belarusian émigrés was cultural and educational. Germany was another important country that supported Belarusian émigrés in various ways. The foundation for Belarusian-German collaboration began soon after the First World War and involved people from various organizations and political orientations. When it became clear that neither Moscow nor Warsaw were interested in offering any concessions to Belarusian nationalists, they turned to the Berlin.[83] German support bolstered Belarusians both in and outside of the country, but for the Germans it was also a means to collect intelligence as they prepared for war, especially into the mid to late 1930s.[84] German-sponsored Belarusian hubs appeared in Germany, Poland, and Austria throughout the interwar period. In addition to sponsoring Belarusian hubs throughout Europe, in 1937 the Germans opened the first Belarusian department at the University of Berlin, under the direction of Gerhard von Mende. Moreover, in Germany, there was an organization called the Belarusian National Union, headquartered in Berlin. The group published the newspaper *Ranitsa,* or "morning" and had smaller chapters in Łódź and Kraków. Another group, referred to as the "Belarusian representation in Germany", was based in Munich.[85]

The first likely contacts between Belarusians and Germans came through Fabian Akinchyts, a prominent member of the Belarusian National Socialist Party (*Belaruskaia natsyianal-satsyialistychnaia partyia,* BNSP). Akinchyts had a radical political trajectory, starting out as socialist revolutionary in 1906, later joining the Belarusian Peasant-Workers' Hramada in Wilno, and then drastically turning to National Socialism.[86] As early as 1933, Akinchyts established contact with the Office of Foreign Affairs of the Nationalist Socialist Party of Germany (*Aussenpolitisches Amt der NSDAP*) and secretly received support to run a newspaper in Wilno called *Novy shliakh,* (the new way).[87] The newspaper reflected many of Akinchyts's beliefs, most notably that it was only through national socialism, and with Germany, that Belarus would be able to develop as a proper nation.[88] The importance and influence of ideology, especially when it comes to antisemitism and radical nationalism, are difficult to ascertain for many of these Belarusian actors. In the case of Akinchyts, however, his position was very much known and made clear. In one of his articles, he stressed that Belarusians were not so naïve as to disapprove of Jews, just because they were Jews or just because they had different customs and a religion. Rather it was because Jews were the biggest exploiters of Belarusian peasants and as such were an enemy to the Belarusian nation.[89] Others close to Akinchyts and in the Belarusian National Socialist Party also began publishing antisemitic articles in the late 1930s from Berlin, primarily in the newspaper *Ranitsa*. In an article from December 1939, an author writing under the name "S. Bulat" remarked that "Jews play a dangerous role in the domestic lives of nations." The German invasion was explained as an effort to defeat the "Jewish capitalists who were controlling Poland."[90] In another article from 1939, the same author ends with a warning, noting that the Belarusian nation does not yet fully understand the threat that Jews present as the latter were preparing to "seize power over all nations."[91]

With the exception of a few small BNSP chapters in Wilno, Lida, and Stołpce, Akinchyts's radical nationalist party did not garner significant support among Belarusian nationalists. Many prominent Belarusians involved in the national movement had little respect for Akinchyts and called him a "middle-aged sect-like fanatic."[92] During the earlier parts of the German occupation of Belarus, the Gestapo, or German state police service, provisionally sponsored him. Despite aligning ideologically, however, it soon became clear that Akinchyts had too many enemies and eventually the Germans saw him as too unstable to work with.[93]

The War Begins

In September 1939, Germany and the Soviet Union invaded Poland. The Soviet Union absorbed the eastern provinces of Poland and began to secure and assimilate those living in these regions. A postwar recollection from a Polish woman on the 1940 anniversary of the Soviet invasion reveals how differently locals experienced the nearly two years of Soviet rule. Though the Soviet invasion and anniversary commemoration were devastating for her personally, they meant different things for others:

> The 17th of September 1940 was approaching. The tragedy's first-year anniversary – but not for everyone. Our Lithuanians, Belarusians and other pseudo-Poles gathered together and were discussing how to commemorate this "liberation day", and how to thank their "saviors."[94]

The woman then went on to sarcastically comment that perhaps they should have also thanked these "saviours" for also imprisoning so many people. Though this recollection was given after the war and in hindsight of what happened later, it still captures a very real experience based on ethno-national background. Indeed, many non-ethnic Poles were satisfied to see Poles removed from their long-held positions of power in various economic and cultural spheres and welcomed changes enacted by Soviet authorities.[95] Furthermore, non-Polish populations formerly living in eastern Poland and now in the Soviet Union had much to be optimistic about. They expected they would be treated better than they had been by Polish authorities, meaning they would get more land and enjoy more privileges.[96] These expectations were bolstered by early Soviet rhetoric, such as this proclamation:

> For nearly twenty years you have been controlled by Polish masters, landowners, and capitalists. They took your land and sentenced you to poverty and hunger. […] They do not recognize your language, forcibly polonize Belarusians, shut down all Belarusian schools, and in doing so deprived your children of a right to be educated in their native language. […] In these terrible days for you, Belarusian brothers, the Great Soviet Nation, whose interests are close and dear to you, lends out its brotherly hand to help you.[97]

In contrast to this enthusiasm, other locals from the eastern parts of Belarus who had been living in the Soviet Union already for over twenty years had different opinions about the unification of Belarusian lands. One veteran noted, "Let those Belarusians live in the Soviet Union, then they'll find out how one lives here. They won't be welcoming the Red Army much longer."[98]

Ultimately, for many inhabitants of these newly absorbed regions, the two years of experience living under Soviet rule proved to be tragic. Soviet authorities seized private property and collectivized farms, while corruption and black marketeering increased.[99] The process of *sovietization* from above drove policies on the ground, which focused on repressing enemies of the state, whether real or alleged. The more violent elements of *sovietization* involved mass operations. The goal for the deportations and arrests was twofold. First, they were intended to physically eliminate people who could potentially become active in any opposition against the state. Second, these arrests, mass deportations, and executions were intended to serve as a psychological blow to potentially dangerous enemies of the state.[100] Because Soviet authorities saw ethnic Poles as "bourgeois" and one of the most dangerous national groups, they targeted this group especially.[101] Simultaneously, Soviet authorities capitalized on local anti-Polish sentiments in an attempt to garner support from the non-Polish population.[102] In the almost two-year period of Soviet rule, there were four deportation waves from the Belarusian regions. The first wave came on 10 February 1940 with a victim count of 51,000 just from the BSSR. These included not only Polish military personnel and their families but also assumed-to-be-wealthier Ukrainians and Belarusians. The second deportation period came on 13 April 1940, affecting between 60,667 and 61,092 people of ethnic Polish, Jewish, Ukrainian, and Belarusian background, from the borderland region. This number included about 21,857 Polish officers and 14,7000 Polish soldiers. They were sent to three prisoner-of-war camps in Kozel'sk, Starobel'sk, and Ostashkov. Later in June 1940, the third group, comprising between 75,267 and 80,653 individuals, was also deported. This group included refugees from now German-occupied Poland, who fled eastward at the beginning of the war. The final wave commenced less than a month prior to the German invasion in May–June 1941. This group included between 86,000 and 91,000 individuals and included "counter-revolutionary" people, including those working in positions of civilian and military administration.[103]

There were also several waves of mass arrests from the newly-annexed regions. The first wave of arrests between September and December 1939 included 2489 Belarusians. In this wave, Belarusians were targeted, following higher numbers of victims including Ukrainians, at 3033, and Poles, at 10,557. In the January to May 1941 period, a total of 12,310 individuals were arrested, of which 1022 were Belarusian. In this second wave, Ukrainians composed the highest number of victims at 5554, followed by Poles at 3459, and Jews at 1084. The most prevalent charge issued by the state during these arrests was participation in counter-revolutionary organizations and groups, as alleged kulaks, employers of the former Tsarist regime, and officers. The majority of those arrested received sentences of five years in prison. Some received higher sentences of ten years, while only a handful were exiled internally. In terms of mass arrests, according to Soviet documents, between September 1939 and May 1941, they arrested 43,000 people from the western regions of Belarus, formerly part of Poland.[104]

Far away from Soviet Belarus, Belarusian nationalists watched the new geopolitical situation with intrigue. For them, September 1939 was an important moment and a positive step in the development of the Belarusian nation with the unification of ethnic Belarusian territory, albeit under Soviet control.[105] Many now focused their efforts on developing a stronger working relationship with Germany, especially into 1940, when rumours of an impending German – Soviet War began circulating.[106] One of the most important sites for Belarusian – German cooperation were POW camps run by the Germans that held approximately 20,000 Belarusian soldiers of the Polish Army already in late September 1939.[107] Initially, the Germans hired Akinchyts to infiltrate POW camps and recruit captured Belarusian soldiers.[108] Others also followed. Usevalad Rodz'ka, for example, served in the Polish Army during the interwar period. On 19 September 1939, Rodz'ka was captured by the Germans and was interned at a camp in Ostrzeszów, Poland. He was recruited as a spy and the following year on 20 August 1940 was released and sent to Brzesko, about fifty-four kilometres east of Kraków.[109] One of his earlier missions included spying on members of the Organization for Ukrainian Nationalists in the region.[110] Most German-sponsored Belarusian espionage activity during the early years of the war focused on anti-Soviet efforts and on recruiting Belarusians to participate in covert activity. Many of these Belarusian participants had military experience, had served in the Polish Army, were captured by the Germans, then released and recruited as agents.[111]

The German-occupied parts of Poland soon became the home to various Belarusian committees that drew potential spies and agents together. Various Belarusians initially reached out to German officials with requests to create organizations in the region. Ivan Ermachėnka was one of these individuals. Ermachėnka had been living in Prague during the interwar years and received his medical degree from Charles University. Already in the spring of 1939, he began negotiations with the Germans regarding the position of Belarusians in the case of a future German-Soviet War.[112] Upon his request and that of his acquaintance, Vasil' Zakharka, the Germans allowed for the creation of a Belarusian committee in November 1939.[113] The Germans also sponsored a Belarusian committee in Warsaw in late 1939, with Nikalaĭ Shchors as its chairman.[114] Later in the spring of 1940, a Belarusian Self-Help organization (*Belaruskaia samapomach'*, BSP) was created in Berlin.[115] Other Belarusian groups, approved in Germany, appeared in Łódź, Poznań, Gdańsk, and other cities in occupied Poland.[116]

During meetings at various Belarusian committees, members discussed and debated what the nature of Belarusian-German collaboration should be. One of the most respected Belarusians during the interwar and wartime period was Father Vintsent Hadleŭski, who initially disapproved of any working relationship with Germany. However, over the course of 1939 and into 1940, he began to change his mind about a potential Belarusian – German relationship.

> Belarus finds itself between Germany and Russia… we must find ourselves in a union with someone. Under Polish conditions, we Belarusians could not achieve anything and were not supported. With the Soviet Union, we have formed particular relations. That is why, we have one possible union left – with Germany.

> Germany maintains comfortable relations with Belarusians, because Belarus is on their path to Russia… in this way Germany supports us and proclaims their support for the creation of an "Independent Belarus". We must utilize this window of opportunity, and essentially stand on the path with the Germans with their resources, to fight against the Soviet Union, to give us the right to an independent life.[117]

Other Belarusians came to similar conclusions. "To fight on two fronts: against communist Moscow and the powerful armed force from Berlin," recalled Dz'mitry Kasmovich, "would have been national suicide."[118] Not surprisingly, this reason would be one referred to frequently by collaborators.

Operation Barbarossa, or the German invasion of the Soviet Union in June 1941, was not merely a German military advance on Soviet territory. Rather it also entailed the coordinated and clandestine cooperation between Germans and other anti-Soviet organizations and individuals, over a series of months. In preparation for the invasion, Belarusian-German planning involved organizing covert missions by parachuting agents into Soviet territory or sending spies directly by crossing the border on foot. These operations were intended to gather intelligence on the ground just before Barbarossa. German authorities hoped to get a sense of what the mood of the population was on the ground and what kind of environment they would be entering into. For Belarusian nationalists, these earlier covert operations saw the beginning of Belarusian armed groups and Belarusian cells infiltrating Soviet territory. Usevalad Rodz'ka and Uladzimir Kachan were some of main Belarusians who coordinated these missions.

To organize these clandestine missions, these Belarusian agents worked more closely with German authorities, particularly in the second half of 1940. One German agent, Jurgis Gerulis, was especially critical in these early operations. He served in the German Army during the First World War. In the postwar period, he taught at the University of Leipzig, as head of the Department of Baltic Languages and later as Rector of the University of Königsberg, and Professor at the University of Berlin. Through his academic career he was known as an expert of the Lithuanian language, focusing on dialects, phonetics, and older texts. He joined the National Socialist Party in 1930. In 1939, he enlisted in the German Army and served as an officer. Early on during the war, he likely met with some Belarusian nationalists and discussed the possibility of military cooperation. As a representative of the Abwehr, or German military intelligence, he worked closely with Belarusian, Ukrainians, and Lithuanians in their anti-Soviet covert operations.[119] Just between January and June of 1941, it is estimated that there were approximately 152 German parachuting operations into Soviet territory, involving various national groups.[120] Different German representatives and institutions, such as the Abwehr, held their own training facilities that operated separately. Some individuals were parachuted in through German planes, which frequently crossed into Soviet territory and therefore were less suspicious to Soviet authorities. Other times, agents simply walked across the border.[121]

The Belarusian Committee in Warsaw was one of the hotspots out of which spies were recruited. Individuals here were taken to train just outside of Warsaw and then dispatched across the border. In one case, the leaders of the Belarusian Committee in Warsaw tasked two local men, Kazimierz Abramowicz and Bolesław Rymsza, with finding good dispatch points from which Belarusian agents could cross the border. Just days before the German invasion of the Soviet Union, Abramowicz and Rymsza waited for cars transporting young Belarusians dressed in civilian clothing. Some agents carried guns with them but most decided to leave their weapons in Poland to avoid getting caught by suspicious Soviet authorities. One Belarusian allegedly insinuated to Abramowicz that returning to Poland was not an option, as the Germans would shoot them, suggesting that such recruitment was not necessarily voluntary. After the war, both Abramowicz and Rymsza testified that most of the individuals they sent over the border were immediately caught by the Soviet border patrol.[122]

One of the better documented Belarusian covert operations just prior to Operation Barbarossa involved the First Belarusian Assault Union (*1-y Belaruski shturmovy z'viaz*). In early May 1941, the Germans opened a training facility for about fifty Belarusians in Lamsdorf, a former camp in present-day Łambinowice, in Poland's southwestern region.[123] The mission of the Assault Union, for the Germans, was similar to other operations; to get a sense of geographic areas in Belarus, to gather some initial information on the population, and to survey places that could be dangerous hiding zones for the enemy.[124]

One participant of the Assault Union was Mikhas' Biartsėvich who began his covert activity through his association with the Belarusian Committee in Warsaw. Biartsėvich had previously been a soldier in the Polish Army, was captured by the Germans on 14 September 1939, but managed to run away. He met Uladzimir Kachan – also a veteran of the Polish Army – who would become the leader of the Assault Union.[125] He and Kachan joined the Committee in Warsaw and knew from the beginning that they would be organizing a Belarusian armed unit, with the help of the Gestapo.[126] In preparation for their mission, Biartsėvich recalled traveling with around 30 recruits to Lamsdorf where they were trained for about one month. There they were taught how to shoot, read maps, and how to set up mines.[127] Their training also included courses on Belarusian studies, such as literature and history, and lessons on proper hygiene, taught by members of the Assault Union.[128] One speech by Kachan during the training programme noted: "We find ourselves as representatives of the people that aim for independence. As representatives [...] we must be worldly people. [...] We must carry ourselves highly so that people will respect us."[129] The Assault Union was supposed to compose the nucleus of future Belarusian armed groups, with training focused on both Belarusian education and military preparation to further develop such groups. After the month of training, Biartsėvich was transported to Pruszków, just outside of Warsaw, where the group remained for a week in a facility and were forbidden to leave. The Assault Union was organized into three groups that were dispatched on separate occasions, with agents dressed in Soviet uniforms. His particular group included ten people, whose task was to monitor the infrastructure and transportation situation in Soviet Belarus. After their mission, they were to join and coordinate their activities with German Army Group B, following the planned invasion.[130]

The first dispatch from the Belarusian Assault Union on 16 June 1941 included seven people with a goal to land and disrupt railway lines in the Baranavichi-Stoŭptsy area, in the western part of present-day Belarus.[131] Soviet security services quickly discovered the group and captured two of its agents. They expected that more spies would attempt to infiltrate Soviet Belarus.[132] Indeed, they were correct and on June 20, Soviet security services caught at least seven more Belarusian spies and took them in for questioning.[133] The information extracted from the agents pointed to more espionage operations taking place in the near future.[134] In the last known group to be sent, two groups of twenty agents total were dispatched including Kachan and Biartsėvich. One group allegedly managed to successfully sabotage a railway line west of Minsk. Biartsėvich was captured by Soviet security forces on the second day of his mission and was sent to prison in Belastok. He remained in prison for five days and was then liberated by the Germans during their invasion of the Soviet Union. Biartsėvich would continue to work with Rodz'ka, Kachan, and others during the war.[135] Many members of the Belarusian Assault Union later joined the Belarusian auxiliary police battalions and armed groups during the German occupation of Belarus.[136] Some even complained that the Germans had not properly repaid them for their work and sacrifice. Others expected to be elevated to high positions of power during the Second World War but were disappointed when they were not.[137]

During this period and throughout the interwar years, Soviet security forces kept a watchful eye on any suspicious activity both in Soviet Belarus and in neighbouring areas. Frequent correspondence between the head of the People's Commissariat for Internal Affairs in Belarus (*Narodny kamisaryiat unutranykh spravaŭ, NKUS, or more commonly known as the NKVD)*, Lavrentii Tsanava, and the secretary of the Central Committee of the Communist Party of Belarus (*Kamunistychnaia partyia (bal'shavikoŭ) Belarusi, KP(b)B)*, Panteleimon Ponomarenko, reveal they had some concerns over state security. However, these concerns, surprisingly, did not include fears of German involvement in these anti-Soviet covert operations nor worries of an imminent plan. What concerned them was seeing increased activity among anti-Soviet nationalist groups. In the beginning of 1940, the border armed patrol noted increased "nationalist, counter-revolutionary insurgent" activity. Moreover, on 13 February 1941, the NKVD representative of the border patrol, General-Lieutenant Bogdanov, reported that as of that date there had been eighty-seven instances of border crossings by German planes. One of these planes, in the Aŭgustoŭski region, was shot down because it appeared to be using weapons. Another report from the Central Committee of the KP(b)B reiterates this concern by noting that there has been a buildup of German agents crossing over to the USSR.[138] Even when captured agents admitted to receiving help from German authorities, these confirmations still did not significantly worry Soviet intelligence officers.[139]

The period between 1921 and 1941 reveals increasing efforts to prepare for an impending war that would hopefully eliminate Soviet rule in Belarus. It also shows the development of a new generation of Belarusians who experienced their earlier, formative years in this interwar setting. Having not experienced war themselves and having lived outside of Soviet Belarus, Barys Rahulia, Mikhal Vitushka, Usevalad Rodz'ka, Uladzimir Kachan and many others saw collaboration with the Germans as an opportunity to do what the previous generation had not. This opportunity, however, would come at the extremely high price of destruction and violence.

3
Opportunities and Limitations in German-occupied Belarus

By the summer and fall of 1941, most of the key Belarusians collaborating with the Germans already found themselves in Belarus. Some arrived through covert missions, but most were simply transported to Minsk by the Germans from whichever Belarusian émigré hub they were operating out of in Europe.[1] The debate about whether or not to work with the Germans quickly subsided and another discussion emerged that strongly pushed for this collaboration.[2] Outside of Minsk, Belarusians began to organize in other cities and towns as well. Frantsishak Kushal′ initially worked in the eastern military occupied regions of Mahilieŭ and Smalensk, where he met with Radaslaŭ Astroŭski.[3] In the region of Belastok, a group of Belarusians took charge already at the end of July 1941 initially as part of a Belarusian committee. Those drawn to these Belarusian committees in now German-occupied Belarus came from a wide variety of backgrounds. Teodor Iliashevich, a Belarusian poet who had studied in Wilno, had operated in an underground Komsomol in Poland and later was a school inspector. Ivan Helda had been part of the Belarusian Hramada in Poland and spent some time in prison. Vasil′ Lukashchyk also was imprisoned, but in Bereza Kartutska. Two other members of the Belarusian Committee traveled to Belastok from Czechoslovakia where they were completing their studies.[4] Some came into these positions in need of jobs, whereas at least one member of this group was confident that "After the war, the Germans will recognize Belarusian independence."[5] Some Belarusians, now more than ever, saw collaboration with the Germans as the only way to become more independent – at least more than they had been under Poland or the Soviet Union. Many, however, saw their participation in such groups as a means of surviving and perhaps moving up professionally.

In retrospect and to a significant extent at the time, the idea that the Germans would offer more autonomy seemed unrealistic and even naïve.

Nevertheless, despite these doubts over German promises, the Belarusians in question used their new positions of power to try to garner more opportunities for themselves and for what they saw was the promotion of Belarusian nationalism. This multi-generational group of Belarusians operated based on their experiences prior to the Second World War and were influenced by the terms and realities of the occupation. They used this period as an opportunity to promote Belarusian language, culture, and history. Some also saw this opportunity to exert their own power. The Belarusian committee in Belastok, for example, started out as an initial gathering point for Belarusian nationalists early during the occupation, but it soon began reorganizing the city, disseminating propaganda, conceptualizing cultural and educational agendas, and handling the security and administrative operations in the area.[6] But more importantly, this was a period during which Belarusian nationalists returned to their Homeland and tried to foment patriotism among their supposed constituents, the local population.

The Germans, too, were in many ways returning to Belarusian territory though with completely different goals and under very different conditions. Starkly opposed to the military occupation during the First World War, the Third Reich's plans for the East, and specifically for Belarus, were much more lethal. Though Nazi ideologues at the top may have varied in their approaches toward Belarus, their intended outcomes were equally violent for the territory and those inhabiting it. Rank and file soldiers of the Wehrmacht and German police may have not all been ideologically motivated to participate in the violence against Jews and other locals, yet many were complicit in it. The Einsatzgruppen specifically targeted Jews through anti-partisan operations and targeted raids and plundering of villages. In some regions of Belarus, the Wehrmacht too was complicit in these murders, especially if they were stationed close by.[7]

Belarusians had to navigate their relationships with the new occupiers, who were not the same as those decades earlier. However, it did not mean that Belarusian nationalists had little authority or influence during these years. In fact, they exerted their positions in local and regional spheres, created numerous organizations, and pushed for the creation of Belarusian armed units. Despite German oversight in their cultural, political, and military organizations, Belarusians were not merely puppets but actually had agency. As Belarusian nationalists procured certain administrative and military privileges over other national groups during the occupation, however, these allowances came with their increased participation in violence against locals. Moreover, the setting for this activity takes place during the most tragic period of Belarusian history in the twentieth century – the Holocaust. The activity of these Belarusians is intimately tied to murder and other forms of violence against Jews and other victims.

The motivations for participating in all of these crimes were manifold, as explorations of "ordinary" men have revealed in other cases. Professional advancement, comradery with one's group members, past bonds and linkages from previous years, and monetary or food concessions were all factors. The role that ideology played, specifically when it comes to race and antisemitism, is more difficult to ascertain, but should not be cast aside as a potential motivation as well. Indeed, combatants' motivations for partaking in any armed group often reflected multifaceted reasons that were negotiated depending on time and context.

New Opportunities at the Dawn of Occupation

From 1941 to 1944, the territory of today's Belarus was divided into separate German-occupied spheres; Bezirk Bialystok, Reichskommissariat Ukraine and Reichskommissariat Ostland.[8] The latter was divided further into Generalkommissariats (GK) of Estland, Lettland, Litauen, and Weißruthenien.[9] The Generalkommissariat Weißruthenien included a population between 2.5 and 3 million people, most of whom were concentrated in Minsk. Though the region was officially under civilian administrative control, the Schutzstaffel (SS) exerted its power in the region as well.[10] The eastern regions of today's Belarus remained under direct military administration throughout the entire occupation period, due to the unstable shifting war front.[11] The Belarusians in positions of leadership were mainly located in the Generalkommissariat Weißruthenien, although some did travel to other parts of eastern Belarusian territory.[12]

There were three intertwining and fundamental factors that drove German policy in the occupied territories of Belarus. These included the Germans' overall approach to the East, the responsibilities and roles of competing German agencies, and finally the main actors in charge of these decisions. There were important differences between various German leaders that affected their approaches in governing, and these differences also reveal tensions within the German leadership. Alfred Rosenberg, referred to by some as an "inefficient philosopher",[13] officially dictated administrative policy in the eastern regions but was often opposed by regional and SS authorities, including those close to Hitler. Personal problems involving power struggles at the top, trickled down to issues of jurisdiction, especially between the military, SS, and civilian administration.[14]

Belarus, moreover, differed from other German-occupied territories. The region lacked critical natural resources, such access to water, grain, or oil, that were important for the war effort and that oftentimes dictated other regions' relationships with the Germans. Also, historically, Belarusian lands had never been home to an ethnic German minority, as for

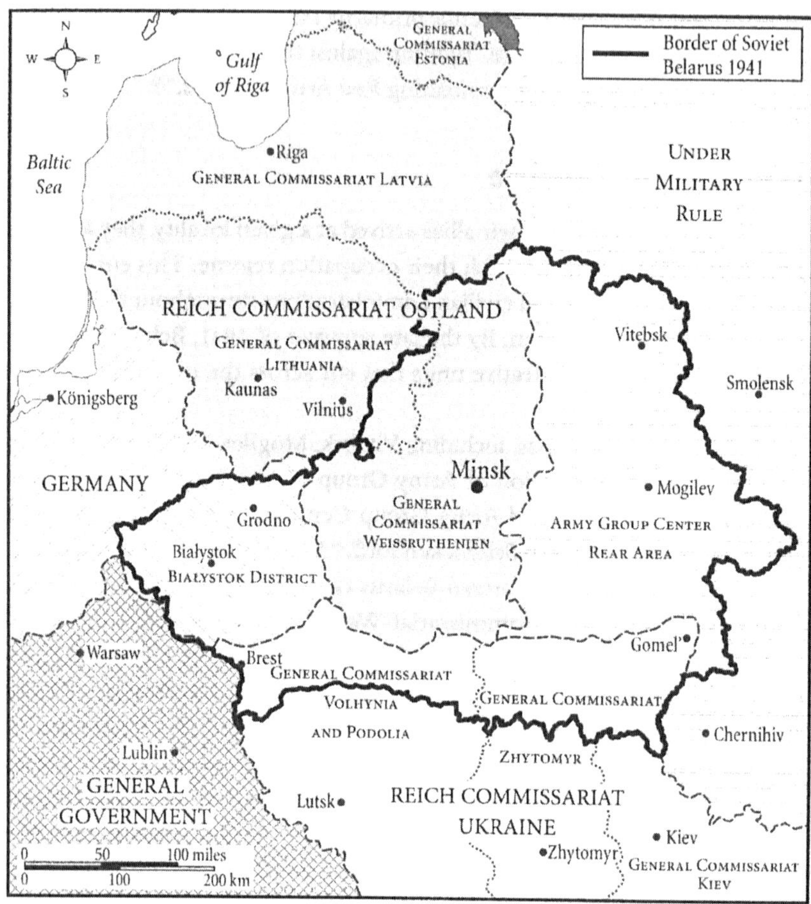

Figure 2: The administrative divisions of the territory of Belarus under German Occupation between June 1941 and July 1944.

Source: Map by Mike Bechthold. By permission of Cornell University Press. From *Ghosts of War: Nazi Occupation and Its Aftermath in Soviet Belarus*, by Franziska Exeler, published by Cornell University Press. Copyright © 2022 by Cornell University. Reprinted by permission of the publisher.

example the Baltic states, Poland, and Ukraine had been. Furthermore, the German experience on Belarusian lands during the First World War planted the idea that Belarusians were the least developed people in Eastern Europe. The Germans, therefore, saw Belarusians as unsuitable for Germanization and the territory open for complete exploitation.[15]

All of these perceptions fueled an especially anti-Slavic sentiment amongst many Germans in occupied Belarus.[16] They envisioned Belarus as a reserve and destination for "undesirable elements" that would become a "wildlife conservation park."[17] One German military report written to the Office of the Reichskommissar Ostland in August 1942 on the "moods of the population in White Russia" noted that,

> The White Ruthenian differs in everything from the Western European... All endeavors, which aim to improve the conditions of life that seem inhumane to a European, are met with incomprehension and rejection... One would think that one was among the most primitive natives.[18]

The report continues on, stating that,

> Minsk leaves a dreary impression... The population is poorly dressed and impoverished. The streets are swarming with abandoned children between the ages of eight and fourteen who, despite the Papyrossi shortage, are smoking, drinking bottom-shelf liquor, and engaging in flourishing barter.[19]

Ultimately, higher ranking German officials envisioned two approaches toward Belarus. One idea advocated making Belarus part of a buffer against Moscow and fostering Belarusian nationalism as an anti-Soviet weapon. The second saw Belarus as a potential dumping ground for people deemed to be "undesirable".[20] Wilhelm Kube, the Gebietskommissar of Belarus, adopted parts of both approaches, wanting to exploit resources and labour as well as develop the area as a buffer.

> We offer the White Russians no parliamentary nonsense and no democratic hypocrisy. We offer them our own destiny: progress, soil, and bread, through labor, discipline, and morals... The White Ruthenians shall become a "nation" only to the extent that they shall be capable of forming a wall against Muscovy and the Eastern steppe.[21]

Despite his candid opinion of Belarus and Belarusians, Wilhelm Kube's rule over occupied parts of Belarus was inconsistent and sometimes conflicting. He protested against the murder of Jews to officials in Berlin, not as a measure of good will but rather because he needed labourers and wanted to avoid production decline and economic chaos.[22] He made proclamations to locals about promising land reforms, but really only to garner support and mobilize individuals to fight Soviet partisans.[23] Some scholarship has been generous to Kube, acknowledging him as a German who supported the development of Belarusian politics, culture, and society.[24] Kube, however, sought to exploit the population to the fullest and ensure every person's participation. Kube favoured Belarusians over other national groups, because he believed them to be the least nationalistically advanced and thus less of a danger to German authorities.[25] Rather, he made concessions as he did not see Belarusian nationalism as a threat but rather something that could be used to offset the stronger Soviet and Polish sentiments.[26] The creation of Belarusian cultural and educational centres under Kube were not goodwill concessions on behalf of the German Gebietskommissar but were intended to benefit the Germans.

Belarusian nationalists, nevertheless, saw the occupation and Kube's measures as a means for development. Starting in September 1941, Belarusians from Vilnius, Warsaw and Berlin arrived in Minsk and in other cities and began putting together organizations, with the Germans' permission. Newspapers that defended Belarusian-German collaboration began circulating, included *Belaruskaia hazeta* (The Belarusian newspaper) and *Holas vioski* (The voice of the village).[27] The articles and pieces published in these and other newspapers were ridden with antisemitic language. Antisemitism was often attached to anti-Soviet and anti-Polish rhetoric, or literally linked together as one label, noting that "the Jewish-Muscovite-Polish bandits still drag on" fighting in Belarus and were impeding efforts to develop the Belarusian nation.[28]

Newspapers also promoted the opening and re-opening of Belarusian organizations intended to "develop" the nation. On 22 October 1941, the Belarusian People's Self-Help was re-created, as a continuation of its predecessor in Berlin before the occupation. It involved the participation of around 80,000 members with the intention to provide welfare services to locals, as well as to organize educational and cultural events for civilians and combatants.[29] The People's Self-Help also coordinated with German authorities for the protection and assistance for local victims of Soviet partisan attacks. Sometimes this help came through food provisions or new living accommodations.[30]

The People's Self-Help's headquarters were located in Minsk, with Ivan Ermachėnka acting as its chairman beginning in October 1941. He was the right person for the job, having essentially done similar work in Prague and Berlin before the war and having lots of contacts within the Belarusian community. Seeing itself as an organization that the Germans needed and relied on, the People's Self-Help presented the Germans with several demands: full independence of Belarus upon defeating the Soviet Union, the creation of a Belarusian government, and the organization of a Belarusian national army. Kube was hoping to groom Ermachėnka into becoming the leader of a future government of

Belarus, of course under German control. Ermachėnka's close relationship with the Germans even got him the nickname "Herr Jawohl Jermachenka", or "Mr. Yes, of course, Ermachėnka".[31]

The creation of Belarusian media outlets and aid organizations was just the beginning of Belarusian-German collaboration during the occupation period. Throughout this time, Belarusians created other cultural, societal, pedagogical, military, and political organizations.[32] A year or so into the occupation period, Kube sanctioned the creation of a "rada doveriia", or council of trustees, consisting of a group of senior Belarusians who would work as his advisors.[33] Later on 21 December 1943, the Belarusian Central Rada (*Belaruskaia tsėntral'naia rada,* BTsR) was created.[34] The establishment of this Belarusian advisory body came with ceremonial celebrations in January 1944, including speeches by some notable individuals followed by theatrical and musical performances.[35]

Of all the tasks and organizations Belarusian nationalists became involved in during the war, none was more important to them than creating a Belarusian national armed force. Very early into German occupation, starting in July 1941, Nikalaĭ Shchors, the former chairman of the Belarusian Committee in Warsaw, began planning and pushing for the creation of a Belarusian Army, backed by the Germans.[36] Initially, the Germans had little desire or need for a Belarusian armed force.[37] This attitude was in part due to the belief that the Germans would sweep through the territory, defeat the Soviet Union in a matter of weeks and, therefore, would not need any additional national units to assist them. During the earlier phases of the war, the Germans felt comfortable and secure both in their administrative and military positions in Belarus. In his own account, Frantsishak Kushal' recalled that during the earlier years of the occupation, the Germans found it comical that Belarusians wanted to create an armed force.[38] However, upon their invasion of the Soviet Union, the Germans encountered some unforeseen challenges. The first major challenge was the capture of millions of Soviet prisoners of war. Some were shot on the spot, but many were kept in POW camps that had to be maintained by additional personnel, for example by local Belarusian guards. The conditions of these camps were abhorrent. Most POWs were left completely exposed to outside conditions, be it the heat or the bitter winter cold. The Germans essentially starved captured soldiers, resulting in the staggering death of around 3.3 million Soviet POWs.

The second challenge the Germans faced were the heavy losses in the winter of 1941 and 1942, due to unforeseen strong resistance by Soviet forces. The loss of Wehrmacht soldiers meant that the Germans had to recruit and rely on other fighters in order to keep up their campaign in the East.[39] The Germans eventually needed and relied on Belarusian personnel in the civilian occupied regions to maintain regional and local order, as German soldiers and resources were prioritized in the eastern military occupied areas. During and after the Soviet victory in Stalingrad in 1942 and into 1943, the Germans became more desperate and gave even more concessions to Belarusians in exchange for their support. These armed groups came to include not only the Belarusian auxiliary police but also the Belarusian Self-Defense Corps (*Belaruski korpus samaakhovy, BKS*), and the Belarusian Home Guard (*Belaruskaia kraiovaia abarona, BKA*).

The first Belarusian armed group to appear during the occupation was the Belarusian auxiliary police, which came to include around 30,000 individuals.[40] In July 1941, Dz'mitry Kasmovich, who had studied in the Belarusian school in Niasvizh, became chief of the Auxiliary Police Department in Minsk.[41] The auxiliary police's primary duties involved maintaining order in the occupied area, monitoring locals, guarding ghettos, keeping track of population numbers, and registering people.[42] Kasmovich himself was responsible for delegating the *Ausweis*, or identification card, to individuals that controlled their movement in and around Minsk.[43] Many policemen were locals from their own towns who volunteered to be in the police. Elizaveta Ainzendorf, a Holocaust survivor, recalled that she knew many people from her town that joined the police, including her former schoolteacher.[44] Local witnesses noted that some individuals eagerly volunteered to be policemen because they had been repressed under the Soviet regime and now sought to harness their energy against the enemy.[45] Some of these volunteers also included children of former "kulaks", as labeled by the Soviet state.[46] Other policemen were former criminals, or even youths who simply were bored and wanted something to do.[47] Though Belarusian leaders wanted these formations to remain Belarusian in ethnic composition, this desire was not always met. In the eastern Belarusian regions, some members of the police battalions were captured non-Belarusian Red Army soldiers. Likewise, in the western part of Belarus, the auxiliary battalions were not strictly Belarusian in ethnic composition; some were Ukrainians, others, Poles. In the Baranavichi district, for example, one fifth of the auxiliary policemen were Polish.[48] The Belarusian leadership repeatedly insisted to the Germans that Poles should be prevented from joining the police units. However, these requests were largely unsuccessful.[49]

In terms of their operation and activity, Belarusians in auxiliary police battalions showed a lack of discipline in performing their duties. Historian Benhard Chiari estimates that more than 70 percent of incoming auxiliary policemen worked in agriculture and lacked military experience.[50]

Furthermore, there were hiccups that affected the relationship between Belarusians and their German superiors, such as language barriers and lack of professionalism on both sides. Some German commanders frequently drank and would physically abuse local non-combatants in order to procure some moonshine, hardly serving as examples to rank-and-file Belarusian policemen.[51] In some cases, the Germans publicly punished and beat up Belarusian policemen because of mistakes they made.[52] There were reports of disorderly conduct, hooliganism, and overall poor behaviour.[53] Kushal′ was especially critical of and embarrassed by the Belarusian auxiliary police and of those in local and regional leadership positions who failed at improving the units. According to his memoir, he arrived in Minsk in mid-September 1941, at the invitation of Tumash, to organize these police battalions. Kushal′ described the head of the Minsk police, Kasmovich, as a decent man with a "spiritual side" but who had no idea about military organizations. When he arrived in Minsk, he was shocked at the state of the recruits who he called a group of undisciplined criminals and drunks.[54]

The Germans believed that the more immediate way of rectifying the poor state of the Belarusian auxiliary police was to bring in non-Belarusian units, such as Estonian, Latvian, Lithuanian, and Ukrainian ones, into Belarus in both Generalbezirk Weißruthenian and the eastern military occupied region.[55] Heinrich Himmler believed that using national police battalions outside of their respective home territory would be more efficient, as foreign armed units would be less likely to sympathize with the local population. German authorities also perceived Belarusian police battalions to be structurally weaker, especially when compared to their Baltic or Ukrainian equivalents.[56] Moreover, the Germans stressed that the Belarusian units were not anti-Jewish enough. One report blames Soviet education as it instilled the idea that Jews were equal to other humans.[57] For both structural and perceived ideological reasons, German authorities brought in numerous non-Belarusian battalions into occupied Belarus. Some of which would gain notoriety for their violence. The 12th battalion of the Lithuanian auxiliary police, together with the Germans, was active in Minsk, Slutsk, Niasvizh, and Kletz already by October 1941, where it murdered Jews and Roma. In Rudzensk, just southeast of Minsk, this battalion also murdered Soviet prisoners of war.[58] In March 1942, the Germans sent another notorious group, the Schutzmannschaften Battalion 201 led by Ukrainian Roman Shukhevych, around Baroŭka in northern Belarus. This battalion, composed of many future fighters in the Ukrainian Insurgent Army, replaced a Latvian Schutzmannschaft battalion that operated in the area previously.[59]

Kushal′, Kasmovich, and other Belarusian nationalists, however, were adamant in creating some form of Belarusian armed force that would prove to be professional and redeem the image of the police. This plan came with the creation of the Belarusian Self-Defense Corps on 29 June 1942, approved by the Germans.[60] Upon its creation, the Belarusian leadership eagerly announced they had the honour to present the first Belarusian formation that had a clear military programme.[61] Seven Belarusians served at the head command of the Self-Defense in Minsk, including Kushal′, as well as former communist during the interwar years, Iulian Sakovich. From the Germans' perspective, the Belarusian Self-Defense Corps was not a generous concession to the Belarusians but an armed force focused on tackling the fight against Soviet partisans. Moreover, the deployment and use of the Self-Defense Corps at any time had to be approved by German police authorities.[62]

To ensure the creation of a more organized and professional armed group than the Belarusian auxiliary police, Belarusian leaders mapped out a more strategic path for the Self-Defense Corps. They decided that Belarusians would organize and recruit suitable candidates, while the Germans would deal with the training, housing, and arming of soldiers.[63] By 9 July 1942, 8,000 people had registered for the Self-Defense Corps and several months after the announcement of its creation, this number rose to 15,000 individuals organized into 20 battalions.[64] Officers up to the age of 50 and junior officers up to the age of 40 were accepted, whereas rank-and-file soldiers born between 1916 and 1923 were welcomed.[65] Initially, both the Belarusian and German leadership agreed that only ethnic Belarusians would be allowed into the fighting units, all on a voluntary basis. A month later, however, the "voluntary" caveat was complemented with an announcement that if no one came forward to join, the area would be combed for "volunteers". Oftentimes, authorities would threaten people with land requisition or family deportation to Germany for forced labour.[66] Similarly as with the "volunteering" method of recruitment, Belarusians eventually had to concede to the German decision of accepting non-Belarusians into the Self-Defense Corps.[67] This factor frustrated and antagonized Belarusian leaders who sought to homogenize their armed groups.

To prepare and train new recruits three officers' schools were organized. The first one, a month-long training camp, was established in Minsk under the leadership of Mikhail Puhachoŭ. Ninety-seven officers graduated from this first training programme on 19 August 1942 and were re-assigned to various regions of occupied Belarus.[68] The second officers' school was completed on 30 September 1942, with seventy-three graduates, and the third, on 14 November of that same year, trained twenty-eight officers. The two other schools also sent their newly trained officers to similar locations, in order to serve as the regional representatives of the Self-Defense and train other soldiers stationed outside of Minsk.[69] The graduating officers were strategically placed in particular cities and towns in occupied Belarus. Belarusian leaders hoped that if local people knew those leading the Self-Defense Corps, they would be more likely to volunteer as soldiers. Barys Rahulia, for example, had experience serving in the Polish Army before the war and was immediately put in charge of the Self-Defense Corps in the Navahrudak region, where he was originally from. Uladzimer Kachan, who also served in the Polish Army and then led the First Belarusian Assault Union, was stationed in Hlybokae, a city close to the village where he grew up in.[70] Thus, the organization of the Self-Defense Corps initiated a system of placement of Belarusian representatives to specific cities and areas that would continue with the development of other Belarusian armed groups during the war. Furthermore, many of these connections made between Belarusian leaders and new recruits from local areas continued well after the war ended.

The tasks of these units would include fighting Soviet partisans and members of the Polish Home Army, as well as collaborating with the Germans in the repression and murder of Jews and other locals.[71] Although several Belarusians, including Ermachënka and Kushal′, held high positions in the Self-Defense, it was ultimately the Germans who mainly controlled and utilized the organization as a network of anti-partisan divisions.[72] The Germans noted that because they had "saved" the Belarusian people from Soviet rule, it was now time for "the peasants to unite, fight the partisans, and destroy them."[73] Of course, these anti-partisan operations did not solely target partisans, but also those with real or alleged ties to them, leading to the killing of many more non-combatants.

Problems quickly arose and persisted during the Self-Defense's one year existence. Though Belarusians were technically in charge of placing their soldiers in certain areas and units, the Germans many times removed fighters from their assigned posts and sent them to fight in other battalions or even to work as forced labourers elsewhere. Though training was intended to better discipline the combatants, the conditions and provisions offered to soldiers were seriously underwhelming. Many Self-Defense Corps soldiers were promised extra food rations for them and their families but failed to receive any.[74] Furthermore, most soldiers were not well armed, nor did they have proper uniforms. Acquiring sufficient weapons for soldiers proved to be a challenge, and obviously, a major inhibitor to successfully fending off partisans. In the Slonim region, for example, there were around 900 soldiers in the Self-Defense, out of which only 340 were armed.[75] In other cases, as with the Rudzianski unit, soldiers even purchased weapons from German soldiers.[76] One local from the Naliboki Forest recalls seeing a Belarusian Self-Defense unit roaming around through the villages, out of which only a few were armed with leftover Polish rifles or with discarded German weapons.[77]

These challenges were not only supply issues, but they also revealed a large disconnect and poor communication between the German and Belarusian leadership. The Germans consistently ignored requests to use Belarusian commanders and refused to grant promotions for qualified Belarusian soldiers. For example, one Belarusian who was successful in managing the 48th battalion was Iazep Dakinevich. Despite his contribution to the organization and effective mobilization of nearly five thousand individuals into the battalion, he was never given the official commander status. Later, the Germans transferred him out and the battalion deteriorated.[78] As the months went by, Belarusian leaders also sent repeated requests to the SS and head of German police asking for more weapons and provisions. German authorities procrastinated in their delivery.[79] Whereas Kube wanted to provide more weapons to Belarusian fighters, Himmler refused to arm Belarusian soldiers as they could be used against the Germans themselves.[80] Because of these poor conditions and lack of necessary provisions, many soldiers stopped showing up for duty and deserted.[81] Holocaust survivor Jack Shepsman recalled that a Belarusian policemen in the Navahrudak ghetto even clandestinely supplied the resistance with weapons.[82] Sometimes entire Belarusian units would desert and join other fighting groups, such as Polish underground cells.[83] Others joined Soviet partisans.[84] One of the Soviet methods used in recruiting Belarusian soldiers was borrowed directly from the Germans. They lulled Belarusians into their ranks by promising to recognize and promote the Belarusian nation. A 1942 report from the Soviet Belarusian Partisan Headquarters stated:

> We have to show the Belarusians that we are ready to accept them as equals [...] We must awaken national feeling and patriotism amongst the Belarusian people, as this will help our victory. After the victorious war, the Belarusians will not pose a danger to us, as we will be strong enough to deal with them.[85]

Eventually, the Belarusian leadership was unable to successfully harness the Self-Defense and the Germans took over full control. Belarusian regional leaders of units were removed and replaced with German policemen stationed there. By April 1943, the Germans completely disbanded the Belarusian Self-Defense Corps. Some soldiers were sent into the local police, others tasked with protecting railroads, and some were sent to Germany as forced labourers.

Though the Belarusian Self-Defense Corps lasted a mere year, its existence was important for several reasons. First, it prompted the beginning of training programmes for Belarusian soldiers which would help in the long run. Kushal′ recalled that many of those serving in the auxiliary police attended training courses, which improved the quality of the police. Another legacy of the Self-Defense Corps was the network foundation it set up through its Belarusian representation in various regions and cities of occupied Belarus. This network allowed for Belarusians to operate locally or regionally and maintain and build connections with local Belarusian fighters, while also staying in touch with other representatives of armed groups in different areas. For Kushal′, Kasmovich, and Sakovich, being in Minsk ensured proximity to the ears of German authorities, but Rahulia, Kachan, and Rodz′ka's positions regionally allowed for them to operate without the immediate oversight of the Germans. It also allowed the latter to develop relations with the younger generations of Belarusian soldiers.

One example of the success of the network placement and recruitment system was Barys Rahulia's armed group in Navahrudak, an area that witnessed some of the most intense partisan activity and fighting. Because of his previous work with the Self-Defense Corps and his likeability among soldiers, Rahulia was granted permission from German authorities to organize the 68th Belarusian Infantry Schuma-Battalion, better known as Rahulia's Navahrudak Eskadron in November 1943.[86] The group operated independently from the police and SS, was comprised of 180 men, and sought to garner support from the Belarusian youth.[87] Kanstantyn Miarliak, who would later be recruited by the Central Intelligence Agency (CIA) in the postwar period, was a member of this squadron and was trained by Rahulia.[88] Miarliak asserted that another incentive to create the Navahrudak Eskadron was to attract as many youths as possible into the armed group and prevent them from being sent to Germany as forced labourers. The group was trained from November 1943 to March 1944 and actively participated in anti-partisan operations. The notoriety of the group was additionally validated by a member of the Polish Home Army, who recalled that Navahrudak was one of the strongest armed, Belarusian-controlled areas.[89]

In terms of the broader experience during the occupation and war, the creation and presence of Belarusian armed groups was especially important. German forces could not feasibly be physically present in all parts of occupied Belarus and, therefore, relied heavily on their collaborators. Local civilians, therefore, felt the presence of Belarusian armed groups much more strongly in the countryside and in small towns, where Germans only passed through momentarily.[90] It was Belarusian soldiers, familiar with their local towns and their neighbours, who identified Jews to the German occupiers.[91] It was also Belarusian soldiers, among others, who rounded up Jews and other victims, moved them to local ghettos or sent them away to be murdered.[92] Holocaust survivor Noakh Mel'nik recalled that it was more difficult to fool the Belarusian police than it was the Germans.[93] Another survivor held prisoner in a forced labour camp, in the town Koldychava, noted that Belarusian female guards were "worse than the men."[94] This intimacy and knowledge of their neighbours, however, also allowed some Belarusian soldiers to warn, hide, or save victims.[95]

Local Ethnic and National Tensions

Throughout the early decades of the twentieth century, German, Polish, and Soviet rule had a tremendous effect on individuals at the local level. The various changeovers of power together with the agrarian and nationality policies of varying states meant that different national groups were privileged or repressed over others. During the German occupation, the local population was further polarized affecting the realities of their everyday lives, both related and unrelated to collaboration.[96] Similarly to preceding Polish and Soviet rule over Belarusian territory, the Germans' agrarian and nationality policies would significantly dictate experiences for locals. However, locals themselves were also responsible for tensions and discord, contributing to a multi-factorial and layered web of conflict.

It was not until February 1942, nearly eight months after the Germans swept through Belarus, that officials in Berlin agreed on an agrarian policy.[97] Proponents of decentralizing the Soviet kolkhoz system argued that allowing independent farming would garner more support from peasants who, during Soviet rule, strongly rebelled against it. This kind of support would be instrumental in the long run and foster good relations between locals and the occupying forces. Opponents of this approach, however, saw a more favourable treatment of locals as going against their colonization vision for the occupied eastern territories. They also claimed that peasants, particularly those from eastern Belarus, would have a difficult time readjusting to independent farming, since they were longer conditioned in the collective farming system. In the end, those in favour of keeping the status quo won and simply renamed kolkhozes as agrarian "communal economies."[98] The lack of changes in the agrarian policy frustrated locals and would foment resentment throughout the occupation period. For Belarusian nationalists, the lack of reform was another lost incentive that could have been used to galvanize the population into their armed groups and anti-Soviet efforts.

German nationality policies also affected local conditions and impacted Belarusian relations with other national groups. Prior to Operation Barbarossa, the Germans were divided in their views regarding the nationality question. Some saw the entire eastern area as just one block to be organized into smaller, more manageable colonies. Others, such as Alfred Rosenberg, suggested separating ethnic Russians from other national groups to create a buffer.[99] Ultimately, one of the biggest fears was the development of any national group that would mobilize large parts of the population against occupying German forces. With the case of Belarus, however, the low level of national self-awareness, especially in comparison to neighbouring national groups, led Germany policy makers to opt for the promotion of "Belarusian-ness" while curbing other nationalities.[100]

Though on paper this plan parallels the German approach during the First World War, the processes of national promotion and demotion in the Second World War were much more violent. It essentially involved pitting various nationality groups, including Poles, Russians, and Belarusians, against each other, in order to prevent any one of them from becoming too strong. Belarusian nationalists welcomed this process, as it promoted Belarusian culture, education, and language while repressing the very same things in Polish and Russian.[101] The process of bolstering Belarusian nationalism while limiting others further antagonized existing ethnic and national tensions at the local level. For some Belarusians having lived in the western regions that were previously part of Poland, resentment against Poles persisted. The situation in eastern Belarus was different, where the population had endured Soviet rule longer and without interruption. Divisions and internal conflicts between people during the war were really a culmination of tensions that existed for many years and were further antagonized starting in the summer of 1941.

To proceed with this process of "equalization", Belarusians were placed in regional and local positions of power. Though the Germans may have ruled from Berlin, or even from Minsk, outside these centres of power it was Belarusians who could largely dictate what the local wartime experience would be. For many inhabitants, the realities of the German occupation were less directly affected by the German forces but more by local individuals who were in power directly there. Far from being merely cogs of the Germans, Belarusians had significant agency and exerted this power over other Belarusian and non-Belarusian locals. Most local and regional Belarusian leaders were placed in positions of power in the western occupied regions that had been previously in Poland and run by ethnic Poles. This change, albeit not uniform, largely flipped the pre-existing power dynamic and contributed to one of the most contentious and violent ethno-national relationships during the German occupation – that between Belarusians and Poles.

Belarusian-Polish tensions were in part fueled by the Germans themselves. Believing that Polish nationalism was the most dangerous in the area, the Germans initially banned Polish education and pedagogy in the occupied territory. One Polish witness recalled that while Belarusian, Lithuanian, and even Russian schools were being built, Polish ones ceased to exist.[102] The Germans also gave Belarusians higher positions of power in administrative posts over Poles who had previously been in these positions.[103] Belarusians, however, were largely inexperienced in administrative matters, having largely never been in such positions before. Poles, on the other hand, had dominated as higher-ups in all sectors of interwar society and many more Poles knew the German language than Belarusians did. Because of these reasons, some administrative and bureaucratic positions were re-assigned to Poles, frustrating many Belarusians.[104] Some sent reports to the Germans complaining that Poles continued to retain some positions of power in the police and local governing committees.[105] The Germans, however, were not the only drivers of Belarusian-Polish tensions. Local rivalries and competition persisted, especially for material concessions. A witness account from the spring of 1942 in Zhirmuny recalled how local Belarusian police controlled rations and registration records in the area, often denying Poles their share.[106] Others noted that Belarusian peasants, working in agriculture during the day, were using their horse carts for bandit activity in the evening, mainly to steal from their Polish neighbours.[107] One man recalled a group of Belarusian youngsters plundering his house, while he and his family were forced to lie face downwards.[108]

The actions by some of these Belarusians were sometimes much more violent and devastating than those perpetrated by the Germans. The *Polenaktion* was one manifestation of this tension, which involved repressing, deporting, and executing Poles. As part of the *Polenaktion,* Belarusians denounced Poles, calling them "Sikorski's agents".[109] Other times, regional Belarusian officials were tasked with selecting people to be sent to Germany as forced labourers and chose to only send ethnic Poles. On 16 November 1942, for example, Ermachėnka himself gave the order to the Belarusian regional representatives to put together a list of such "volunteers". The announcement specified that these were to include individuals of Polish nationality who did not contribute to the development of Belarusian nationalism.[110] Another Belarusian later admitted that as part of Ermachėnka's order, he and others also submitted the names of

Polish intelligentsia to the German Police. These actions resulted in the deaths of dozens of people.[111] In another instance on 13 March 1943, an operation against "undesirable elements" by the Belarusian Self-Defense Corps resulted in the massacre of twelve Poles.[112] Even Polish clergymen sent reports to the Vatican reporting on the gravity of the situation. One report noted that:

> "the [Catholic] church has become the battleground for Belarusian nationalists supported by the Germans against the Polish element. The vast majority of Polish priests were murdered by the Germans as a result of Belarusian denunciations. In many districts of the Navahrudak province, there was barely a Polish priest left."[113]

These measures were often met with repercussions against Belarusians living as neighbours next to the victims' families.

The biggest site of Belarusian-Polish contention was the city of Lida and the surrounding area, located west of Minsk.[114] The region was overwhelmingly inhabited by ethnic Poles and was especially notorious for the strong presence of members of the Polish Home Army there – who were fighting the Germans and Soviet partisan groups – in addition to members of the right-wing National Armed Forces (Narodowe Siły Zbrojne).[115] Just in the city of Lida itself, there were six Polish Home Army companies actively fighting.[116] It was the Poles who knew the area well and could navigate the thick forests and swamps, whereas the Germans were typically afraid to go in and avoided them whenever possible.[117] Because of the strong Polish armed presence and a desire by Belarusian nationalists to better control the area, the violence perpetrated by both groups in Lida was especially intense. In the summer of 1942, the Belarusian auxiliary police arrested approximately three hundred Poles on random charges, of which fifty received the death penalty. Similar arrests and executions continued until at least the fall of 1943.[118] In retaliation, members of the Polish Home Army targeted their attacks on Belarusian representatives and commanders who passed through the area. For example, in June 1943, Iulian Sakovich was killed in broad daylight in an ambush near the town of Vasilishki, some 30 km from Lida.[119] The murder of Sakovich finally prompted Belarusian armed groups to refrain from fighting in the area or from sending Belarusians soldiers there. Kushal′ himself recalled stopping in Lida during his tour around occupied Belarus to try to attract soldiers into armed groups. During his stop in Lida, Kushal′ asked a group of policemen to raise their hands if they were Belarusian. He noted that only 20 percent of the group did so, and that the group was largely dominated by ethnic Poles. To avoid more tension, Kushal′ toned down his Belarusian motivational speech and eventually left the city.[120]

Despite deep tensions between Poles and Belarusians, some points of cooperation did exist especially when it pertained to mutual survival. In his recollections of his time in the Polish Home Army, Stanisław Sędziak stressed that discord at the upper level did not necessarily trickle down to all locals.[121] He recalled having good relations even with members of the Belarusian auxiliary police, who often gave the Home Army fighters safe passage in exchange for things. "Of this kind of police, we could not complain", he noted.[122] Another account of a Home Army fighter noted that in the areas where he was active, around the Naliboki Forest region 73 km west of Minsk, the Polish fighters maintained good relations with the Belarusian police. He recalled an occasion in Rakaŭ, after a heavy Soviet raid, when the Belarusian police offered the Home Army fighters two cases of ammunition, which allowed them to survive.[123] In another situation, the same individual claimed that the Belarusian police convinced the Germans to uphold a ceasefire with the Poles.[124] Good relations also stemmed from shared interests. Medical staff from different national backgrounds including Poles, Russians, and Belarusians worked together.[125] Also, after deserting from their respective units, Belarusians were sometimes accepted into Polish groups, albeit with some suspicion.[126]

For some Belarusians who had lived in the territories that were formerly part of Poland, their attitudes and actions toward Poles were largely driven by their early experiences. Once they acquired power as commanders of military units, bureaucrats, and administrators, some Belarusians abused their positions more than others. Though the framework of the occupation certainly put them in these positions of relative power, the Belarusians in question also exerted control without German influence. They selected who could be rounded up and sent as forced labourers, they distributed ration cards and travel permits, and affected other aspects of people's everyday lives. Moreover, these conflicts at the local level hardly reflected well on Belarusian nationalists who were trying to garner support and respect.

Violence, Mass Murder, and Anti-Partisan Operations

The systematic killing of Jews in Belarus began a few months after the German invasion, in October and November of 1941. The Einsatzgruppen B increased its killing of Jews in the eastern regions of Belarus under direct military rule. These mobile killing units rounded up and shot Jews in the regions of Babruĭsk, Homel′, Mahilieŭ, Vorsha, Polatsk, and Vitsebsk. The systematic mass murder of Jews and others in Generalbezirk Weißruthenien entailed the collaboration of various national auxiliary police battalions, including Belarusian ones. Local Belarusians who joined the auxiliary police knew their neighbours and could identify to the Germans who was Jewish.[127] In Niasvizh, on 29 October 1941, German forces together with the Lithuanian and Belarusian auxiliary police battalions arrived. They selected Jews who were skilled workers and separated them from the rest. The Belarusian auxiliary police took the skilled workers and guarded them in a school. The rest of the 4000 Jews were taken to the outskirts of the Niasvizh castle where they were shot by the Germans and Lithuanian auxiliary policemen. The local Belarusian auxiliary police then moved the surviving Jews from the school and into the ghetto, which they guarded. In other cases of mass murder, however, members of the Belarusian auxiliary police were directly involved such as in Mir, Turets, and Yeremichi in November 1941. Later outside of Stoŭbtsy, local witnesses testified that it was Belarusian policemen who shot Jews after they were forced to strip their clothes and lay face down in pits.[128]

From the early onset of the occupation period, Belarusians were also involved in the ghettoization process that occurred predominantly in the summer and fall of 1941. The formation of ghettos in Belarus varied from city to town. Most of the time, the Germans selected a specific area to guard with barbed wire and fences. Sometimes ghettos were established immediately upon the arrival of German authorities, whereas other times it took several months. Some ghettos were open, allowing for people to move more easily in and out of the ghetto, whereas others were sealed. The establishment and maintenance of ghettos relied heavily on members of the Belarusian auxiliary police. Testimonies from Holocaust survivors reveal that Belarusian policemen in the ghettos oftentimes beat people up or even killed Jews, frequently visited homes to look for any valuables, but could also be bribed in exchange for better treatment or even transport out of the ghetto. Eduard Fridman recalled that in the Minsk ghetto, members of the Belarusian police were young, came from poor families, and were often intoxicated. His brother was on one occasion beaten up by three Belarusian police officers and thrown in an outhouse, while the latter three continued to drink and laugh.[129] Other Jewish witnesses in the Minsk ghetto reiterate similar observations, adding that policemen often stole from locals and were sometimes even more cruel than the Germans themselves.[130] However, others survivors recall more benevolent treatment, noting Belarusian policemen warned them when a roundup was to happen and on occasion would let people go.[131] Belarusian city and town mayors were tasked with organizing both the creation and the eventual dismantling of ghettos. Emmanuel Iasiuk became the mayor of Kletsk and Stanislaŭ Stankevich the mayor of Borisaŭ.[132] The young man who looked up to Kushal′ and joined him as a Belarusian activist, Vitaŭt Tumash, served as mayor of Belarus's capital and co-signed the order for the establishment of the Minsk ghetto.[133] Tumash survived the war and escaped west, later moving to the United States.[134]

Starting in 1942, a second wave of mass murder began, targeting Jews in ghettos. In March 1942, the Germans and collaborating auxiliary policemen transported Jews out of the ghetto in Baranovichi, just southwest of Minsk, and murdered them.[135] More waves of violence followed in late spring and summer of 1942, with the deportation or murder of Jews living in ghettos in Braslaŭ, Disna, Druya, Daŭhinava, Hlybokae, Kryvichi, Miory, Niasvizh, Slonim, Valozhin, Vialeĭka, and many other cities. Belarusian policemen were tasked with securing the premises and ensuring there were no escapees. Following the murder of Jews in the ghetto, the local Belarusian police continued to look for Jews in hiding and were expected to kill any they found. This second wave of mass murder continued until the end of 1942, when smaller towns and villages became the targets of these attacks. In exchange for their participation, the Germans sometimes allowed Belarusian policemen to move into former Jewish homes or seize any possessions.[136] One Holocaust survivor recalled that in Slutsk, the children of Belarusian policemen lived just outside of the ghetto in the best houses and even had dogs and bikes to play with.[137]

What would also link Belarusian nationalists through continually violent ways was their participation in anti-partisan operations. Soviet partisans, many of whom identified as Belarusian, were fairly successful in their fight against German and collaborationist forces, particularly after this resistance was centralized and formally supported by the Soviet state. This Soviet partisan movement served as the largest form of resistance during the Second World War, involving approximately half a million people. Indeed, on the broader European scale, partisan activity was the strongest in Belarus and in what was Yugoslavia.[138]

The strength of the Soviet partisan movement in Belarus picked up in 1942 and proved to be too much for the Germans to handle singlehandedly. What began as approximately 56,700 Soviet partisans in the territory of Belarus at the beginning of 1943 swelled to 153,500 by December of that year, according to the Soviet Belarusian Partisan Headquarters.[139] Initially, Soviet authorities were hesitant to support and use partisans for fears that they would turn against the state.[140] However, as more German soldiers from behind the front were sent to engage directly with the Red Army, they left behind poorly protected transportation and communication lines, now exposed to the partisans.[141] Soviet authorities saw this as a window of opportunity and began to provide material support for partisans, whose activity would dramatically shape the course of the war in Belarus.[142]

The German reference to "anti-partisan operations", however, meant more than just preventing the spread of Soviet partisan activity. Anti-partisan operations became euphemisms for targeted attacks against Jews and entire villages. Already in the fall of 1941, German officials were emphasizing the direct link between Jews and Soviet partisans: all Jews were Soviet sympathizers, and Soviet sympathizers were partisans. German officials played upon this connection to justify their military goals and their genocidal ones. Furthermore, masking the murder of Jews as anti-partisan operations made the issue a security and military one, which subsequently entailed the participation of the Wehrmacht.[143] Between 24 and 26 September 1941, a conference and training session was organized in the eastern Belarusian city of Mahilieŭ. Most of the participants came from the Wehrmacht but also in attendance were members of the Einsatzgruppe B. General Max von Schenckendorff, the commander of the Army Group Rear Area from March 1941 until July 1943, invited the conference's participants, many of whom already had records of mass murder. Though comprehensive details about the conference's minutes are not available, there is evidence to suggest that the organizers and presenters stressed the direct link between Jews and Soviet partisans. Therefore, the responsibility of all parties, including the Wehrmacht, was to handle anti-partisan operations. The most damning evidence, as historian Waitman Beorn notes, was the round up and murder of all Jews living in the town of Krucha, committed by the Wehrmacht. Some of those responsible for the massacre had attended the Mahilieŭ Conference nearly two weeks earlier.[144]

Over the next year, more discussions took place as to how to better address Soviet partisan activity. In the spring of 1942, German officials began to rethink their approach in their fight against the partisans. On 6 June 1942, a meeting between notable Nazi German authorities – including Heinrich Himmler, Max von Schenckendorff, and Carl Zenner – took place.[145] One of the biggest obstacles in dealing with the partisans was the density and German unfamiliarity with local forests and terrain. Good portions of Belarusian territory occupied by the Germans included the Belavezhskaia and Naliboki woodlands, in addition to parts of the Prypiatskiia Marshes – the largest wetland in continental Europe.[146] Some suggested clearing and draining some of these difficult areas, which would allow for increased mobility. One German official even suggested the complete deforestation of areas "contaminated by partisans".[147] However, any plans to significantly shape or alter the terrain turned out to be very unrealistic.[148] As thick forests and marshes would continue to be a problem for the Germans, it was part of the reason why Soviet partisans and members of the Polish Home Army operated successfully.

The only realistic solution in dealing with local terrain was to use Belarusian collaborating fighters who knew the land better than the Germans. Schenckendorff insisted that effective measures against Soviet partisans could only occur with the use of local collaborators.[149] Belarusian battalions, in addition to those from neighbouring nations, participated in the mass murder of Jews and other locals through anti-partisan operations.[150] Just in Minsk for example, those active in security forces in 1943 included 1,100 Belarusians and only 150 Germans.[151] In other parts of the occupied area, Belarusians were active in battalions and armed groups that killed Jews and other locals and that also devasted villages and towns. One example was a coordinated operation of the 3rd regiment of 91st police battalion and the 3rd regiment of the 13th police battalion in the forests of Ruzhany – an operation that resulted in the death of 36 people.[152] Another account from a Polish Home Army soldier discusses the heavy anti-partisan two-week campaign in the Naliboki Forest in July 1943, consisting of five German SS divisions in addition to units of Ukrainians, Lithuanians, Latvians, and Belarusians. This operation resulted in 250 casualties of the Polish Home Army battalion; some were killed by bullets, and some were drowned in the swamps. In addition, the collaborating armed groups captured 100 civilians and sent around 25,000 people for forced labour work to Germany.[153]

One armed group, the 13th Belarusian Battalion, had a particularly notorious reputation when it came to anti-partisan operations. Officially co-organized by Kushal′ and Sakovich, along with the Germans in December 1942, it was intended to be a Belarusian fighting force specifically for the purpose of combatting partisans.[154] Kushal′ coordinated the mobilization of soldiers with Ermachėnka and brought in former fighters of the Self-Defense Corps into the 13th battalion. The composition of the soldiers was not uniformly Belarusian and, like in other armed groups, those involved had often served in the Polish, Tsarist, or Red Army.[155] In his memoir, Kushal′ insists on the voluntary nature of mobilization into the battalion, yet other accounts counter this claim.[156] Upon its inception, the battalion was commemorated with much fanfare in Minsk, and its fallen soldiers memorialized with all the honours by Belarusians and Germans.[157] When compared to some other Belarusian armed groups, the 13th Battalion was more effective, organized and, according to Kushal′, even more popular among Belarusians. Its co-organization by the Germans and Belarusians at times caused problems between the two.

Kushal′ frequently protested the Germans' decision to replace Belarusian commanders of certain companies in the 13th Battalion. On occasions when Kushal′ refused to remove people from command positions, the Germans would simply send those commanders away to Germany.[158]

The 13th Belarusian battalion actively participated in anti-partisan operations and the destruction of ghettos, particularly in the areas of Hlybokae and Vialeĭka located roughly northwest of Minsk. Part of its notoriety came during *Operation Cottbus,* an anti-partisan campaign carried out between May and June of 1943 in the Vitsebsk region located in the northern region of Belarus. Though officially intended to target partisans, this operation became more of a complete demolition mission. From the supposedly 4500 dead Soviet partisans, only 492 rifles were found, suggesting there was a high volume of civilian casualties.[159] The same can be seen the other way around, during Soviet partisan attacks. Between April and November 1942, the Slonim region suffered 1024 casualties at the hands of Soviet partisans, of which only 20 percent were members of the German or Belarusian armed groups.[160]

In exchange for their participation in anti-partisan operations, the Germans made promises to bolster support for Belarusian nationalism.[161] Those fighting in armed groups were also promised better food provisions and job opportunities for their family members. The Germans also invited higher-ranking Belarusians, such as Kushal′ and others, to propose plans and ways to deal with the partisans. Discussions between the Germans and Belarusians, however, revealed points of contention rather than agreement. Belarusian leaders did not fully agree with the German method of attacking towns and civilians. Over the months during which they organized and participated in anti-partisan operations, Belarusian nationalists stressed the negative impact this violence had on their relations with locals and especially wanted to eliminate repressive measures against non-combatants.[162] Indeed, the biggest victims of these operations and retaliations were the locals themselves.[163] Out of the 1.7 million people killed during the occupation period, 345,000 stemmed from anti-partisan operations.[164] The collective anti-partisan struggle fostered a cyclical progression of violence and killing. When Germans and Belarusians would participate in anti-partisan operations, Soviet partisans would retaliate and vice versa. Rather, Belarusians suggested monitoring residents and maintaining updated censuses of local towns. Keeping a close track of local residents, they argued, would make it easier to identify roaming partisans trying to pass as locals.[165] To do this, the Belarusians recommended creating more Belarusian formations under the German SD in each region and city and even a Belarusian secret police that would be able to track and monitor local residents and potential partisans. They also proposed disseminating more anti-Soviet propaganda among the locals.[166] Ultimately, neither the German nor Belarusian approach would prove successful. Despite repeated plans to tackle Soviet partisans offensively, as the war progressed the Germans and Belarusians found themselves largely on the defensive and limited in their control just to the Minsk region. In historian Czesław Madajczyk's words, "Minsk was a German fortress in a partisan country."[167]

Belarusian armed groups, whether it be the auxiliary police, the Self-Defense Corps, or more specialized battalions such as Barys Rahulia's Navahrudak group and the 13th Battalion were involved in this killing, many times masked through anti-partisan campaigns. Higher-ranking Belarusians led these armed formations, and they recruited younger Belarusians into these groups. Ianka Filistovich, for example, was merely a teenager when he served in the 13th Battalion in Vialeĭka in the fall of 1943. His life before this point is not well known, nor is the context for his either forced or voluntary mobilization into the battalion. In the postwar period, he operated in covert operations sponsored by Belarusians and US intelligence services. Much of his experience of the terrain and fighting in Belarus was fostered during his time serving in the battalion during the war.[168] He would have witnessed this cyclical, vicious cycle of intense Soviet partisan attacks followed by cruel anti-partisan attacks, whose victims were many times local non-combatants rather than fighters. According to Soviet sources, the number of policemen and collaborators killed on Belarusian soil during the occupation was 27, 977. Other sources put the number at 78,788, a number which, if correct, would very likely include many innocent locals.[169]

The participation of Belarusian nationalists in anti-partisan operations and in the murder and violence against Jews and other locals is, not surprisingly, largely absent in their memories, interviews, and writings. In the memory and recollections of Belarusian nationalists, their involvement in anti-partisan operations was seen as a necessary means for the creation of an independent or at least more autonomous Belarus. According to these Belarusians, they participated in the hopes of garnering more favour with the Germans and also to acquire weapons and supplies.[170] These recollections spend little time discussing how the operations actually occurred and fail to mention the individuals involved. However sparsely their crimes appear in their postwar memoirs, many Belarusians did participate in these operations and broader violence. Their role in the Holocaust came predominantly through anti-partisan operations, the creation and dismantling of ghettos, and murder of Jews and other locals in camps but also by bullets.

The Relevance of the Occupation Period

Far from being controlled fully by the Germans, these Belarusian actors had agency and exerted power and judgement within spaces they operated in. They believed that having a proper Belarusian fighting force would be a way to legitimize themselves in the eyes of locals. However, the shortcomings of the Belarusian police, the Belarusian Self-Defense Corps, and other battalions ultimately soured relations between locals and Belarusian nationalists. Two ways in which this failure can be seen is by examining the anti-partisan operations and the relationship between Belarusians and Poles. Other things also prevented the success of Belarusian armed groups. A lack of experience by Belarusians in both administrative and military affairs, as well as the strength of other groups, including the Soviet partisans and Polish Home Army, challenged Belarusian power. The lack of proper German provisioning, of course, also exacerbated the situation.

For these Belarusians, the occupation was a critical juncture during which their engagement with locals in places of authority reached a peak. Years of subordination under Soviet and Polish rule created a yearning to develop their national identity, as well as their political and military power. They were willing to use their positions to do so, at least as much as they could under the occupation, and they utilized opportunities to leverage the Germans when possible. Their positions became increasingly more important in 1943 when the tide of war witnessed Soviet partisans and the Red Army increasingly devouring Belarusian territory.

For Belarusian nationalists, the occupation was more complicated than just a fight between the Soviet and German states; it was an opportunity to recruit more Belarusians into their cause and to broaden their appeal on Belarusian territory. In the end, though they attained heightened positions of power, they ultimately failed to garner support from their most important constituents – the locals. Though they had experienced exclusion earlier in their lives by authorities or by the state, this new form of rejection by their very own potential supporters would be the most damaging. In the later phases of the war, they would continue to push for a Belarusian armed force and for the development of Belarusian nationalism. This renewed push also came in the wake of new German leadership over occupied Belarus. On 22 September 1943, Kube was assassinated by Elena Mazanik, who worked as a housekeeper in his residence in Minsk. Mazanik was one of the few workers in Kube's home that was allowed to live outside of the premises. Hours prior, she went to work as usual and successfully brought in a bomb, which she planted under his mattress. Miraculously, the bomb killed Kube, yet left his wife unscathed who was close to him. As in other cases of successful, or attempted, assassination attempts against German officials, this event instigated German reprisals, which cost the lives of one thousand locals in Minsk.[171] General-Lieutenant of the Police, Gruppenführer SS Kurt von Gottberg, subsequently took up the position of Generalkommissar. This new German leadership now faced the changing movement of war, as evidenced by recent military defeats, the increasing partisan movement, and underground resistance that successfully took out Kube. Moreover, for Belarusians too, the last phase of the war became a realization that they were failing in their wartime efforts and now had to prepare for a new, postwar world.

4
In the Twilight of War

It was not until the end of the occupation period when Frantsishak Kushal′ finally got what he wanted – a Belarusian armed force. On 23 February 1944, Generalkommissar Kurt von Gottberg officially allowed for the creation of the Belarusian Home Guard (*Belaruskaia kraiovaia abarona,* BKA).[1] By this point in his life, Kushal′ had a lot of experience in the military, in different states and organizations. But at this moment, he felt that the creation of the BKA, though still subordinate to the Germans, represented a new phase for Belarusians and their armed struggle.

> Every nation that leans toward an independent life, always attempts, through one way or another, to create its own armed force. Depending on the circumstances in which this nation finds itself, realizing these desires comes about in different ways. Some form illegal organizations that prepare armed personnel, others mask these formations under some other legal organizations.[2]

According to the BKA commander, the Belarusian leadership, even this late into the occupation period, did not see the Belarusian – German relationship as collaboration but as an "involuntary necessity" that would lead to the foundation of a Belarusian army.[3] Another announcement by Barys Rahulia also addressed the importance of the Belarusian Home Guard stating that, "the Belarusian Home Guard is our first military formation that stands as a purely Belarusian national group and fights, not for German interests as propaganda rumours state, but for the Belarusian people's will."[4] The creation of the BKA was intended to be a clean slate for Belarusian military ambitions, especially in light of previously, poorly organized armed groups.

For the Germans, the creation of the BKA was a concession given at a critical turning point in the war, when Soviet troops were inching ever closer to Belarusian civilian-occupied territory and as the struggle against the Soviet partisans in the east was increasingly disastrous. The BKA was to be another fighting force to be used against encroaching Soviet partisans and the Red Army.

For the Belarusian leadership, the Belarusian Home Guard was created with the idea that it would serve as the nucleus of an independent Belarusian army after the conflict was over. With the momentum of war turning, Belarusian nationalists thought more about the postwar era, after German defeat when they would then be fighting the Soviet Union.[5] For these reasons, Belarusian leaders hoped the BKA would be stronger than the other armed units, in terms of the Belarusian quality of its soldiers, their discipline, and in its longevity. Despite these hopes and expectations, the BKA only lasted from February 1944 until April 1945. Moreover, when thinking about its counterparts in neighbouring regions, such as the Ukrainian Insurgent Army or the Lithuanian Partisan Front, the Home Guard's existence seems embryonic. Yet its period of operation represents a key moment in the war for many of these Belarusians: the period of scrambled and chaotic escape, of continued fighting, and of transition to what the new postwar world would bring.

This critical period of the war is one of the murkiest in terms of understanding the whereabouts of these Belarusians. Many individuals changed their names and assumed different identities in order to bypass their enemies and escape westward. Their names may appear in Displaced Persons' camps under different spellings and nationalities. Many of these individuals disappeared into the postwar period unscathed without leaving any archival, written, or testimonial footprint.

Some of the Belarusians in question, however, managed to leave enough of a trace. For them, the war took a different turn with the creation of the Belarusian Home Guard. Even this late into the conflict when defeat was in sight, they still persisted in organizing, mobilizing and training soldiers. Moreover, their relationship with the Germans continued during their evacuation westward and precipitated in the organization of Belarusian training schools, armed groups, and covert operations outside of Belarusian territory. In this last period of the war, Belarusian nationalists tried to leverage the Germans for more concessions. However, these heightened moments came at the expense of their relationship with locals, who were at the receiving end of violence. The history of the Belarusian Home Guard, however embryonic, represents this turbulent and critical transition period.

The Belarusian Home Guard

In 1944, the Belarusian Central Rada announced the creation of the BKA, insisting that, more than ever, Belarusians had to participate in the anti-Soviet armed struggle. These proclamations stressed that through this struggle, the goal of independence and a future, "happier" Belarus could be possible.[6] The media frenzy surrounding the BKA was paired with the leadership's advertisement of the new armed force around occupied Belarus. The president of the Belarusian collaborationist regime, Radaslaŭ Astroŭski, traveled with other individuals to get a sense of how locals would react to a potential Belarusian Army.[7] According to his recollections – which continually stressed the strength of local support toward the Belarusian cause – the only complaint locals had was that the BKA was being organized too late in the war. To that Astroŭski allegedly responded with, "It is never too late to fight for your family and nation!"[8] Because of his experience organizing other armed groups during the German occupation of Belarus and because of his personal military background, Kushal′ became the commander of the BKA. Other prominent Belarusians, including Usevalad Rodz′ka, Mikhal Vitushka, and Barys Rahulia, maintained positions of power within the BKA's administration.[9] By early March, sufficient preparations were made, and the recruitment effort began.[10]

The mobilization effort targeted men born between the years of 1908 to 1924.[11] Those born between 1925 and 1927 were to be mobilized into the Belarusian Youth Union, though later into the war, boys aged 15 and 16 would also be moved into the ranks of the Home Guard.[12] The Rada mobilized soldiers through its regional representatives as well as in newspapers. Some of these calls appealed to national sentiments and to anti-Soviet attitudes. Other announcements emphasized the need to protect and fight for one's family to encourage volunteers. Articles appeared about proud mothers allegedly taking their sons to BKA recruitment centres or encouraging their sons to enlist.[13] Initially, the leadership was wary of the number of volunteer recruits they would have and subsequently made tentative plans for forced mobilization should enough people not enlist.[14] To the shock of German and Belarusian officials, their expectations for mobilization were greatly surpassed. Based on a combination of sources, the number of volunteers reached around 40,000 thousand, of which 29,000 were accepted into the BKA.[15] German officials justified the scaling down of recruits by claiming that mobilizing such a large number of men would take away from the labour force they needed to maintain the local economy. The Belarusian leadership organized the 29,000 soldiers into 50 BKA battalions with headquarters in Baranavichi, Hlybokae,

Navahrudak, Minsk, Slutsk, Vialeĭka, and Slonim, located in the western regions of Belarus.[16]

Though the number of people volunteering to join the ranks of the BKA exceeded expectations, the Belarusian leadership realized it lacked people with actual military experience.[17] For this reason, the Belarusian leadership accepted Russians and Poles into the BKA if they had former military experience, yet they prohibited non-Belarusians from assuming any leadership positions in the Home Guard.[18] Far from being strictly motivated by the Belarusian cause, the majority of soldiers came from poorer or peasant backgrounds and joined the BKA as a means of survival. Opportunities for rank-and-file soldiers created incentives and motivations for those choosing to join the BKA. Home Guard soldiers and their families had access to better medical facilities and services over others.[19] Furthermore, soldiers received a monthly salary, and their families were protected from Soviet partisans and were compensated in the event of any attack. Soldiers' families could also be evacuated and relocated to another town for their protection.[20] Indeed, Soviet partisan attacks appeared to be the root reason for many of the requests that soldiers made. One petition from the BKA representative of the Minsk region to the local meat processing plant requested that extra meat be delivered to a particular soldier's family, because Soviet partisans had stolen their cows.[21] Other requests indicated that because Soviet "bandits" had kidnapped or killed other viable working members of the family, the soldier now needed to return to their farm and help with the work.[22]

Having made the decision to enlist in the BKA, volunteers had to report to their designated locations with their passports, several sets of undergarments, warm clothes, a cot for sleeping, pillows, and some utensils.[23] The BKA organizers then categorized the recruits based on a medical examination. Those labeled "A" were fit for service and cleared to partake in any military tasks. Recruits labeled "B" needed some medical attention, after which they could reapply and take another medical exam. Category "C" indicated they were cleared for certain non-military duties, and "D" meant they were not fit at all.[24] The BKA's official military ranking system included: lieutenant (*leĭtenant*), senior lieutenant (*starshy leĭtenant*), captain (*kapitan*), major (*maior*), lieutenant colonel (*padpalkoŭnik*), and colonel (*palkoŭnik*).[25]

After acceptance, the recruits pledged an oath:

> I, a soldier of the Belarusian Home Guard, swear on the Almighty God and soldier's honour, that I will loyally serve my Belarusian people. [...] I promise that I would sooner die a heroic death, than let my wife and children, parents and sisters, brothers and everyone else do so.[26]

It was no secret to anyone that Belarusians collaborating with the Germans during the Second World War had problems in the organization and operation of armed groups. The Belarusian auxiliary police and Belarusian Self-Defense Corps both suffered structural problems making them less efficient than the Germans would have wanted and making the Belarusians in charge of them look incompetent. Kushal′ admitted that one of the biggest issues stemmed from the lack of experience of the Belarusian leadership in charge of these armed units. Once in these units, another problem in these earlier formations was a lack of discipline and of proper preparation and training. Drawing from his preceding experience organizing Belarusian armed groups, Kushal′ wanted to prove the BKA's worthiness by better structuring the training and command of battalions, while also improving the composition of soldiers.[27]

To create more professional fighting groups, Kushal′ and other Belarusian nationalists organized officer and non-commissioned officer (NCO) training programmes. Not only did they organize these training camps, but the Belarusian leadership did so more quickly than they had with the previous armed groups. For example, the first training school for the Belarusian auxiliary police was not organized until 1 December 1941, nearly five months after the initial formations were created.[28] When training the Self-Defense Corps, there were some improvements made from the auxiliary police. The first officer's training school was created one month after the Self-Defense Corps was created, in July 1942.[29] Nevertheless, internal and external issues developed and persisted, which led to the premature conclusion of the first training school on 19 August 1942.[30] Furthermore, higher-ranking officials dismissed both the Germans and Belarusians in charge of the Self-Defense Corps from their posts.

The efforts put into the BKA revealed some organizational improvements from the preceding two attempts. The coordinated Belarusian – German leadership organized the first officers' training school in mid-March 1944, less than a month after the BKA's official announcement, far quicker than they had done with the auxiliary police or the Self-Defense. Moreover, the BKA leadership was composed of individuals who, by the spring of 1944, had acquired the experience needed to better lead and organize such formations. Though the Belarusian leadership became very experienced in military affairs by this point in the war, the quality of rank-and-file recruits continued to be a problem. Several regional BKA leaders described the recruits as being immature and lacking seriousness in their training.[31]

To address this problem, a significant portion of the training school programme lectures were devoted to Belarusian history, culture, and politics in order to mould these young men. It was believed that if these soldiers harnessed their Belarusian identity, they would be more dedicated to the struggle.[32] Because the Germans were largely indifferent to this portion of the training, the Belarusian leadership was largely free to do what it wanted when it came to "belarusifying" its soldiers. During a typical day, officers in training were required to exercise physically and familiarize themselves with weapons.[33] In the afternoons, they read newspapers or discussed politics and culture. By the beginning of June 1944, the BKA leadership was still concerned that there were too little Belarusian national sentiment among soldiers. To remedy this issue, one proclamation declared that all non-Belarusian activities should be eliminated, such as the singing and reading of Russian or Polish songs and texts. The leadership also pushed for increased promotion of Belarusian culture and literature during the training period.[34] They encouraged this involvement in Belarusian affairs by opening cultural centres in various towns.[35]

Commemoration and memorialization played a critical role in the training of soldiers and the promotion of Belarusian affairs. The 25th of March, which commemorated the 1918 declaration of the Belarusian People's Republic, was declared an official holiday and celebrated with lectures on Belarusian history, theatre performances, film screenings, and concerts.[36] Even though the BKA was created late in the war, its organizers saw it, and themselves, as part of a larger history of the Belarusian armed national struggle. Moreover, the BKA was interpreted as a continuation of the Belarusian units that had fought against the Bolsheviks in the Slutsk insurrection in November 1920.[37] Two surviving fighters of the November insurrection, Todar Daniliuk and Anton Sokol-Kutyloŭski, gave many talks stressing the connections between soldiers of the Slutsk insurrection and those of the BKA. In one of his speeches, Belarusian nationalist Stsiapan Shnėk remarked on the quality of the Slutsk fighters, noting they "gave us an example of an armed national fight."[38] Radaslaŭ Astroŭski also made public appearances and noted that the "Slutsk spirit" lived within the BKA fighters.[39] The BKA would certainly last longer than the 1920s Slutsk Brigades did, if only by a few months. What rank-and-file soldiers in both scenarios had in common was their varied backgrounds and motivations, not necessarily inspired by Belarusian patriotism.

Also important to the construction of a proper Belarusian army were aesthetics and more tangibly, uniforms. Belarusian leaders saw the issue of uniforms as particularly important and one necessary to ensure the BKA's success. They strongly believed that proper uniforms would contribute to positive morale amongst soldiers and would ensure their productivity, unlike fighters from previous Belarusian groups. It was not merely an issue of having uniforms but of having Belarusian ones that would be distinct from German attire utilized by other Belarusian armed groups most of the time.[40] There was even a special BKA commission set up for the acquisition of uniforms and other military necessities.[41] However, any Belarusian insistence on acquiring uniforms was met with pushback by the Germans. Soldiers who were lucky were given the black uniform of the Belarusian auxiliary police and some received the Belarusian "Pahonia" insignia to be patched onto the uniform. Others, if they could, would wrap the Belarusian People's Republic white-red-white flag around their left arm, above the elbow.[42] Most BKA soldiers, however, wore civilian attire, while fighters of six of the railway battalions wore engineering uniforms used in the German Army.[43]

The Belarusian leadership targeted potential and existing soldiers, but they it also recruited people of different professions, such as physicians or academics into the ranks of the BKA. To expand its reach, the BKA created jobs for those who were too old or too young to serve, as well as for women. The involvement of women was especially true in May and June of 1944, when the tides of war were turning increasingly faster. Zinaida Cherniavskaia, for example, worked in the BKA as a railway employee. During the earlier years of the war, she had trained and worked as a teacher in various towns in the Maladzechna county. In the postwar period, Chernavskaia told Soviet Lithuanian authorities that she had never had any interest in Belarusian affairs and was merely interested in procuring a job.[44] Her possible lack of investment in the Belarusian cause suggests that she and perhaps many others used these institutions as a means to survive, similarly to soldiers. Though her postwar account should most definitely be taken critically, stories like Chernavskaia's demystify much of the romanticized and patriotic descriptions Belarusian nationalists gave during and after the war pertaining to the galvanizing enthusiasm around these armed groups.

Despite improvements in the organization, mobilization, and training of BKA soldiers, it ultimately did not exude the Belarusian military prowess its leaders hoped it would be. What weakened the BKA – similarly to preceding armed groups – were the poor conditions offered to soldiers, which only deteriorated as the war progressed. There continued to be shortages during actual fighting that inhibited the ability of soldiers to defend themselves against Soviet partisans. In late May 1944, one BKA leader in the Minsk region reported on the state of his troops, noting that there were six individuals who deserted and had joined Soviet partisans, six who were severely ill and given a leave of absence, more than twenty who were barefoot, and that the battalion lacked weapons and ammunition.[45] The lack of sufficient weapons was one of the most pressing issues and was something Home Guard soldiers consistently complained about. Officially, it was the Germans' responsibility to provide weapons to the battalions. The Germans, however, refused to properly arm soldiers and sometimes even refused such access during the weapon's training portion of BKA schools.[46] Even this late into the war when the Germans were desperately trying to fend off Soviet partisans and an approaching Red Army, they were still wary of arming any Belarusian armed groups, or any perceived to be racially inferior soldiers.[47] During the later stages of the war, this hesitation was compounded by the fact that the BKA had garnered more support than anticipated during the recruitment process. Moreover, a weapons shortage beginning in 1944 guaranteed that German soldiers would receive weapons over Belarusian fighters. A battalion in the Vialeĭka county, for example, which comprised around 15,000 BKA soldiers, received weapons for only 3,000 men.[48] During a meeting with the German SD unit in Vialeĭka in March 1944, Astroŭski further insisted on the need to arm Belarusian units. The Germans assured him that they would fully arm and provide uniforms for the troops in three weeks but ultimately did not.[49] Soviet intelligence reports at the time also commented on the embarrassing weapons shortage among Belarusian soldiers. In one report, Soviet officials estimated that in the town of Dziarzhynsk, the 17th BKA battalion had 545 fighters but only 40 rifles.[50]

Even when not fighting, provisions in BKA camp sites were so scarce that soldiers were responsible for bringing even the most basic essentials.[51] They lacked sufficient medical supplies and food. Many fighters were affected by diseases, particularly typhoid, and they had little understanding of how to maintain sanitation and hygiene.[52] These shortages led soldiers to be less productive, drink heavily, and be written up for disorderly conduct.[53] Beginning in the spring of 1944, the number of requests for "temporary" release from work spiked.[54] One main reason for leave requests also stemmed from the dire situations soldiers' families found themselves in. The conditions of war forced women, children, and the elderly to fend for themselves and work the land without the help of able-bodied men. The Belarusian leadership had little choice but to grant requests for temporary leave so that soldiers could work on their family farms. These leave requests typically led to desertions toward the latter years of the war which increased steadily.[55]

Other desertions were motivated due to enemy infiltration into BKA units. The Polish Home Army on several occasions managed to infiltrate BKA groups and convince the commanders to disband their group and let the soldiers join them.[56] The 35th BKA battalion, stationed in Pastavy, was reported to have been heavily influenced by Polish propaganda; so much so, that two of the battalion's companies joined the Polish Home Army. Another similar case occurred in Baranavichi where forty soldiers of the 1st BKA battalion joined the Home Army. Among these were both

Poles and Belarusians.[57] By late April 1944, the problem with deserters was so grim that a report from the BKA command itself suggested offering pardons to deserters in order to win them back.[58] This extension of forgiveness was also offered to any Soviet partisans who defected their unit to join the BKA.[59] Increased desertions and defections also meant that the BKA leadership now had to turn to forced mobilization, employing methods that became quite violent.[60]

The poor behaviour and lack of discipline among rank-and-file soldiers also soured their relationship with locals and reflected poorly on the Belarusian leadership. The conduct of soldiers, as Kushal' admitted, was inappropriate and, despite the additional training, was reminiscent of the Belarusian auxiliary police and Self-Defense Corps.[61] Locals not only witnessed this violence, but by the summer of 1944, their surroundings had drastically changed. Villages had been burnt down during operations and the situation continually exacerbated with the incoming Red Army. Industrial capacity by the end of the war reached 20 percent of prewar levels and the quantity of livestock was down to 31 percent – hardly enough to meet the food demands of both the occupiers and those being occupied.[62] All of these factors reflected very poorly on Belarusian armed groups and on the Belarusian leaders in positions of power during the occupation.

Secret Networks and Clandestine Activity

The beginning of the proliferation of myths and anecdotal stories pertaining to these Belarusian actors begins at this latter stage in the war. Namely, many of them claim to have been secretly active in clandestine organizations out of German oversight. They allege that the legitimate Belarusian armed groups, training camps, and meetings served as sites and opportunities for clandestine activity without German knowledge or support. Hence, a meeting between Belarusian leaders under pretenses that they were discussing issues related to anti-partisan operations, for example, served as an excuse to draw Belarusians together for other purposes.[63] Dz'mitry Kasmovich, in his recollections, asserted that networks of Belarusians often met without permission from the Germans. He insisted that he himself was involved in the secret recruitment of Belarusians for a future national armed force that would be independent of German rule and would unite with parts of the BKA. Beginning in late summer of 1941, he noted that he and Michal Vitushka travelled to the eastern parts of Belarus to establish more contacts and recruit more people.[64] In the postwar period, Kushal' even told the Central Intelligence Agency (CIA) that the BKA leadership had been divided into two groups; one being official and subordinate to the Germans, whereas the other, the "illegal" part, aimed at creating an independent Belarus and at preparing for the postwar period.[65] Though the possibility of such clandestine activity and secret gatherings is plausible, how pervasive was it and should we believe the words of those claimed to be involved?

A more likely scenario is that though there may have been Belarusian clandestine organizations, groups, gatherings, and even parties during the war, the existence of a strong movement, independent of foreign support, is unlikely. One such clandestine organization was the Belarusian Independence Party (*Belaruskaia Nezalezhniskaia Partyia*, BNP). The party was founded as early as 1940 and was likely co-organized by Father Vintsent Hadleŭski and Usevalad Rodz'ka, with responsibility falling entirely on Rodz'ka after the Germans killed Hadleŭski in December 1942.[66] There was a secret central committee for the Independence Party, and its regional representatives were matched with their official posts as members of German-sponsored Belarusians armed groups. As regional representatives, the Belarusians were then in charge of official Belarusian-German armed groups in their respective cities, in addition to any clandestine work there that needed to be done. Some notable members of this network included Rodz'ka, Vitushka, Sakovich, and Kasmovich.[67] However, it is unclear how much widespread knowledge there was about its existence by higher-up Belarusians. The official party programme called for the creation of an independent Belarus by means of armed resistance that would exist entirely free from either German or Soviet rule.

One of the goals of the BNP was to create a Belarusian armed force that would be able to fight both the Soviet and German regimes. Rodz'ka organized some smaller Belarusian anti – German partisans at the onset of the German occupation but these fighters were hardly significant or substantial in numbers.[68] Later on throughout the war, as Soviet partisans became an increasing threat, the Germans allowed Belarusian leaders to travel around the territory and mobilize soldiers into German – sponsored units. The members of the BNP took advantage of these travel opportunities to do their own recruiting for their clandestine group. Rodz'ka and Sakovich were to organize armed groups in western Belarus, while Kasmovich and Vitushka would do the equivalent in the eastern Belarusian region.[69] A Soviet report from the time affirmed that Kasmovich, Astroŭski, and Vitushka indeed traveled to the eastern Belarusian regions of Mahilieŭ, Smalensk, and Briansk, for some secret and unknown business.[70] For Belarusian nationalists, more intimate collaboration with the Germans ensured more autonomy for them to pursue their secret plans.[71]

If such a network, and other conspiratorial groups, did indeed exist, the logistics of them would have paralleled existing operations. BKA leaders and Belarusian representatives of armed groups were in the ideal position to engage in clandestine activity, while officially maintaining their posts under the Germans. Kushal', for example, frequently traveled around occupied Belarus to try to recruit soldiers into the BKA. Under such auspices he would have been able to engage in subversive activity, just as Vitushka, Kasmovich, and others. Similarly to the way in which soldiers were recruited, Belarusian leaders drew in potential agents from their region where they were stationed. On one occasion, one young Belarusian officer, Iazėp Sazhych, noted that Kushal' instructed him to gather fifty men from Navahrudak and to go to Lida, where they would meet other trained officers and create a battalion. Sazhych argued with his commander, stressing that the Germans would not tolerate any form of subversive or clandestine activity, but Kushal' insisted that they "had to gather weapons, however possible."[72]

Barys Rahulia was another leading Belarusian that could have been capable of engaging in clandestine activity, through his established position in Navahrudak.[73] In memoirs and later interviews, individuals close to him recalled that, "Barys often traveled somewhere (Minsk, Vilnius), but did not always share with us where he was and what he felt."[74] In an interview taken in the 1990s, Mikola Rulinski recalled that Rahulia secretly recruited him to join the Belarusian Independence Party despite the fact that the existence and discovery of such a party by the Germans could have cost him his life.[75] Another interview during the same time provides a similar story. Viktar Sikora, a young Belarusian during the war, claimed that Usevalad Rodz'ka recruited him into the Independence Party in 1944. Rodz'ka allegedly told him to ignore the fact that he was working with the Germans, as the most important thing was to use their platforms given to them by the occupiers and create networks to prepare for the next phase of the Belarusian struggle against the Soviet Union.[76]

Another Belarusian clandestine group, which may have been organized by the Belarusian Independence Party, was the Belarusian Home Army, sometimes referred to as the Belarusian Liberation Army, commanded by Rodz'ka.[77] One of the more interesting aspects of this organization was its attempt to coordinate armed activity with other non-Belarusian groups in the area. Kasmovich recalls attempting to forge ties with General Vlasov, the leader of the Russian Liberation Army that collaborated with the Germans, in order to coordinate a collective anti-Soviet front that would be able to survive in the event of German defeat. According to Kasmovich's account, Vlasov was intrigued with the idea but was only interested in absorbing the Belarusian Liberation Army into his own group rather than coordinating efforts.[78]

Another possible point of cooperation was that between these Belarusians and their Ukrainian counterparts. Even prior to Operation Barbarossa, Rodz'ka had connections with the Organization of Ukrainian Nationalists (*Orhanizatsiia ukraïns'kykh natsionalistiv*, OUN) in Kraków, when the Germans sent him there for espionage work. Rodz'ka was apparently quite inspired by the OUN's programme and hoped to borrow from it to create a future organization of Belarusian nationalists.[79] During the war, Rodz'ka, Vitushka and others were allegedly in contact with Ukrainian nationalists such Taras Bul'ba-Borovets' and Stepan Bandera.[80] In his memoir, Bul'ba-Borovets' does confirm that his group, the Polissian Sich, and Belarusians commanded by Rodz'ka and Vitushka maintained relations.[81] However, the exact nature of Belarusian – Ukrainian collaboration is unknown and the amount of ideological cross-over between OUN and the Belarusians is also murky.[82] Bulba-Borovets and his group controlled the town of Olevsk, presently in the Zhytomyr region of Ukraine, where they tortured and murdered Jews without any German presence in the area.[83] If they had been close, Rodz'ka and Vitushka would have likely been very aware of this activity.

Much of what is known about these clandestine networks is found in personal memoirs and interviews. The little hard evidence that does exists suggests there may have been an increase in Belarusian subversive activity just before the evacuation westward. BKA activity, as well as that of the Belarusian Independence Party and Belarusian Liberation Army all attest to this possibility. Some of the last cases of insurgency organized on Belarusian territory, came as late as July 1944 when Rodz'ka organized five armed groups in the regions of Vilnius, Baranavichi, Lida, Pastavy, and Hlybokae, with the Abwehr's support, called *kalinoŭshiki*. These groups were supposed to remain on Belarusian territory after the Red Army took over and were to serve as anti-Soviet partisan hubs. However, Soviet security forces ultimately dismantled all of these these armed resistance cells by 1945.[84] Though the specifics of these alleged clandestine groups can certainly be seen with scepticism, the fact that there was a continued desire to recruit, gather, and unite Belarusians is important. It is precisely these connections, whether open or clandestine, that would ensure the continued existence of a network of Belarusians after the end of the war.

Leaving the Bats'kaŭshchyna

Merely a few days prior to the Soviet arrival in Minsk, the Second All-Belarusian Congress took place on 27 June 1944, in the same place where its predecessors gathered nearly 27 years earlier. If there was any feeling of concern or fear due to the incoming Red Army, it was certainly not reflected in the Congress minutes. The Congress reaffirmed its Belarusian goals and aspirations, committed itself to continuing the armed struggle for its cause and recognized the Belarusian Central Rada as the legitimate government of the Belarusian people.[85] There was no contingency plan for resistance forces that were to remain behind in Belarus nor anything concrete about an army in the postwar period. The document that published the proceedings of the meeting several years later, highlighted the continued struggle against bolshevism, Stalinist bandits, and Polish landlords. Just as their predecessors of the First All-Belarusian Congress in late December 1917, the members of the Second Congress soon fled Minsk as the Red Army entered the city on 3 July 1944.

Not only did members of the Congress leave westward, but the summer of 1944 saw the evacuation of approximately 35,000 individuals who collaborated and participated in German-Belarusian organizations and armed formations, including between 10,000 and 15,000 BKA soldiers.[86] Each Belarusian soldier and unit pursued different trajectories and met different fates in the aftermath of evacuation. This variety of experiences was frustrating for Belarusian leaders who wanted to reorganize the BKA in Germany and struggled to track people and units. Even by November 1944, the Rada, which was now based in Berlin, was still trying to trace the remnants of its Home Guard.[87]

One Belarusian soldier, Neaniŭ Kakhanavich, recalled his journey from the Vitsebsk area with a group of Belarusians. Some of them were taken by the Red Army, some were injured and were left behind, and still some managed to make it to Kaunas. Those that made it to Kaunas were mobilized into German units under the pretense that they would eventually link up with other Belarusian battalions. Indeed, for many, Kaunas became one of several stops en route to western Europe. Kakhanavich traveled to Kaunas while injured, then from Kaunas to Soldau (currently Działdowo, Poland), then to Weimar, and eventually to Berlin where he gave his testimony to the Belarusian leadership in October 1944.[88]

Other fighters, such as Belarusian soldiers from the Slonim BKA battalion, were recruited by the Germans and used in battle against the Allies in Italy. During the later phases of the Battle of Monte Cassino in May 1944, Belarusians fought on both sides of the conflict; some under General Anders's Second Polish Corps and others for the Germans. Some figures indicate that, by late summer of 1944, twenty percent of those fighting in Anders's army were Belarusian or Ukrainian.[89] Those fighting for the Germans are assumed to have perished somewhere in the Apennines.[90] Other Belarusians, such as Kanstantyn Miarliak, joined the Polish Army directly in order to avoid capture by the Red Army.[91] In later interviews with the CIA, Miarliak alleged that the Abwehr approached him and asked him to join the Polish Army in Italy to convince Belarusians to stop fighting against the Germans.[92]

Though some individuals' motivations may have been the continued struggle for Belarus, more than likely, many fighters sought to end up in an Allied sphere of influence because they knew their chances of survival were much higher – whether as collaborators or as ordinary, unidentifiable soldiers. Many rank-and-file Belarusian soldiers especially hoped to reach US – controlled parts of Germany.[93] In the East, those captured by the Red Army were more likely be punished for their activity during the war, not to mention more likely to be recognized by their victims or locals.

Reviving Belarusian-German Units

In November 1944, there were between 16,000 and 19,000 former Belarusian fighters living in Germany, who had escaped westward during the evacuation.[94] For these soldiers that made it to Berlin and reported to the Rada, conditions were difficult. They were living with untreated wounds, diseases, and insufficient food. They struggled to communicate in German. Nevertheless, reports from the leadership of the Belarusian Central Rada in Berlin stressed that there was still enthusiasm to continue fighting "against Judeo-bolshevism and for a better future in Europe".[95]

Unlike the BKA, the organizational structure of the post-evacuation period of Belarusian armed groups consisted of a network of armed cells entirely dependent on the Germans. The Germans absorbed Belarusian fighting groups directly under their command mainly because the Rada lacked the organizational and administrative ability to do much. The Rada did not formally announce its presence in Berlin, on 28 Gumbinner Straße, nor make a mobilization call for Belarusian troops until October 1944, nearly three months after it had left Belarus.[96] During this three-month hiatus many stranded Belarusian armed groups were unaware of where the Rada leadership was located and were unable to rejoin even if they had wanted. By October 1944, there were no concrete plans or blueprints for a Belarusian Army. Rather Kushal' and other leaders began organizing a more or less, provisional battalion, which would serve as the basis for a Belarusian Legion.[97]

The slow and cautious resurrection of Belarusian armed groups reflected the weakness of the Rada at this point in time. Because its leaders had no idea of where BKA units and other Belarusian soldiers were scattered, they organized a tentative battalion in order to get a sense of how many people they could mobilize. By mid-October, a total of 157 people volunteered for the battalion and only a few more would continue to do so in the next months.[98] The Rada elected a Belarusian Chief of Staff for Military Affairs (*Haloŭnae Kiraŭnitstva Vaiskovykh Spraŭ,* HKVS) that would be in charge of Belarusian – German armed activity in this last phase of the war, with Kanstanty Ezavitaŭ at its head.[99] During the post-evacuation period, the Belarusian units included: a Belarusian Legion, the ongoing remnants of the Belarusian Home Guard, and a "Dalwitz" Group which would later be referred to as the "Special Belarusian Battalion Dalwitz".[100] Training camps and plans were established for the latter groups. Ultimately, however the collective units came to include merely a few hundred soldiers who were, once again, poorly provisioned.[101]

Another armed group in which Belarusian soldiers fought was the 30th Waffen-Grenadier Division of the SS. This presented the last serious attempt at training and dispatching soldiers against the enemy, though this time against the Allies much to the soldiers' dismay. As with preceding German-controlled Belarusian units, the Division was poorly equipped; its soldiers poorly fed and clothed. Part of the reason for this problem came from a shortage of supplies, but another major part had to do with persistent German ideological superiority attitudes. Moreover, the soldiers in this Division suffered from physical and verbal abuse by the commanding Germans, and their family members were oftentimes sent to work as forced labourers. These unfavourable conditions and attitudes worsened when the Division was sent to fight in France against the much better equipped Free French Army. Morale suffered, drunkenness and insubordination were ubiquitous, leading to more desertions by rank-and-file soldiers who joined the French posing as Poles.[102] The remaining soldiers were recalled by the end of 1944.[103]

The remains of the 30th Waffen-Grenadier Division were disbanded and merged into the Belarusian Sturm-Division, under the nominal command of Kushal′, but in reality subordinated to Lt. Colonel Siegling.[104] This division had one brigade, the SS-Grenadier Brigade "Belarus" consisting of three battalions: two under German command and one under Belarusian command.[105] After a series of meetings, on 15 January 1945 the Rada made the official announcement and called for volunteers to join the "Belarus" Waffen-SS Division.[106] The German -Belarusian leadership provided some form of housing and financial support, as well as the possibility for professional advancement through officer training courses.[107] There was an agreement that Belarusians would be promoted within the Belarusian brigade. Officers' social clubs officially welcomed both Belarusians and Germans, while the divisional staff was shared as well. The Division, however, was dissolved three months later in April 1945. By this point, the Belarusian leadership had resorted to mobilizing fourteen and fifteen-year old boys into their formations. The German command wanted to directly absorb the remaining Belarusian soldiers into the Wehrmacht, but the Belarusian leadership strongly rejected this call, fearing their soldiers would be used as forced labour for the Germans. Instead, any Belarusian soldiers still active were sent to General Aleksei Vlasov's army.[108]

Throughout the post-evacuation period, the Belarusian leadership continued to be frustrated over the progress in organizing Belarusian armed groups, particularly when compared with other national groups. A report by the Rada remarked on this matter, stating that for the entire Belarusian population, of allegedly 12 million, there were only 200 officers, whereas there were some 3,000 Estonian officers out of a population of 1.5 million.[109] The numbers of Belarusian officers also paled in comparison to those of the Latvians and Lithuanians. The Rada report indicated that this low representation existed because Belarusians were not recognized in certain positions of leadership as other national groups were. They saw this discrimination as a major offense to them and to the sacrifice they had made in their collaboration with the Germans. Aside from a lack of professional promotion, Belarusian soldiers, along with Ukrainian ones, received lower wages than their counterparts from the Baltic states.[110] Belarusian leaders worried that these problems could negatively impact the number of volunteers that joined the Belarusian military formations.[111]

This period of the war represents the height of Belarusian armed group organization, but it also reveals its fast dismantling and chaotic process. Desperation and uncertainties regarding the end of the war and postwar period fueled Belarusians' decisions to flee and try to escape, attempt to reorganize groups, switch to the enemy side, or go underground. During this time, younger Belarusians were recruited by more seasoned activists in the hopes of continuing to foment anti-Soviet activity into the postwar period and continue the Belarusian struggle. The multi-generational group of Belarusians had learned to work with each other, and they had also recruited the third, younger generation of soldiers during the German occupation. Just as Kushal', Astroŭski, and others had recruited Rodz'ka, Rahulia, and Kasmovich, so too did the latter individuals train the next generation of Belarusians. Most would never actually return to Belarus. Moreover, the biggest legacy they left as they escaped westward was the violence and destruction they were complicit in toward their own population and land. The Belarus they escaped from had lost approximately one fifth of its inhabitants; not to mention witnessed the permanent disappearance of many villages and towns that would never appear again.[112]

The Beginnings of Covert Missions

The ultimate collapse of the German armed forces from their evacuation in the summer of 1944 until the end of the war the following spring represented a big transition point. This retreat not only marked a stark change in the progression of war, but it also signaled to those collaborating with the Germans that they too would have to change and adapt. More importantly, collaborationist forces had to think about how they would proceed in a newly re-defined geopolitical order. The Belarusians collaborating with the Germans hoped to continue their anti-Soviet struggle, albeit clandestinely and through partisan activity. Beginning in the fall of 1944 the Belarusian – German leadership organized schools where they trained spies and insurgents, who were to be sent back to what was now Soviet-controlled territory. The organization of such sabotage operations fell under the umbrella of the SS – Jagdverbände programme run by Otto Skorzeny.[113] The programme involved two different schools, of which the "Agent" school (*Agenten-Schulen*) focused on training sabotage agents.[114] These groups were sent out in October and November 1944 from East Prussia, and also in the Spring of 1945 from other locations. Altogether, there were a total of four saboteur groups; one that returned to Germany, two that were never heard of again, and one with which only radio contact had been established. The last alleged radio contact made with a stranded group in Belarus occurred between late January and early February 1945, just before the end of the war.[115]

From the Belarusian side, Vitushka and Rodz'ka were intimately involved in the organization of these covert operations, which formed part of the Dalwtiz programme. The programme was named after its initial training location, Dalwitz, located at the time in Insterburg, East Prussia, today's Cherniakhovsk in Kaliningrad. The program's goal was to make connections with other anti-Soviet underground networks in Belarus and prepare Belarusian anti-Soviet partisan units for the continuation of war.[116] Selected agents trained in Dalwitz, and later the training site moved to around present-day Bydgoszcz, Poland and then once again, in April 1945, to Schwarzenberg, Germany.[117] The individuals who participated in these missions came from Belarusian armed groups, including the Home Guard, various police battalions, and the Belarusian Youth Union.[118] At least nine women were also involved in the Dalwitz group, mainly training as radio operators.[119]

In popular culture, the Dalwitz covert operations are referred as the "Black Cat" (*Chorny kot*) missions. There is a lot of mystery and uncertainty surrounding the missions and individuals involved, largely due to a lack of concrete information that is available. Émigré literature and

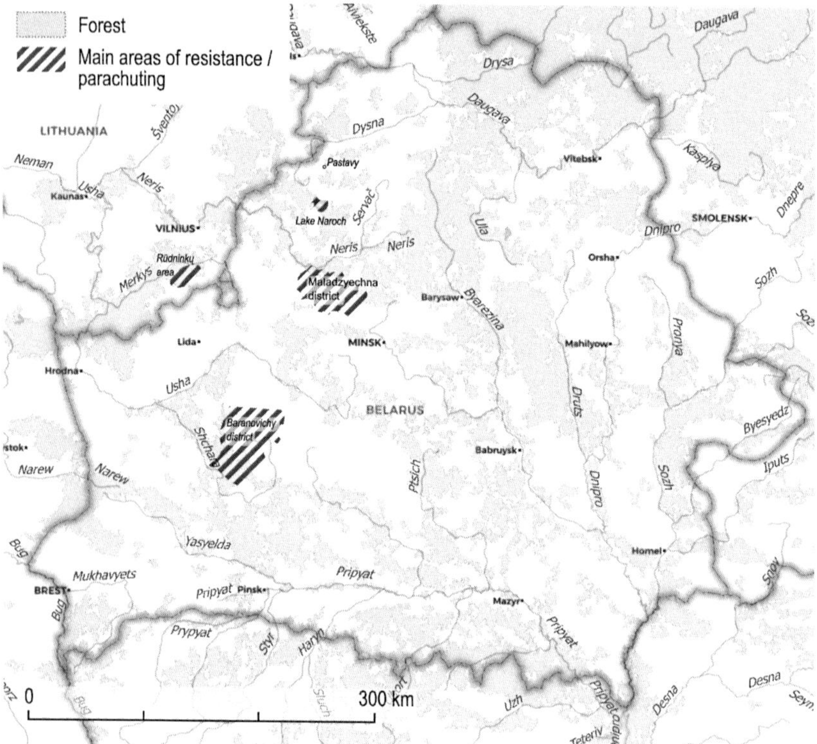

Figure 3: Areas of anti-Soviet resistance in Belarus between 1944 and 1953.

Source: Map by Ivo Offenthaler. By permission of Brill, in Michael Gehler and David Schriffl, eds., *Violent Resistance from the Baltics to Central, Eastern and South Eastern Europe* (Paderborn: Verlag Ferdinand Schöningh, 2020). "Sources: Relief: ESRI Hillshade 2019 [Esri, Airbus DS, USGS, NGA, NASA, CGIAR, N Robinson, NCEAS, NLS, OS, NMA, Geodatastyrelsen, Rijkswaterstaat, GSA, Geoland, FEMA, Intermap and the GIS user community]; Place names: CC-BY-SA (OpenStreetmap user community); Waterbodies: public domain (Natural Earth); Forest cover: free use for research, education and other non-profit use (EC: EEA Global Land Cover 2000)"

interviews of Belarusians who survived the war talk about the individuals and alleged missions, yet much of what is written is difficult to confirm. Information from Soviet sources suggests that there were a handful of such missions in the fall and winter of 1944. The first involved four men from the allegedly clandestine Belarusian Independence Party, but officially members of the BKA as far as the Germans believed. In September 1944, they were sent to Diatlava, in the present-day Hrodna region of western Belarus. Soviet security forces quickly discovered this group.[120]

The second dispatch involved a larger group of 27 individuals, including two women, under the leadership of Mikhal Vitushka.[121] This group was dispatched to the Vilnius region on the night of 17 to 18 November 1944. Their mission was to make contact with anti-Soviet organizations and set up partisan cells. Once again, Soviet authorities apprehended many of these individuals, though some, including Vitushka, managed to escape. In early December 1944, Vitushka and four other surviving members of the dispatched group joined a Polish Home Army group, under the leadership of Czesław Stankiewicz (pseudonym "Komar").[122]

For years after this operation, scholars and popular historians continued to debate Vitushka's fate. Some alleged that he managed to escape to West Germany and live under a pseudonym until as late as 2006.[123] The only archival documentation of Vitushka's fate comes from the Lithuanian Extraordinary Archive, stating he was killed on 7 January 1945 during an encounter between Soviet security forces and the Polish Home Army "Komar" group, in the Rūdninkai forest in Lithuania. Both Polish and Soviet sources confirm that on 7 January 1945, there was a fatal encounter between members of this Home Army group and Soviet security forces.[124] This skirmish is confirmed to have occurred in the same Rūdninkai region, around Kernavas, where Vitushka died.[125] He was buried around Lake Kernavas, approximately 35 kilometres from Vilnius. The other members of the AK group were killed as well, as were the other Belarusian agents who had originally been dispatched with Vitushka.[126]

At the time, the uncertainty of Vitushka and the other agents' whereabouts served as a source of hope for Belarusian nationalists in the early postwar period. They utilized the possible existence of active agents in the BSSR as a way to justify more covert missions after the war. Throughout the years, people claimed to have seen Vitushka in Minsk at the end of 1946 and at the beginning of 1947.[127] The same was true of sightings of others in Warsaw and Białystok after the war. The utilization of alleged active agents, but especially of Vitushka, continued in Belarus and in the West. Indeed, the mystery surrounding him became more important than his actual actions during the war. In 1967, a group of people opened a café in Hrodna, in western Belarus, with the name "Black Cat". Soviet authorities were so concerned that this café would mobilize nationalist sympathizers in the name of Vitushka, that it arrested the organizers and shut it down.[128]

After Vitushka's group landed on Soviet territory, another much smaller, four-man group was being prepared. The four men were dispatched in December 1944. They were not heard from again and were assumed to have been caught by Soviet authorities.[129] As the months went by and the front moved westward, it became increasingly more difficult to send agents into Soviet territory and so they were dispatched into Poland as the Red Army passed through. One group of Belarusian insurgents connected to Dalwitz was parachuted at the rear end of the Red Army in Poland, on the night of 27 March 1945. One of the insurgents, Filip Moroz, like so many other Belarusians, had initially fled westward with Germans. It is unclear what happened once they were in Poland, but even into the mid-1950s, the Polish Ministry of Internal Affairs was still looking for these individuals.[130]

With the rapid advance of the Red Army westwards, the remaining Belarusians involved in the Dalwitz programme, along with other members of Jagdverband Ost, fled to the Czech city of Jablonec nad Nisou, nestled in the Jizera Mountains.[131] Rodz′ka was among those who fled to Jablonec, where Czech partisans discovered and disarmed them.[132] Upon being released Rodz′ka traveled to Warsaw and met with other individuals, attempting to once again re-organize some Belarusian armed group. The group decided that he would go to Białystok, in eastern Poland close to the border with Belarus, with some former Dalwitz training school participants. Their plan was to clandestinely recruit and operate in the territory, in the hopes of joining with other partisan groups that were thought to still be active in Belarus. In July 1945, however, Soviet security forces arrested Rodz′ka and his men. He was presumably killed.[133]

Regardless of the individual anecdotes surrounding members of the Dalwitz group or how the memory of them continued in the postwar period, ultimately these Belarusian agents failed to foment any strong resistance. More broadly, it is unclear whether or not the activity of these Belarusians during the latter portion of the occupation fomented any surge in Belarusian nationalism among locals. By the end of the war, many surviving BKA soldiers or Dalwitz insurgents tried to assimilate to postwar life as quietly as possible. Many remained in the BSSR or Poland, where they managed to lay low for many years. Others ended up moving to western Europe or across the Atlantic Ocean. But for some, the conclusion of the war did not signify an end to the Belarusian cause but merely the conclusion of Belarusian – German collaboration as a vehicle to pursue their aims.

5

Belarusian Émigrés and Covert Activity after the War

A few years after the Second World War, Frantsishak Kushal′ emerges in the documents of US intelligence services, across the ocean and in a new country. In December 1949, a man known by the name "Monitch" presented himself to US intelligence officers in Germany, stating he had a message from some Belarusian insurgents for Kushal′. The fighters, allegedly organized into three groups under Mikhal Vitushka himself, were "well supplied with German and Soviet weapons and even have sufficient ammunition for the foreseeable future."[1] Though Kushal′ had not returned to Belarus since his evacuation, nor had heard from Vitushka since then, he still saw promising potential for the continued development of anti-Soviet activity in Belarus and enthusiastically shared this message with US intelligence officers. The case officer who received the news from Kushal′ relayed this message to the Central Intelligence Agency (CIA):

> Kushal′ believes that the partisan movement in Byelorussia has a considerable potential both for immediate intelligence purposes and for military purposes in case of an East-West conflict because Byelorussia lies astride the main supply route for Soviet troops in the West. He is convinced that contact with them would be of great importance for the US… In furtherance of long-range plans, he proposes to enlist up to one hundred young Byelorussian patriots […] to be sent to the BSSR in time of war, as cadres both for intelligence and paramilitary purposes.[2]

In the end however, Monitch's fantastical narration of his journey, which included smuggling his way into Belarus, clandestinely contacting insurgents with the help of locals, and escaping attacks by Polish soldiers, soon became a source of embarrassment for Kushal′, when it became known that Monitch had actually been taken and turned by Soviet authorities.[3]

Monitch's story captures the murkiness and patterns involving Belarusian anti-Soviet activity in the postwar period. Some continued to fight in what was once again the Belarusian Soviet Socialist Republic (BSSR). Of these individuals some would be killed for their collaboration, or alleged collaboration, with Nazi Germany. Other times Soviet security forces apprehended and sent these individuals to forced labour camps in other parts of the Soviet Union. Others would manage to escape to western Europe, North America, South America, and Australia either continuing their anti-Soviet activity within émigré circles or disappearing into the background of their new lives and off the pages of history. For a select number of Belarusians, the struggle for their cause was not over and the new Cold War period offered promise for their efforts through collaboration with western states. But just like with Monitch's case, parsing through what was real or fabricated became a serious challenge for all parties involved. The new battlegrounds for this Belarusian armed struggle after the Second World War were organized mainly in two spaces; first in Belarus, driven by Belarusians who remained in the region and fought in small guerrilla groups, and second, in the West, involving operations that were supported by foreign states, the United States being the most significant.[4]

Following the Living and the Dead in the Postwar Period

On 3 July 1944, the Red Army arrived in Minsk. The now, "liberated" BSSR would be heavily monitored by Soviet security forces looking to find those who were anti-Soviet in political orientation or who had collaborated with the Germans. However, the extent of anti-Soviet armed activity in this area after the evacuation remains ambiguous. According to Soviet records, in January 1945 there were 2385 individuals active in eighty-two "bandit" groups in the region. In 1945, Soviet security forces arrested 106,814 people in the BSSR, accusing them of engaging in espionage, saboteur activity, desertion, evading conscription, being traitors to the homeland, and of being German escapees from POW camps.[5] There were two Soviet security agencies tasked with fighting anti-Soviet activity, or "banditry" as it was called. These were the Main Directorate for the Struggle against Banditry (*Glavnoe upravlenie po bor'be s banditismom*) and the Main Directorate for the NKVD Security Troops (*Glavnoe upravlenie vnutrennikh voisk NKVD*).[6] The state also employed military and police groups in the apprehension of suspicious individuals.[7] From the time the Red Army overran Belarus in the summer of 1944, the Soviet state dispatched counterinsurgency units to combat nationalist groups and remnants of German soldiers who had not been evacuated.[8]

The territory of the BSSR, however, was really one theatre of much larger anti-Soviet insurgent activity. To the north, the Baltic states had anti-Soviet partisan groups fighting the Red Army and Soviet Security forces, as was the case to the west in Poland, and in the south in Ukrainian territory. Indeed, anti-Soviet resistance in Belarus shared some features with its neighbours. For example, the Belarusians' lack of organization and decentralized structure was a feature paralleled among Estonian and Lithuanian groups.[9] Similarly, the composition of Belarusian anti-Soviet resistance was predominantly peasant, something familiar to its Ukrainian counterpart.[10] Many participants of anti-Soviet groups were raised in anti-communist households during the interwar period, which conditioned their activity after the Second World War.[11]

Because Belarus was at the crossroads of all these anti-Soviet movements, the territory itself was occupied by different, non-Belarusian insurgent groups. These included the Lithuanian Freedom Army (*Lietuvos laisvės armija*, LLA), the Polish Home Army (*Armia Krajowa*, AK), and the Ukrainian Insurgent Army (*Ukraïns'ka povstans'ka armiia*, UPA). Both in quantity and organizational capacity, Polish armed units dominated anti-Soviet fighting in Belarus, particularly in the western regions.[12] Soviet reports assessed the strengths and weaknesses of the different national partisan groups. In one Soviet report on insurgency, the number of Belarusians killed in 1945 was zero and forty arrested, whereas for UPA members it was seventy-six and eighty-nine respectively. The number of Poles killed or arrested consisted of 257 and 564 respectively.[13] However, some scholars emphasize that proper figures for Belarusian anti-Soviet cases are unreliable because they were not accounted for by Soviet authorities. This detail is very possible, as Belarusian resistance was comparatively so small that Soviet security forces considered it negligible and perhaps not important to account for separately.[14]

The remains of the Belarusian Home Guard, Dalwitz insurgents, auxiliary police, and other armed groups organized during the war, were the principal agents behind anti-Soviet, Belarusian armed resistance. However, Monitch's 1948 information claiming to have encountered a well-organized partisan group led by Vitushka is questionable. This doubt stems not only from the fact that Monitch's testimony was unreliable but also because the Home Guard had only existed for about four months before the Red Army swept into Belarus. The Dalwitz programme similarly operated for only a handful of months. With this short amount of time, under extreme pressure and resource shortages, and with the escape or death of some of major Belarusian leaders, it is unlikely that there was a well-organized and developed anti-Soviet, Belarusian partisan movement. Furthermore, most of those left behind were lower ranking

Belarusian soldiers, who had little leadership experience to organize a substantial anti-Soviet resistance.

Despite the conditions and limitations to any substantial Belarusian anti-Soviet movement, Belarusian memoirs, testimonies, and newspapers indicate that there were several smaller points of resistance on the ground. Something Belarusian insurgents remarked on extensively was the belief that there would soon be a Soviet-US conflict. The belief that another war would erupt motivated many Belarusians to continue fighting, believing that they would soon be backed by US and western forces. The prospect of a future war prompted some Belarusians, including members of the Dalwitz group, to agree to fight in the interim, after which they expected foreign aid. In the April 1981 issue of *Belaruski holas* (The Belarusian Voice), Belarusian activist Iurka Stasevich described the existence of various Belarusian anti-Soviet groups. The article makes allegations about the existence of groups some of which were corroborated by other state security documents.[15] One such group was an organization called the "Belarusian People's Partisans" (*Belaruskaia Narodnaia Partyzanka*). According to Stasevich, this group was entirely disbanded by Soviet authorities.[16] After this unit, two anti-Soviet partisan groups temporarily remained in the Palesse region, under the leadership of two individuals referred to as Khareŭski and Perahud. These groups hid in the thick Belavezha and Aŭgustoŭski forests. According to the article, Khareŭski and Perahud ended up in Brazil and Paraguay respectively.[17]

More significantly, the available sources reveal that resistance on the ground, even if small, lasted many years after the Second World War. Ivan Ramanchuk is one such example. During the Second World War, he was initially a teacher in the town of Iaskevichi, in today's Hrodna region, from November 1941 to July 1942 but later worked as an inspector and a representative of the Belarusian Self-Help organization in Niasvizh.[18] Toward the latter part of the occupation period, he was in charge of the Belarusian cultural centre there as well. In the postwar period he sought employment but after three weeks of working he became the suspect of a Soviet security search. He subsequently went underground and was later joined by other individuals including Nikolaĭ Demukh and Bronislav Buko. Between 1947 and 1949 the group perpetrated a series of crimes. These included robberies – on one occasion amounting to a total of 154 thousand stolen rubles – the torture of Soviet officials, the killing of a village council chairman, and the murder of an employee of the ministry of state security in Niasvizh. The group's survival rested significantly in the hands of locals and family members who provided shelter and food. When this generosity was exhausted or unavailable, they turned to theft and armed robberies. In May of 1949, Ramanchuk, along with Demukh and Buko, was caught and arrested by Soviet security forces. On 17 November of that year, they were sentenced to twenty-five years in prison.[19]

Another case of extended anti-Soviet armed struggle concerned one Aŭhien Ivanovich Zhykhar. He had been a member of the Belarusian Youth Union in Pastavy during the Second World War and completed the Dalwitz training programme. Zhykhar returned to Belarus but soon after went into hiding as Soviet security forces began to look for him. Between 1946 and 1955 he and his armed group were responsible for twenty-three terrorist acts, forty-two robberies, and nine ambushes on Soviet village councils. A local from the town of Karpavichy eventually tipped off Soviet security forces and indicated where Zykhar was hiding.[20] After an armed ambush, the body of a dead man was found.[21] When going through the belongings, security forces indeed found the identity documents of an Aŭhien Ivanovich Zhykhar born in 1925. However, later interviews with those that knew Zhykhar doubted his death. There were also stories indicating he had fled to Poland in the 1950s and garnered a reputation there for being a local "Robin Hood".[22] During an interview in the 1990s, Viktar Sikora, a member of the Belarusian Independence Party from Pastavy, indicated that Zhykhar was the last to "fight against the Bolsheviks". Sikora recalled recruiting Zhykhar to the Belarusian Independence Party after which he was sent to Belarus as part of one of the parachuting Dalwitz teams.[23] His partisan group was mainly active in the Pastavy district in northern Belarus. Sikora cites the end of summer 1955 as the time of Zhykhar's apprehension by the Soviets, about seven kilometres from Pastavy. Finding himself surrounded by the security forces, Sikora alleged that Zhykhar took his own life.[24]

Though Romanchuk and Zhykhar did not organize substantial partisan movements, their existence and activity were very significant for a few reasons. Both Romanchuk and Zhykhar had collaborated in some way during the occupation. They were not members of the Belarusian nationalist elite and perhaps were not even interested in the Belarusian cause at all. Nevertheless, versions of Romanchuk's and Zhykhar's stories were politicized by both the émigrés and the Soviet state; the former elevated their activity to show there was anti-Soviet Belarusian nationalist resistance against the state, whereas the state also over emphasized their actions in order to justify more surveillance and repression of citizens and to amplify the threat of foreign influence on domestic terror. These two cases also show how important it was to have local support. Some locals were sympathetic, helped these individuals with directions, and provided shelter and supplies.[25] Indeed, it was local support that typically dictated the length and survival chances of these anti-Soviet groups.

Whereas those fighting in Belarus met a more disastrous fate, those Belarusians who managed to escape west led much different lives. Some of the main Belarusian nationalists found themselves in Displaced Person's camps and managed to escape to western Europe, North and South America, and Australia. Kushal's life during this time is one example of successful escape. After evacuating Belarus in the summer of 1944 and unsuccessfully training armed groups with the Germans, he ended up in a camp in Amberg, occupied by the US military. He remained there, at times passing as a stateless person, as a Pole, and as a "White Russian", listing his occupation as a teacher and making no mention of his military career. Later he was transferred to another camp in Regensburg and finally moved to the United States in June 1950.[26] Barys Rahulia similarly escaped and ended up in Belgium for a few years completing medical school and then subsequently moving to North America. In his application for assistance through the "Care and Maintenance Programme", he indicated that he had been a teacher during the war years, omitting any mention of his involvement in the Navahrudak Battalion he commanded.[27]

For those Belarusian nationalists who managed to avoid Soviet capture, they were united in their pursuit to continue engaging in anti-Soviet activity. However, this phase also witnessed internal conflict among the émigré community. The Belarusian Central Rada continued to operate for some time, after a brief retirement, but many of its members realized that the group's reputation had been soiled through its collaboration with Germany.[28] Alternatively, the Belarusian People's Republic, which had officially existed since 1918, drew in many Belarusian émigrés and former collaborators into its ranks.[29] The primary driver of the Rada and its supporters would continue to be Radaslaŭ Astroŭski, whereas prominent members of the People's Republic would include Kushal', Rahulia, and Mykola Abramchyk. Until at least the mid-1950s, both of these organizations and their members would work with western intelligence services to pursue their anti-Soviet activity. One of the most important partners for Belarusian émigré nationalists in their postwar efforts was the United States.

US – sponsored Covert Operations with East European Émigrés

The United States' process of recruiting anti-Communist groups began during the Second World War, though some scholars note that the ideological precondition for this process existed since 1917, following the Russian Revolutions.[30] US officials, including Allen Dulles, the future Central Intelligence Agency (CIA) director, made contacts with German officials and with collaborators of various nationalities and began embryonic espionage attempts in the Central and East European region.[31] George Kennan's Long Telegram in 1946 also contributed to US intelligence seeking out and working with former collaborators.[32] In order to destabilize the Soviet Union, Kennan argued that the United States had to foment nationalism in the Soviet republics and communist satellite states.[33] Administratively, the Office of Policy Coordination (OPC) took on the role of carrying out espionage and sabotage, under the umbrella of the CIA.

US intelligence officials recruited and brought in Nazis and collaborators for several reasons. One was to bring experts into the United States who had critical or highly-desired skills. Operation Paperclip, for example, was essentially a mission to find and bring in German scientific experts, who would eventually work on rocket building projects for NASA.[34] Another reason for working with such individuals was because of their knowledge and expertise of the lands which they came from. In this case, former collaborators in Eastern Europe and the Soviet Union piqued US interest because it lacked sufficient knowledge on the region. More importantly for intelligence efforts, they knew little of the people residing in these regions and had no eyes on the ground to assess the level of any anti-Soviet sentiment. In exchange for their services, the United States offered such individuals protection, legalization, and a safe haven in their eventual relocation to the United States. In terms of logistics and practicalities, a few postwar realities rendered the use of collaborators almost inevitable. The war had left anywhere between seven and eleven million displaced persons in Europe as of May 1945.[35] Some historians estimate that between 75,000 and 100,000 former residents did not return to the BSSR after the war. Of these, only 5,147 individuals identified themselves as being "Belarusian" and registered with the International Refugee Organization (IRO).[36] Some, like Kushal′, passed through various camps and countries under different nationalities. The resources to properly vet and investigate former collaborators were just not enough to keep up with the number of displaced persons. Furthermore, many people passed as "refugees" and were given safe haven in certain countries. This terminological and legal grey-area allowed for former collaborators to move more fluidly through institutions and states.

The other important factor that enabled the recruitment of former collaborators was the lack of institutional oversight in the United States. Legal agencies were created for the recruitment of agents, admitting candidates they thought were viable, and turning a blind eye to any potential damaging past by foregoing any additional investigation into their backgrounds.[37] The institutions that participated in this process included the International Refugee Organization, the State Department, the National

Security Council (NSC), and the Central Intelligence Agency through the Office of Policy Coordination.[38] Sometimes these institutions intervened directly by naturalizing former Nazis and collaborators or by overturning earlier deportation decisions. These institutions stressed that the selected candidates were at risk of being repatriated to the Soviet Union. In some cases, even providing false information on one's application for fear of being deported was considered a legitimate excuse by the Bureau of Immigration Appeals Court.[39] Through these channels, thousands of former Nazis and collaborators from the region in question entered the United States legally.[40]

These legal loopholes only persisted as the years went on, in part due to a Cold War atmosphere that quickly forgot or diminished the significance of collaborators in favour of forming a stronger anti-Communist front.[41] Between 1946 and 1947, the US intelligence community began fostering and strengthening its clandestine attempts with Eastern and Southern European émigré organizations. In 1948, the Displaced Persons Act announced that those who had served as Nazi collaborators would be ineligible for a US visa, yet by 1952 this law expired and was replaced with a new one allowing suspected individuals to enter more easily.[42] The United States accepted between 400,000 and 500,000 European refugees after the Second World War.[43] Some of these included individuals who would be dispatched to Belarus, Latvia, Lithuania, and Ukraine as part of anti-Soviet intelligence missions.[44] In a memorandum discussing the background of a potential Belarusian agent, one report stated that "Americans will not try as war criminals those members of the resistance who collaborated with the Germans."[45] There was no explanation as to what "resistance" meant.

Belarusian – US Collaboration

Most connections between anti-Soviet Belarusian agents and US intelligence services initially occurred in Displaced Person's camps. Kushal' was staying in a camp in Amberg in June 1945 and later in Regensburg in December of the same year.[46] Also finding himself in the camp in Amberg was Stanislaŭ Stankevich, the former mayor of German-occupied Barysaŭ during the war. Both men came into direct contact with US intelligence agents here.[47] A little further away, Barys Rahulia, had some contact with US intelligence officers in June 1946 at the latest, living in Marburg at the time.[48]

According to CIA documents, one of the earliest cases of wartime recruitment that piqued US intelligence services occurred in late fall 1944. It involved Youri Vinogradov "a 21-year old White Russian born in

Germany and educated in France… who proved to be a valuable source of information on life in Germany… Vinogradov opened the eyes of OSS [Office of Strategic Services] to the existence of an entire underground network of Eastern Europeans who supported the Nazi cause."[49] Another valuable intelligence agent was a Georgian by the name of Kedia who offered this insight:

> With regard to the people of Eastern Europe including non-Russians in the USSR who number 90 million, the Baltic states, White Ruthenia, the Ukraine, the Caucasus, Turkestan, Volga-Tatar, and the Taxus people of the Crimea… their organization and direction will be simple. These people all want to separate from Russia and establish the independence of their countries… [they] cannot of course be organized on a policy based on a concept of the 'sub-human' out of the east, but with a democratic policy of Liberty and the self-determination of peoples.[50]

Despite such promising claims, some US intelligence workers were initially apprehensive about investing in potential Belarusian agents. This hesitation stemmed from uncertainty about the potential of anti-Soviet activity in Belarus and in light of Monitch's falsified story that Kushal′ had conveyed to intelligence services.[51] Furthermore, US officials knew next to nothing about Belarus, as reflected in the many reports and briefings that contained a basic outline history. Sometimes meetings between case officers and Belarusians were held just to "learn" about the region.[52]

By July of 1951, however, the OPC was confident that there was some sort of anti-Soviet partisan group in Belarus that could be developed and could survive a long time due to the prevalence of swamps and heavy forests, which catered well to such activity. The CIA, with Frank Wisner as its first chief of clandestine operations, hoped to develop Belarusian partisan and intelligence cells in the BSSR that would connect with the already existing Lithuanian and Ukrainian cells – essentially creating a larger anti-Soviet net. Putting aside Monitch's story, the CIA decided that "the republic is a sufficiently strategic area to make cultivation of this nationalism worthwhile."[53] In addition to geography, the CIA believed that Belarusians would be excellent agents to undertake these missions because of their language skills: "Probably no other group, except perhaps the Galician Ukrainians, are so well equipped in terms of language and background to work well and effectively […].[54] The use of former war criminals did not present any moral issues for the Agency. For example, Stanislaŭ Stankevich, who was connected to the mass murder of six thousand Jews in Barysaŭ, was put under consideration, even though living witnesses attested to his involvement in the atrocity. Ultimately, he was dismissed as a potential agent; not for his crimes, but rather because of his problematic drinking, which could lead to vital information being divulged. Another concern was that Stankevich had potential ties to Soviet intelligence services in Germany who had asked him to gather intelligence on anti-Bolshevik activity.[55]

Though Belarusians wanted to be considered as agents sponsored by the US, they envisioned a more ambitious and integrated partnership than merely being connectors of existing Lithuanian and Ukrainian partisan groups. They hoped to not only gather intelligence but to bolster any anti-Soviet resistance on the ground in Belarus.[56] In a letter sent to General Matthew Ridgway, who served as Supreme Allied Commander of Europe in 1952 and was a senior officer of the US Army, Dz'mitry Kasmovich expressed:

> What can we do to help the Western democracies to maintain their independence and freedom, and what positive and definite action can we take in the struggle against communism to win back our own freedom and independence stolen by Bolsheviks? [...] Here in exile we have organized cadres for guerilla warfare behind the Soviet lines that can help the Western democracies in case of war with Russia. We are prepared and able to organize in the near future, or, in case of need, even now in the territory of our country Byelorussia, the revolutionary underground movement which can help future guerilla units and the Western troops, if there is war.[57]

Kasmovich went as far as to ask that NATO create a specialized "Guerilla Warfare" branch, which would fund, train, and deploy Belarusian and Ukrainian officers who specialized in such fighting in the region. He sent a similar appeal directly to Dwight Eisenhower afterward. Throughout the postwar period, he continued to make appeals to western governments, organizations, and intelligence services.[58]

From the start of this Belarusian-US collaboration, Abramchyk, who became an integral part of this postwar story despite being absent from Belarus during the war, suggested to intelligence officers that Rahulia be in charge of recruiting and spotting potential candidates. He stressed that Rahulia was younger and better suited to the job than an older, traditional military man like Kushal'.[59] Rahulia also had connections with people from his Navahrudak armed group and was well-connected with Belarusian émigrés in western Europe. Though Kushal' would continue to have close relationships with intelligence officers and Belarusian agents, a new generation was taking charge of the new postwar Belarusian struggle.

This collective Belarusian-US mission was referred to as the AEQUOR project and approved by the Department of State and Department of Defense.[60] There were two main components of this project. The first was the cultural aspect, which would manifest through US financial sponsorship of the Belarusian émigré newspaper *Bats'kaŭshchyna* (The Homeland), and later of the satirical paper *The Hornet*.[61] The second element involved the organization of anti-Soviet covert operations, referred to as the Cadre programme. This activity involved operations in the BSSR for the purposes of intelligence gathering and potentially creating partisan units. The latter portion of the plan proved to be the more challenging part of Belarusian-US collaboration. Intelligence documents, memoirs, and correspondence all reveal that the Belarusians pushed strongly for more involvement on their part in these missions and wanted the programme to include more of the saboteur training for its candidates. However, US intelligence agents were wary of pursuing such plans, which contributed to tension between both parties that built up as the years passed.

The US attitude vis-à-vis the Cadre programme is also reflected in a statement pertaining to the building of a training facility for Belarusian candidates:

> not necessary that the plant be anything beyond the simplest – a house for classes, with the students living in lodgings nearby, would be ample. [...] The school will be financed by the United States; however, in every other aspect, it must be completely a product of the BNR [Belarusian People's Republic]. The United States can provide absolutely no assistance, supervision, or other help beyond the financial assistance.[62]

US officials were simply interested in covert missions as a form of intelligence gathering in the BSSR itself, not in systematically developing a more home-grown programme with serious investment.[63] They would often pay lip service to many of Rahulia's proposals while always pursuing different intelligence avenues and seeking alternative Belarusian contacts – even if it caused internal rifts within the Belarusian émigré community.[64]

Nevertheless, the fact that Belarusians were making such plans for saboteur activity reveals important aspects of their postwar activity. They certainly felt comfortable making such demands, either because they thought they had little to lose or because they saw themselves critical partners in this collaboration. Drawing from his experience, Rahulia drafted detailed guides and suggestions that entailed serious organization and forethought. These proposals also show how well connected and aware Rahulia and others were of the operation, activity, and existence of

Belarusian nationalists all over the world. Rahulia, Kushal', and Abramchyk kept in contact regularly with different Belarusian émigré communities and hoped that those agents would organize anti-Soviet groups and spread anti-communist propaganda.[65] Rahulia spent a lot of time putting together dossiers of willing and competent Belarusians, which he passed on to US officials. It appears the latter also hoped that this information would allow them to expand their connections with other Belarusians, making them less reliant on the content creator himself.[66] Though Belarusian nationalists welcomed the prospect of having financial support, they too were wary of US intelligence promises.

In the context of these hidden and unsettled expectations from both parties, Belarusians and US officials began systematically recruiting candidates as early as the late 1940s. Over the course of their collaboration, the Belarusian leadership spotted and recruited candidates primarily in Europe and North America.[67] Rahulia forwarded lists of potential candidates and their backgrounds to US officials. If they passed initial verification, the candidate in Europe went to the US Zone in Germany for a follow up interview. Only after CIA approval could candidates then begin their "technical training, indoctrination and briefing".[68] US officials were in charge of training recruits but also convinced Rahulia to be part of this process because of his athleticism, intelligence, medical knowledge, and, most importantly, his experience as a military commander.[69] Furthermore, because Rahulia was living in Belgium and completing his medical degree at the University of Louvain, Belgium seemed to be a good place to train candidates.[70] In this way, the University of Louvain became a critical hub for Belarusian recruitment, training, and education, sponsored by Belarusian émigré organizations who offered scholarships.

Ideal candidates for the Cadre programme were those who were ideologically in line with the Belarusian cause, and specifically to the Belarusian People's Republic (BNR), because they would likely be more loyal to Abramchyk, Kushal', and Rahulia. Another important element included having connections in Belarus. Having friends and family still living in particular regions, increased the likelihood for an operative's survival and the mission's sustainability in the BSSR.[71] Having connections also meant these candidates were more familiar with the area, which would equip them with the tools to find existing partisans as well as to maintain a convincing cover as civilians.[72]

Once recruited and successfully vetted, candidates underwent political and military training. The political portion included taking courses on Belarusian history and language, the history of the United States, Marxism-Leninism, Fascism, the Stalin constitution, and Bolshevist propaganda and methods of combatting it. Military training would involve courses on the organization of both the Soviet and American armies, topography, partisan tactics, first aid, and a course called "life in the forest".[73] The entire training programme lasted between seven and ten months.[74] The candidates that went through the programme, both successfully and unsuccessfully, were enthusiastic and proud of their work but also had a lot of doubt, fear, and apprehension, even until the very end of their training. Some of them were unquestionably loyal to Kushal', Rahulia, and Abramchyk whereas others were doubtful of their leaders and handlers. These individuals were younger than the latter three and had their first formative experiences during the Second World War. Some of them were born in the western parts of Belarus that had been in Poland, whereas others were born in Soviet Belarus. Collectively, Belarusian nationalists and US intelligence officers organized two covert operations involving Belarusians. The first was a one-man mission in 1951, and the second involved a four-man team in 1952. The members of both missions had worked hard to escape Belarus in the summer of 1944 and now were returning to their homeland, which would look very different from what they remembered.

The Case of Ianka Filistovich

Nationalist émigrés perceived individuals who participated in anti-Soviet partisan activity as heroes who contributed to the Belarusian cause.[75] In the postwar Belarusian case, no one was heroized more than Ianka Filistovich. Filistovich was born in the village of Paniatsichy (Vialeĭka district, Minsk region) in 1926 to a family of farmers. His father was arrested as a kulak by Soviet authorities in 1939 but released in 1941. When he was sixteen years old, Filistovich claimed to have been forced to work for the Germans, mostly beginning with delivery jobs and writing reports in the areas of Il'ia and Al'kovichy, about 60 kilometres north of Minsk.[76] In the fall of 1943, he was mobilized for service into the notorious 13th Belarusian Police Battalion in Vialeĭka, as well as being used to guard a labour camp in Koldychevo, around Baranavichi.[77] When the Red Army moved into Belarusian territory in the summer of 1944, Filistovich travelled westward through Poland and, in January 1945, ended up in Ústi nad Orlici, now in the Czech Republic. There he was arrested by the Germans and sent to a prison around sixty kilometres west in the town of Pardubice. His life was spared when, on 8 May 1945, the Germans abandoned the town. Because of his knowledge of Polish, he worked in an administrative position on the Czech-Polish border until October of that year. Eventually Filistovich made his way to Paris, where he began his studies at the Sorbonne in February 1948. In Paris, he was active in the Belarusian community, including the Belarusian Independent Youth Organization.[78] It is at this point that he met and built a connection with Mykola Abramchyk. Abramchyk made Filistovich a member of the Belarusian People's Republic and even gave him a position in the party's council.[79] He also spent some time in the University of Louvain, where Rahulia was predominantly active.

CIA documents reveal that after his recruitment in June 1951, US officials transported Filistovich to a town outside of Munich for training.[80] Rahulia recommended him to US intelligence officers because of his discipline, his physicality, and his education. Though he was bright, Rahulia stressed that Filistovich was not too intellectual, suggesting he would follow orders and not question his duties during his training and the mission.[81] During his preparation for the mission in Germany, he studied topography, learned how to use a compass, read coordinates, and jump from a plane with a parachute. Filistovich also prepared by reading Soviet literature and newspapers. In CIA documents from early July 1951, Filistovich is referred to as CAMPOSANTO 1, whose mission was to commence operations in the BSSR, specifically in the Maladzechna region. His more ambitious tasks were to:

> establish contact with Byelorussian partisan groups [...] and, with their aid, to establish support bases for us for future operations. Besides knowing the area in which he is to operate as well as knowing the people and the alleged partisans there, CAMPOSANTO 1 will be provided with the leads by CAMBISTA II as well as photographs and documents of the BNR with which to establish his bonifides [sic] with those he is to contact... CAMPOSANTO 1 feels certain that he will be able to contact the partisans, but in the event he fails, feels certain that he can fulfill his mission of setting up a support base and remaining in the area indefinitely.[82]

Filistovich was to make the journey from Belgium to the French Zone of Occupation under the name John Dupont, with a cover of working as an US administrative assistant. His residence was ten miles from where he would train, to which he would be taken by a case officer, sometimes blindfolded, depending on what type of training they were doing. He was discouraged from fraternizing with locals or making himself more noticeable than seemed appropriate by his case officer.[83]

On paper and throughout his training, Filistovich was the ideal candidate to undertake such a mission. He was patriotic enough to be motivated by reasons beyond financial compensation and he had, what one report noted, a "fanatic devotion" to Abramchyk and Rahulia.[84] Furthermore, from the same report it appears that Filistovich took his responsibilities seriously, understanding that the preparation and result of this mission would impact US continued support for the Belarusians. Everything was going smoothly, until US officials postponed the mission in late August 1951. After rescheduling his dispatch for the following month in September, Filistovich became increasingly agitated and expressed his hesitation about going to the BSSR. US intelligence officers even brought in Rahulia to see Filistovich and reassure him that the mission had to continue and dissuade him from thinking otherwise.[85] Filistovich's last briefing occurred on 10 September 1951, and he was reminded of the mission's goals: to assess the anti-Soviet partisan situation in western Belarus and, if possible, to make contact with this resistance. After a month of this covert activity, he was to exfiltrate himself out of the BSSR. With a plan put in place, finally, on 21 September 1951, Filistovich was dispatched.[86]

Several months after he had been scheduled to return, intelligence officials began to worry. On 28 January 1952 concern over Filistovich and his mission surfaced in a semi-monthly report on the AEQUOR mission.[87] And yet despite Filistovich's lack of any communication with case officers since leaving for the BSSR, the CIA still believed he would exfiltrate successfully and that he was merely facing some hiccups. Indeed, other Belarusian candidates were already training in order to follow Filistovich's path on a subsequent mission. During the same month, even Abramchyk noted that he was optimistic that Filistovich would return in the spring.[88] A few months later, another report mentions Filistovich, yet this time more grim in its discussion about any outstanding personal commitments and remuneration in the event of his death. Whereas intelligence officers now continued to doubt the success of the mission, Rahulia and other Belarusians continued to believe, or at least insist, that he was still alive.[89]

It is still not entirely certain what exactly happened to Filistovich. Information about his whereabouts in Belarus comes from interviews with family members, an article from 1957 published in *Zviazda* acknowledging his capture by Soviet authorities, and in the work of Aliaksandar Lukashuk who had an opportunity to look at some pages of the BSSR trial transcript.[90] Piecing these fragments of information together, it appears that Filistovich spent an entire year organizing underground anti-Soviet groups in Belarus and also managed to distribute illegal literature published abroad to locals.[91] He lived in the forest among locals he knew from his childhood. One of his older sisters, Vera, recalled visiting him at some point in the town of Perasloŭka, now in the Vitsebsk region of northern Belarus.[92] Filistovich also managed to join an existing partisan group organized by a man by the name of Siargeĭ Mikulich. He eventually reorganized the latter into a more efficient underground cell called the "Belarusian National-Liberation Armed Forces".[93]

Filistovich's activity came to an end in September 1952 when he was captured by Soviet security forces.[94] He had been injured earlier in a scuffle and escaped deeper into the forest. However, with a growing infection and fever, he was forced to find refuge. He ultimately chose to go to the remote village of Iarmolichi, about 80 kilometres north of Minsk, where he knew an acquaintance from primary school whose father had been sent to the Gulag. Filistovich thus assumed that his former friend would not have any allegiance to Soviet authorities. Being caught harbouring a fugitive, however, came with serious repercussions.[95] In the end, under the pretenses that he was going to get medication to heal Filistovich's wounds, his childhood friend betrayed him to Soviet security forces.[96] For nearly a year, having local connections had helped Filistovich, but in the end they led to his capture.

Details of his capture and trial, if there was one, are unclear. Filistovich's sister claims that a witness testified that Filistovich never hurt nor stole from locals, and though he was a "natural enemy" of the state, he was not a terrible person and did not deserve to be shot. Those that had aided Filistovich, or were suspected of having done so, were also arrested and tried but their fates are not entirely known.[97]

There are different dates for Filistovich's death, with one pointing to 1953. However, other stories circulated, indicating that Filistovich was never executed.[98] In an interview from 2001, his older sister, Halina, provided a document from the Executive Committee of the City of Minsk (*Mingorispolkom*) in response to her earlier request to find out about her brother's fate. The document, dated on 14 February 1992, states that Filistovich's trial took place from 4 to 5 November 1953 by military tribunal. He was accused of voluntarily joining the 13th Belarusian battalion during the Second World War and of engaging in US-backed saboteur and espionage work against the Soviet Union. The accusation further notes that Filistovich founded and commanded an underground organization in the region that took part in terrorist activity.[99] His sister also cited another document she received from the Soviet Red Cross in Moscow indicating her brother died in the Soviet Union on 19 March 1954.

At the time of the supposed trial, US intelligence agents knew nothing about Filistovich's fate. It was not until January 1957 that US officials and Belarusian émigrés finally understood what had happened. This news first came secretly from a Belarusian woman who had emigrated to England recently and informed Abramchyk that Filistovich had been caught. She also claimed that all those helping and abetting him, about forty people, were executed.[100] A few months later, a version of the woman's story was confirmed by the publication of Filistovich's mission and fate in the May and June 1957 articles from *Zviazda* (The Star) – the official newspaper of the Communist Party of Belarus. All of the things that the CIA and Belarusians had wanted to keep secret came out in the article, including references to particular case officers, US training facilities, and Abramchyk's and Rahulia's direct involvement in these operations.[101] Over the years, Soviet security forces continued to use Filistovich as an example to show the threat the United States posed to the Soviet Union.

Belarusian émigrés remember Filistovich for his ardent patriotism and for his sacrifice which legitimized Belarus's fight for independence. Others, however, claimed that Filistovich would have been more efficient and productive had he remained in the West.[102] In his contribution to the memory of Filistovich, Rahulia wrote, "I don't know if there would be a Pahonia, or a White-Red-White flag, if it were not for people like Ianka Filistovich… I would like to think that his sacrifice was not in vain."[103] As for Filistovich's own opinion in the matter, he had been quoted for saying he appreciated his mentors, Kushal′, Abramchyk, and Rahulia, and that:

> Independence of one's nation can never be asked for, can never be sought diplomatically; it can only be achieved through armed struggle […] with their character, the Belarusian people have very useful knowledge and quality of being fighters. This is evidenced by our past and history of war of those nations, whose armies Belarusians were forced to serve in.[104]

Though in the early 1950s, the fate of the mission was uncertain, US intelligence officers recognized Filistovich's capabilities as a good agent. Therefore, they were confident they would be able to recruit more individuals like him. This hopeful belief was soon shattered by shortcomings from both the Belarusians and US officials, which affected their future collaboration. Equally impactful were larger, international political developments that shaped the nature of the relationship.

The Creation and Dissolution of AEQUOR Team I

While Filistovich was just finishing his training in the summer of 1951, Belarusians and US intelligence officers were already discussing plans for more dispatches and picked out a few candidates. However, whereas Filistovich's training went relatively smoothly, preparing the group of agents who would be known as the AEQUOR team proved to be more challenging. These problems were related to specific details of their operation and training, as well as personal issues the candidates were experiencing.

These challenges offer insight into what the candidates may have been experiencing and they also reveal growing points of contention between US officials and Belarusians.

The AEQUOR plan was organized into five phases, starting in April 1952. The first phase, extending from April to July 1952, was to begin with the group being airdropped to the Naliboki Forest, where they would engage in reconnaissance. Two of the individuals, who were trained as wireless telegraphy (w/t) operators, would remain on the makeshift base, whereas the other two would gather intelligence in the western Belarusian towns of Maladzechna, Navahrudak, and Lida.[105] In the following phase, they were to continue their work from the previous period and also fortify four separate drop zones (DZ). During this time, they were to also integrate one individual in a local town so that the agent could operate openly as a normal citizen.[106] The third phase covered the colder months from November 1952 to April 1953. By this point, those agents who had been unable to integrate themselves into nearby towns were to lay low and dig in for winter. After winter, it was proposed that the agents should attempt to recruit local residents, if it was deemed possible. If this was successful, the agents were to continue to expand their clandestine group.[107]

To prepare for this multi-phase mission, the selected agents trained on a daily basis from 8:30 am to 10:00 pm and were taught courses in tradecraft – including selecting dead drops, using recognition signals, and acquiring information from individuals – survival techniques, in addition to practical skills such as document falsification, observation, and reporting.[108] Some candidates were better at these skills than others. Based on their strengths, the group was divided into two: those specializing in wireless telegraphy (w/t) and those specializing in intelligence gathering in the field. The original AEQUOR I team consisted of individuals with the cryptonyms Camposantos 2, 4, 6, and 7. Camposantos 2 and 4 were trained as w/t operators, whereas Camposantos 6 and 7 were trained more in the field.[109] One of the first major hurdles for the AEQUOR team came with Camposanto 7. A week into his training, he refused to jump off a parachute tower during three consecutive attempts. This hesitation was a critical issue, considering that the candidates were suppose to be parachuted into the Naliboki Forest. In an attempt to motivate the man, US intelligence officers, once again, brought in Rahulia to try to convince Camposanto 7 to jump. These conversations failed. Some intelligence officers initially suspected Camposanto 7 of being a Soviet agent, however further talks with other AEQUOR team members made no indication that he was a spy but that he merely "chickened out".[110] The CIA and Belarusian leadership organized his release from the programme and reintegration into civilian life. He continued to be monitored for some time afterward.[111]

Fortunately for the mission, there was another individual, Camposanto 5, who quickly replaced Camposanto 7 and would prove more competent. Intelligence officers recruited Camposanto 5 earlier, in December 1951, but he had failed to show up for his training. With Camposanto 7's dismissal, intelligence officers approached him once again. This time, he agreed to join the mission and begin his training within the month.[112] Although Camposanto 5's decision was important from a practical point, the Belarusian leadership also considered him the most qualified member of the team.[113]

From here on out the training portion of the preparation went relatively smoothly, however other issues arose. Though case officers noted that the group's morale was good, there were personal differences and issues. One root of this problem stemmed from the agents' backgrounds. They were born and raised in the interwar period when Belarusian territory was divided, coming from either western Belarus that had been part of Poland or eastern Belarus that was the Belarusian Soviet Socialist Republic. This difference was important because it shaped their memories, motivations, and attitudes toward the mission. For example, Camposanto 4 was from eastern Belarus. His driving reason for volunteering for the mission was a "hatred of the Soviets and, to a lesser extent, of the Russians – for what they have done to him and his family."[114] Similar in background, Camposanto 6 was also a former Soviet citizen.[115]

Whereas Camposantos 4 and 6 were from eastern Belarus, Camposanto 2 and 5 were from western Belarus. Camposanto 2, was reportedly, "the most intelligent, better educated, and stands slightly higher in the social scale."[116] He had also been training longer than anyone else on the team, as he had started the programme at the same time as Filistovich. He was given the leadership position of the team for these reasons, yet there were still many doubts about him. Because he was originally from western Belarus, there were concerns that he did not inherently "belly feel" Soviet mentality beyond an intellectual level.[117] This difference could result in his inability to successfully assimilate when in Soviet Belarus.

The newest member of the team, Camposanto 5, was from the western Belarusian area where the AEQUOR I mission was to take place.[118] Curiously, he was also the only individual on the team who was a member of the Belarusian Central Rada, unlike others who were affiliated with the foundational 1918 Belarusian People's Republic.[119] His quiet and solitary behaviour was attributed to difference in party affiliation, as well as to his delay in joining the group. In the 1950s, the Rada's hub was in Manchester, England but it is unclear how close Camposanto 5 was to the party. Also unknown was whether or not the Rada knew of Camposanto 5's participation in the mission.

It would be Camposantos 2 and 5 who would prove the most difficult to work with. In the winter of 1951, during the last holiday season before the team was to be dispatched, intelligence officers had to persuade Camposanto 2 not to abandon his training to go see his fiancée over Christmas.[120] He became more agitated and unpredictable, yet intelligence officers still decided to give him the position of group leader to motivate him and out of concern that he would abandon the mission altogether.[121] However, these efforts did little to appease Camposanto 2. He continued to make last-minute lists of demands just prior to the group's dispatch, and his outbursts caused a lot of distress for the rest of team. Most of his demands were about money. The original financial agreement was a net sum to be delivered to agents after their return from the mission or to their selected beneficiaries should they not survive. Camposanto 2 demanded his financial sum be doubled and transferred immediately to his bankers in London prior to the team's departure.[122] This demand was brought up even during the team's final meeting before their planned dispatch, on 26 April 1952. Despite Rahulia's pleading and visible disappointment, Camposanto 2 refused to let this issue go. He seems to have been alone in his demands, as the other members of the group refrained from partaking in the argument. In the end, Camposanto 5 asked to be dismissed from the mission because he was concerned about Camposanto 2's leadership ability and did not trust him.[123] The final report by the US case officer describing the situation stated that the driving reason for the mission's collapse was not only Camposanto 2's demands but also his egotistical behaviour and disregard for the cause or efforts put into the mission. By this point, the other two candidates insisted that they no longer trusted Camposanto 2.[124] The CIA had no choice but to dissolve the AEQUOR Team I and delay the mission indefinitely.

The experience with the first AEQUOR project inevitably soured relations between Belarusian nationalists and US intelligence officials. They soon put together a new AEQUOR team and its members followed a similar training programme to the first. However, the sense of optimism during Filistovich's training and dispatch had dissipated with the first AEQUOR project and saw no revival. What pushed the new mission forward was a sense of urgency and a continued lack of intelligence about the BSSR's underground activity, especially not yet knowing about Filistovich's fate.

A Renewed Attempt: the Dispatch of AEQUOR Team II

In an attempt to start fresh, US intelligence services dismissed Camposantos 2 and 5, and began looking for two more candidates. While Camposantos 4 and 6 were given some time off, the new members of AEQUOR Team II, Camposantos 8 and 9, trained in preparation for a four-man mission to be launched in August 1952.[125] The responsibilities of Camposanto 4 and Camposanto 9 included to continue working as w/t operators, whereas Camposantos 6 and Camposantos 8 would be scouts and eventually integrate themselves as residents in nearby towns.[126] The operational area was the western Belarusian region between Minsk, Ashmiany, and Baranavichi. The four men assigned to the mission included Mikhail Ivanovich Kal′nitskii (Camposanto 4, aka "Joe"), Tsimafei Akimovich Vostrykaŭ (Camposanto 6, aka "Carl"), Gennadii Adamovich Kastsiuk (Camposanto 8, aka "Ben"), and Mikhail Pavlovich Artsiusheŭski (Camposanto 9, aka "Finn"). Kal′nitskii and Vostrykaŭ were members from the original AEQUOR I team.

How did these four men end up on a four-man mission to infiltrate the BSSR, sponsored by the United States and organized by Belarusians? In the immediate postwar period, the latter four men, like Kushal′, Rahulia and other Belarusians, escaped westward and moved around camps. Artsiusheŭski identified as a Pole in the immediate postwar era, moving between Höchstadt an der Aisch to Amberg in the American zone of occupation and finally to England in 1948.[127] Kal′nitskii passed as a Russian, a Pole, and a Ukrainian and spent some time in a Displaced Persons camp in Germany, where he attempted to get some employment. In 1947, he was resettled in Belgium, at which point he may have developed connections with other Belarusians there.[128] Kastsiuk knew Rahulia from Navahrudak, where he served in various armed groups, and later escaped westward. He claimed Polish nationality and spent some time in Denmark, later resettling in France in 1948.[129] It is very likely that it is in France where Kastsiuk also met Abramchyk as well as Ianka Filistovich, as they all appear on various lists pertaining to Belarusians living in France.[130] Last, but not least, Vostrykaŭ passed as a Russian at Düsseldorf and Iserlohn in the British occupied zone.[131] The point of contact between these individuals with higher up members of Belarusian organizations remains unclear, but based on Rahulia's memoir, it appears collective relief efforts and admission to university in Belgium brought these individuals together.

Unike the first AEQUOR team, reports indicated that the AEQUOR Team II preparations and training were going smoothly in the summer of 1952. Part of this was possibly due to more pressing restrictions by the training programme in an effort to reduce the chance of repeated problems suffered with the first team. Other reasons may be attributed to the personalities of the new candidates who worked well together.[132] The men seemed comfortable with their cover stories, which they were to use when assimilating in Belarus.[133] According to their covers, the four men were born in Soviet Belarus in 1924, with the exception of Kastsiuk whose supposed date of birth was 1923 in Wilno. All had moved a lot during the war, been displaced, and were finally making their way back to Belarus in 1952. These identitites were used for their falsified passports and military service records. In general, their cover stories did not differ much from reality.[134] US intelligence officers instructed the four agents to make contact with the American base in Germany at least once in a forty-five day period, not exceeding three times during that time frame.[135]

After their training in late July, the team was sent to the staging area but was forced to stall their dispatch for twenty-six days due to poor weather conditions.[136] This period of waiting, which weighed heavily on the minds of the candidates, was noted by the case officer preparing the report. The case officer noted that they were

> forced into an admiring recognition of the team members' courage. It is one thing for a soldier in time of war [...] to undertake an heroic action; it is, however, quite something else, and requires a higher order of courage, for a clandestine activist to undertake such an action in time of peace – knowing, as he does, that he will remain unrecognized no matter what its outcome.[137]

Finally, on the night of 27 August 1952, the team was parachuted into Soviet Belarus from unmarked American planes.[138] Putting it in perspective, this dispatch came only a few days or weeks before Filistovich's capture, yet this information was not known at the time.

To the relief of the Belarusians and US officials in western Europe and across the pond, the AEQUOR II team did manage to send a series of messages to the base in Germany. The first message from the team noted that they had landed between ten to fifteen miles from their intended drop point, and the second communication was sent from one of the agents, Kal'nitskii, on 31 August 1952. However, nothing was heard after this second message for several months. By November of that year, the US intelligence base in Munich was beginning to show concern. Some case officers reasoned that a possible explanation for this silence may have been some w/t equipment malfunction. Others believed the team had been caught by Soviet security forces.[139]

In the end, Soviet capture ultimately proved to be the reason for the group's silence. After the communication made in August, the following day the group made a temporary base around the village of Krasnaia Gorka, splitting into two teams. Kal'nitskii and Artsiusheŭski remained on base, whereas Vostrykaŭ and Kastsiuk headed towards Navahrudak, in western Belarus, and Rahulia's home town. They travelled to Navahrudak under the pretenses that they were forest workers returning home from another towm.[140] Vostrykaŭ and Kastsiuk went to meet Rahulia's mother-in-law, who was supposed to help them find someone who could arrange legal documentation. A man named Gutor later gave Vostrykaŭ the name of a contact in Minsk. Gutor turned out to be an agent of the BSSR security services, and immediately after meeting with Vostrykaŭ, passed on everything he had been told to security forces. Vostrykaŭ was subsequently arrested at the train station in Minsk. According to Soviet security documents, during his interrogation he revealed the location of the team, their descent date, and their pseudonyms. On 10 September 1952, Soviet security forces found the remaining three team members; capturing Artsiusheŭskii and Kastsiuk and mortally wounding Kal'nitskii who died two days later.[141]

US intelligence agents, however, did not know the entire group had been captured at this time as they continued to receive messages at the base in Munich. From CIA reports, it appears that US officials believed that while Vostrykaŭ had gone to meet one of Rahulia's contacts, Soviet security forces ambushed the other three men. They believed that two of the men, Kastsiuk and Artsiusheŭskii, had fled and retreated deeper into the forests where they continued to communicate to the intelligence base in Munich. According to a message sent to the base in early October, Vostrykaŭ joined the latter two in a prearranged location, where they communicated their coordinates to the base in Germany indicating their location was in a bunker on the outskirts of a village. The message asserted that Vostrykaŭ was still meeting with Rahulia's contact and was to go to Minsk to visit people at the contact's suggestions.[142] According to w/t messages from the team members, as of November 1953 they had not been successful in finding any type of collective resistance, besides occasional individuals living clandestinely.[143]

These later messages sent by the team concerned US case officers and the Belarusian leadership. They remarked on the tone of the messages and warned that "there have been some disturbing indications in certain of Artsiusheŭskii's messages." What was meant by that was not explained in the report, but it certainly was important enough to mention.[144] A later addendum to another w/t message suggested that the team may have been compromised and was being controlled by the Soviet authorities.[145]

The last time contact made with the team was on 9 January 1955, and US intelligence officers did not expect that they would re-establish communication.[146]

Similarly with Filistovich's end, the fates of the four men were loudly published in a Soviet paper and subsequently republished in a Belarusian émigré paper in Toronto, two years after the last w/t message.[147] An article in *Belaruski holas* (The Belarusian Voice) from March 1957 cites the Soviet paper, *Kolkhoznaia pravda* (The Collective Farm Truth) from January 1957, which claimed that "American" parachuters were found, along with their equipment, in the area of Baranavichi, in western Belarus.[148] In subsequent pieces, *Bielaruski holas* explicitly named Abramchyk and Rahulia as the organizers of the operations.[149]

Back in the BSSR and prior to the publication of these newspaper articles, a trial was held for Vostrykaŭ and Kastsiuk between 10 and 14 November 1955. The verdict, announced on 23 January 1956, gave both men twenty-five-year prison sentences.[150] The fate of Artsiusheŭskii remains a bit murky. According to a testimony by a local, he surrendered himself and was allowed to remain and study in Minsk. It appears that he was pardoned and relieved of criminal liability, suggesting he may have been a Soviet agent or at the very least did something in exchange for his freedom.[151]

The Decline of Belarusian-American Relations and End of Covert Operations

The rise and ultimate fall of Belarusian-US covert operations had as much to do with the failure of the dispatches as it did with personality issues between case officers and the Belarusians in charge. Early on in this relationship, in the Fall of 1950, US intelligence officers described Rahulia as a man of "above average intelligence, strongly anti-Communist and [who] had considerable experience in anti-Soviet counterintelligence work with White Ruthenian groups."[152] His only fault seemed to be that he was ambitiously trying to further Belarusian nationalism. By February 1954, however, the description of Rahulia would be that of someone who:

> has come to be of increasingly less value to Project AEQUOR during the past year [...] He has displayed a gross lack of understanding of operational matters which require his full attention [...] This state of affairs has undoubtedly been exacerbated as a result of AECAMBISTA 2's [Rahulia's] undertaking too many activities but is basically attributable to his impatience, temperament, and inability to grasp the need for clandestine mentality.[153]

During the early to late 1950s, Belarusian-US intelligence collaboration suffered for a few reasons, and the unsuccessful covert missions were symptoms of deeper issues. The failure of the AEQUOR project was due to the deteriorating relationship between Belarusians in charge and US intelligence officers and because of the poor quality of recruits, or lack thereof, as time went on. As the US invested more money and other resources without good results, the rift with the Belarusians became bigger.[154] Figures reveal that between October 1951 and February 1952, Rahulia found and recommended twenty-nine candidates, of which sixteen were rejected. By July 1952, the sentiment was that Rahulia, or "Cambista 2's work in recruiting in Europe have been extremely unsatisfactory [...] a greater effort and a more intelligent approach to the problem by Cambista 2 would have produced better results. In the face of this poor showing, we are unwilling to 'reward' Cambista 2 by permitting him to travel as Cambista 1 [BNR] recruiting representative to North America."[155] Abramchyk, too, was increasingly criticized in reports with case officers who often dismissed his opinion reasoning that he had not been in Belarus since 1943 and therefore, had lost touch with the reality of life there.[156]

Procuring capable candidates to partake in covert activity proved to be challenging. US intelligence officers increasingly criticized Rahulia's recruitment style noting that he was confident "he could tell whether the man was good 'by looking in his eyes.'"[157] By February 1953, the recruiting situation was both so dire and embarrassing that US officials considered using non-Belarusian agents.[158] Finally, on 8 February 1954, Rahulia admitted that he could no longer secure potential candidates in Europe.[159] It is difficult to assess, however, whether this shortage in recruits was due to Rahulia's incompetence or because of a lack of individual interest to partake in missions.

Moreover, US intelligence officers were also responsible for some of the failures during their collaboration with Belarusians. Problems with potential candidates arose with some Belarusians who were drafted to the US military but who the Agency forbade to participate in these covert operations. Despite repeated requests by Abramchyk to allow these individuals to be part of the AEQUOR programme, US intelligence officers procrastinated in their response and ultimately never addressed them.[160] Furthermore, there was a lot of miscommunication, or complete lack of it. At several points, US intelligence officers assured Rahulia that his candidates were viable, and he would subsequently begin transferring them to training locations. Rahulia would then be told that the Agency had changed its mind and would postpone training, or that it was no longer invested in that particular operation or candidate. This last-minute decision-making process caused a lot of embarrassment for Rahulia, which, he expressed to US intelligence officers, could damage his reputation among Belarusian émigrés and agents. US intelligence officers saw Rahulia's concerns as nothing more than his unpleasant personality and ambition to rise up politically among Belarusian émigré ranks.[161] Such observations about Rahulia became more frequent in the years following.

Another layer to the candidate procurement problem had to do with time and place. Many of the emigres who had fled to the West were now assimilating quite well into western society and few would risk their comfortable situation for a life of espionage, hiding, and possible capture, incarceration, or death.[162] Indeed, Rahulia, Abramchyk, Kushal', and others benefited from the comforts of assimilation and their lives in Canada, Australia, and the United States respectively. Some case officers even noted that Belarusian émigré leaders had increasing political and personal aspirations, rather than focusing on US intelligence efforts.[163] They argued that because of other distractions and ambitions, Belarusian leaders were becoming increasingly careless. They had especially serious doubts about Rahulia's professionalism stemming from his disclosure of secret operational details to some individuals. Eventually, Rahulia's indiscretion resulted in a major security breach at the University of Louvain in Belgium that hosted and recruited many Belarusians.[164] A group called the "Inner Circle of Twelve" got access to information regarding US involvement with the BNR, as well as ongoing operations and the role of Rahulia with the CIA.[165] Two days later, the US intelligence officers made the decision to completely get rid of the Louvain recruiting hub and to eliminate Rahulia's role, due to his lack of security understanding, inefficient handling, and general disregard for his responsibilities.[166]

The disintegrating Belarusian-US relationship and failure of covert operations are not necessarily unique to this partnership. Much of the CIA's collaboration with other nationalists and national groups fell short of procuring credible and consistent intelligence.[167] Furthermore, Soviet counterintelligence practices of turning individuals seriously undermined US efforts. In total, US intelligence services dispatched around eighty-five agents of which 75 percent failed in their intended missions.[168] The souring of these relations and anti-Soviet intelligence gathering efforts also came with the changing postwar atmosphere that made a direct and physical war between the United States with the Soviet Union increasingly unlikely. This shift in war potential disappointed Belarusian nationalists, who hoped they could depend on US support, if not for covert operations then at least for Belarusian cultural programmes and an émigré paper. When requesting further aid or funding for the

Belarusian cause, these individuals often insisted that cutting off support would put Belarusians in physical harm and expose them to Soviet security forces[169]

Rahulia's relationship with US intelligence officers ended swiftly by the end of the 1950s. Abramchyk's relationship continued until the early 1960s, with his insistence on continued sponsorship of the Belarusian newspaper. Although we have more information now about the fate of the AEQUOR teams, US intelligence officers were left largely in the dark about the end of these operations. More embarrassingly, the Belarusians who had been in charge of covert activity were losing credibility in the eyes of the Belarusian émigré community. Rahulia expressed these concerns in a letter written to an individual, discovered by the CIA. In it, he writes:

> It must not be forgotten that we are dealing with people who have undergone a number of occupations, and who have been betrayed by a number of occupying powers [...] Among them are also people who have been betrayed by the Americans – immediately after the occupation of Germany. Continual procrastination elicits their distrust, and sooner or later we will have to give them a definite answer and to explain our reasons [...] in order not to lose confidence, to explain the actual reasons for the failure and to admit our naive confidence in the Americans was too great.[170]

Not surprisingly, Rahulia made no mention of his work for the CIA in his memoirs. He attributes his move from Belgium to Canada in December 1954 as a shift in political climate resulting from the Korean War. Along with other Belarusian émigrés, he hoped that the United States would see the cruelties of Soviet rule and engage in direct confrontation. When this did not happen, he and his wife made the decision to go to Canada, where he was offered a job as a physician.[171] This decision came rather abruptly, considering that, according to his memoir, he and his family were settling well in Belgium and had gone through all the effort to legalize their permanent stay there. Their quick move to Canada came around the time of the University of Louvain security breach, though this too is omitted in his memoir.

Interaction with Other Foreign Intelligence Services

Some Belarusians worked with US intelligence services after the Second World War, whereas others operated out of different countries and may have worked with other intelligence organizations. Still others even worked with multiple intelligence agencies, either consecutively or at the same time.

A secret document from the Polish Ministry of Internal affairs in 1954 notes that there were ongoing clandestine operations and Belarusian agents operating out of West Germany, France, Belgium, Sweden, Italy, Great Britain, and the Vatican.[172] If true, this pattern reflects not only a potential interest of western countries in anti-Soviet espionage, but it also reflects the rupture, or ruptures, among Belarusian nationalists who strived to become relevant to intelligence services in their own parts of the world.[173] Just as Rahulia managed things for US intelligence services, other notable Belarusians were tasked with doing similar things for other espionage agencies.

Aside from the Belarusian-US cooperation, the other strong relationship was between Belarusians and British intelligence services. For reasons, in part, similar to those in the United States, the United Kingdom became a place many former war criminals and collaborators called home. There was relatively little oversight and proper vetting of individuals entering the UK, which allowed many questionable figures to enter the country. The UK stood behind its policy of offering refuge to political exiles who would otherwise be persecuted by other regimes, and it relied on immigration screening to prevent the influx of war criminals. Even though the USSR demanded that war criminals be extradited back, UK authorities largely refused to do so noting that it doubted Soviet judicial procedures would handle such cases accordingly. Moreover, the political situation and struggle over the British mandate of Palestine between 1945 and 1948 made matters worse, especially after a series of attacks by Jewish underground groups on British forces. This anti-British violence in Palestine was met with increased antisemitism in the UK which hardly motivated the apprehension of war criminals.[174] All of these factors collectively contributed to Britain's attitude toward former collaborators and war criminals. By some estimates, there were at least seventy-eight alleged war criminals living in Britain in 1989.[175]

Twice in the early 1990s the House of Lords and Commons rejected a proposed bill to apprehend and try war criminals living in the United Kingdom.[176] With the exception of one individual, no other former collaborator or perpetrator of war crimes was tried and prosecuted by in the UK. The exception surrounds the case of Andrei Sawoniuk, a native of present-day Damachava in the western Brėst region of Belarus. Sawoniuk served in the auxiliary police in the area during the war, until he escaped and joined the Polish Army. Following the end of the war, he passed as a native Pole and moved to the UK, where he worked as a ticket collector for British rail services. The case against Sawoniuk involved members of the jury actually traveling to Belarus, as well as survivors and other witnesses of Sawoniuk's actions, who traveled to the UK for the actual trial. The charges against Sawoniuk included two counts for the murder of Jews. He was tried, convicted, and served six years in prison until his death.[177] The Sawoniuk case was an exception in Britain's record of prosecuting war criminals. Sawoniuk himself never claimed to have been a Belarusian patriot or nationalist.

Similarly to US intelligence services, MI6 saw East European collaborators as allies in a potential fight against the Soviet Union. This necessity came, in part, due to the lack of knowledge regarding the region in question. British authorities in various camps often designated such questionable individuals as Displaced Persons, without any additional screening and usually separately from United Nations relief authorities. Another reason for harbouring such individuals was driven by a shortage of man labour in the UK who were then recruited for work.[178] In these ways, British intelligence services worked with notable Belarusians, both in England and also in West Germany. However, in other ways, British intelligence services differed from their US counterparts, in that the practice of intelligence gathering as part of a state institution long predated such work in the United States. Soon after the Second World War, British intelligence services were capable of using their pre-war, anti-Soviet points of contact that had existed since the days of the Russian Revolution. These points of contact were largely concentrated in the Baltic states. From these areas further links were made with other western regions of the Soviet Union.[179]

Most notably, MI6 recruited Dz'mitry Kasmovich, the former chief of the Belarusian auxiliary police, who had changed his name to Liubovik Zarechny in the postwar period.[180] There were also suspicions that Barys Rahulia was also an agent working for MI6.[181] The process by which Belarusians ended up working with British intelligence services differed from those working with the United States, because whereas US intelligence services set up training programmes and missions to plan for dispatches, UK intelligence services largely sent resources and support to existing anti-Soviet Belarusian networks on the ground. For example, several individuals escaped Belarus and eventually made their way to the UK where they allegedly informed intelligence services of active Belarusian cells in Poland, largely including former members of the auxiliary police, Home Guard, and Dalwitz group. This pool of contacts included both men and women operating in cities such as Łódź, Poznań, and Gdańsk. One of the more notable espionage cases, supported by the UK, was a group run by a man named Vasil' Zavadzki. He had served in the Belarusian auxiliary police and the Home Guard during the war, later escaping with the Germans to western Poland. He somehow managed to get to England, receive some support there, and then return to Poland in the early fifties to try to organize a spy ring. The individuals he was allegedly in contact with included many rank-and-file former soldiers of the Belarusian auxiliary police and of the Home Guard. Many of these individuals knew of each other prior to the war because they grew up in the same area and subsequently served in the same battalions or units during the war. In 1952, Polish authorities reported the arrest of a UK-sponsored group of agents who were sent to Poland from Germany and were planning to infiltrate the BSSR. Zavadzki managed to return to England where he lived until his death.[182] Similarly to this group, many real or alleged UK-sponsored spies were arrested by Polish authorities in the mid-1950s.

The overall extent of Belarusian-British collaboration is unclear. In US documents, there is mention of British interest in sponsoring a Belarusian covert mission into the USSR in 1949. However, the source of the information cannot confirm that such coordinated efforts went beyond mere discussion.[183] The same source also indicates that there may have been British training camps for Belarusians in Hanover, yet it does not elaborate on the purpose of these programmes nor confirms their actual existence. Later in 1952, Abramchyk communicated with his US case officer that he received a "small signal" indicating that British Intelligence Services were organizing clandestine operations focused on the BSSR. There was no follow-up or further detail to this suggestion.[184]

Other reports made mention of an officer's training course being put together in Manchester, England, directly by Kasmovich, aka Zarechny.[185] The course was part of an effort to strengthen the Belarusian Liberation Movement, a military organization created in March 1952 that claimed to be receiving support from the British and would be officially subordinate to the Rada, with Astroŭski as the leader.[186] The informant, reporting on Kasmovich's group to the United States, attended one of these gatherings that included men, women, and children. They noted that Kasmovich's speech was passionate and even threatened to have Abramchyk and Rahulia "shot in the future if they were selling out the Belorussians to the Americans."[187] The loud speech, however, was foiled with a small audience in attendance – a mere fifteen people.[188]

Though far from comprehensive, these reports indicate two larger points of contention. The first speaks to the competition between different Belarusian émigrés living in different parts of the West. This competition was mainly organized behind the two driving political factions, the Belarusian People's Republic and the Belarusian Central Rada. Denunciations of members came from both sides. Kushal', Abramchyk, and

Rahulia criticized the Rada's existence as a deterrent to the Belarusian cause because of its past collaboration with Germany, whereas members of the Rada stressed the legitimacy of their group.[189] The other point of contention came through competition between US and British intelligence services. US intelligence reports repeatedly showed concern that the British were poaching their agents.[190] In the end, however, it appears MI6 was distrustful of Astroŭski and the Rada group, due to their compromising past and were concerned that they had been infiltrated by Soviet security agents.[191] This understanding is the same conclusion US officials came to when they established contact with Astroŭski for potential collaboration, stating that he was "at best, an opportunist; at the very worst, it is possible that he might be probably unwittingly – an instrument of the RIS [Russian intelligence services]."[192] Aside from these more direct engagements, there were potentially also indirect intelligence relations between various Belarusians with notable British citizens, though these remain murky.[193]

In addition to Great Britain, Belgium was another site involved in Belarusian clandestine activity. In addition to the establishment of Belarusian networks and organizations nestled at the University of Louvain, it also appears that connections manifested outside the university setting. Most prominently was the Union of Belarusian Combatants (*Zuviaz' belaruskikh kambatantaŭ*, ZBK), an organization led by Kushal', Rahulia, and a few others out of Louvain. At some point during the organization's existence in Louvain, Kushal' even made several efforts to enlist individuals into espionage work.[194] The organization published a newspaper and also participated in various ceremonies, namely ones commemorating the Slutsk insurrection of 1920.[195] Aside from this organization, Belarusians, allegedly had contacts at various governmental levels in Belgium.[196] The extent and reach of these connections, however, is unclear.[197] There were also rumblings of continued Belarusian ties with German intelligence services in the immediate postwar period prior to US support.[198] All of these alleged connections reflect a significant lacuna in understanding these networks, and of the relationship and coordination of various intelligence services with Belarusians and other émigré groups. At the same time, the uncertainty in the tone of CIA documents reveals concern about not only the agents operating for the United States but the US position within the larger global espionage community.

Regardless of whatever real or murky connections these Belarusian may have had with various intelligence organizations, what is certain is that these individuals were in constant communication with each other. The continued existence and restructuring of various organizations, such as the Belarusian People's Republic, entailed significant communication by all actors, regardless of where they were in the world.[199] There were also gatherings of Belarusian veterans, including former members of the Home Guard and other auxiliary police battalions, that took place throughout the postwar period. In the official programme of the world meeting of the Belarusian veterans from 1974, a message from a former Home Guard member was published. It was signed as "your BKA member", and stated:

> For me, 65 years have passed in this stormy life, but I am most proud, that I was a member of the BKA, even though I spent little time in that army. I thank you for inviting me to celebrate the 30-year anniversary of the BKA! [...] Unfortunately, I am unable to travel to England for the meeting. However, I am always ready to help the cause from abroad. I wish you success and I heartily declare: Long live Belarus![200]

Indeed, such an open admission and declaration, albeit anonymous, is still a bit surprising to see on an official proclamation of this organization. Though the BKA operated after most Jews in Belarus had already been murdered, it was still an organization created through German collaboration. And yet such admissions of participating in the BKA and other Belarusian collaborationist armed groups did appear. Moreover, many of these meetings of former collaborators took place openly in various countries without prompting authorities to react in any way.

Just as there were points of meeting and coordination, there were also rifts between Belarusian actors in the postwar period. Most notably, the once president of the Belarusian Central Rada of occupied Belarus, Astroŭski, struggled to retain a significant position of power in the postwar period. Operating for many years in Germany and eventually settling in the United States, he unsuccessfully tried to revive the Central Rada and even renamed it the Belarusian National Centre to disassociate the organization from its tainted wartime reputation. His efforts could not compete with the much stronger BNR, which he disassociated from and whose members referred to Astroŭski as stubborn, not trustworthy, and as being motivated by "presidential ambitions". Similar observations were made in London by members of the Belarusian Greek Catholic Clergy about Rahulia. Indeed, it appeared some Belarusians prioritized their political ambitions over broader Belarusian community-driven needs.[201]

Disconnecting from the Homeland

Although these networks of Belarusians received substantial foreign support, at least in the beginning of the 1950s, their relationship with the homeland waned. Furthermore, the influence and involvement of other states and intelligence services provoked more rifts among the émigré community. Geography, time, and global politics and diplomacy played a crucial role in the development of Belarusian anti-Soviet activity. These factors affected the ability to scout and recruit good candidates for covert activity, the motivations various Belarusians had to continue their anti-Soviet activity, and the relationship between Belarusians and intelligence services.

The older generation of Belarusians continued to underscore their desire for Belarusian independence and promoted this as part of an anti-Soviet struggle to appeal to powerful states and garner protection, security, and personal benefits. To do so they had to make themselves relevant and useful to foreign intelligence services, sometimes sabotaging other Belarusians in the process. Although they ultimately failed to extend the anti-Soviet fight in Belarus, what these individuals did achieve was protection from prosecution and punishment for their activities during the Second World War.

A few more years and archival volumes later another piece of the past resurfaces. Just when it seemed that the Belarusian-US story had ended, a man appeared at the US Embassy in Minsk in 1995. His name was Mikhail Artsiusheŭski, the very same agent who had suspiciously not been tried and imprisoned by Soviet authorities after the AEQUOR II Team's capture. He arrived at the Embassy and was seeking financial remuneration for his work in the AEQUOR II Team. A case officer subsequently debriefed him and indeed confirmed his identity as Camposanto 9. Artsiusheŭski recounted the fate of the AEQUOR II Team, which until that point had not been fully known. He confirmed that one of the men had indeed been killed in an armed ambush, while the others were forced to work for Soviet security forces and send compromised messages back to the US base in Germany. Artsiusheŭski then stated that Kastsiuk and Vostrykaŭ had both died in prison. More confusion arose when, sometime after Artsiusheŭski's reappearance, a Tsimafei Vostrykaŭ, formerly Camposanto 6, also appeared at the US embassy and told his own version of events. The case officer's report revealed confusion and curiosity. Were both men unaware of each other's existence? Or were they working together and had they "orchestrated" their reappearance?[202]

Conclusion

Three years after his appearance at the US Embassy in Minsk, Tsimafei Vostrykaŭ gave an interview to a Belarusian journalist working for the newspaper, *Nasha niva*. Parts of the interview were published in June 1998. Vostrykaŭ discussed his upbringing in Soviet Belarus, his father's dislike of the kolkhoz system, and his father's subsequent incarceration by Soviet security forces. When asked about his experiences during the Second World War, Vostrykaŭ talked about his involuntary mobilization into the Red Army. He said that he had been blacklisted, due to his father's anti-communist beliefs, and was sent to dig trenches around Smalensk. He tried to escape but was caught, sent to fight for the Red Army once again, and then captured by the Germans. The Germans took him to a POW camp, where, he recalled, people were already starving, and he knew he would not survive if he stayed. He managed to escape by passing for an officer, as a group of them was being transported out of the camp. On the transport out of the POW camp, he ran away and ended up joining a group of Soviet soldiers. He eventually returned to his home, in the small village of Khal'chy, in the Homel' region in south-eastern Belarus. Vostrykaŭ decided to volunteer as a labourer to be sent to Germany, noting that he wanted to "see how life was there." He spent some time in Germany and back in Belarus and claims he was never part of any Belarusian or collaborationist armed group.

In 1948, Vostrykaŭ moved to England, along with some other Belarusians, to work in the coal mines. According to his story, it was in 1950 when Barys Rahulia contacted him and invited him to go to Belgium. In his conversation with the journalist who was interviewing him, he insisted that the idea for the covert missions into Soviet Belarus was entirely that of the Belarusians and that they were just using US officials for transport into Soviet Belarus. Of the failed four-man AEQUOR II mission, he said:

> I can offer many facts: they told us to signal on the radio immediately upon arrival, they did not train us, and there was no secret apartment, and they sent us to the very place where the Soviet security agents were waiting for us, and they sent with us a person who sold us out – Artiusheŭski [sic]. They were supposed to have checked him. He turned out to be anti-Belarusian.

Vostrykaŭ confirmed that he was arrested in September 1952 and was imprisoned for three years in Minsk awaiting trial. In 1955, he was sentenced to 23 years of hard labour, most of which he spent in Mordovia in the Soviet Union. After serving almost his entire sentence, in 1975, he returned to Homel′. He died in 2007, without ever being re-habilitated.[1]

If what Vostrykaŭ said about Artsiusheŭski is true, it would clarify a few things. It would certainly explain the bizarre messages intelligence officers received from him. It would also very much explain why Artsiusheŭski was released by the Soviet state, whereas the other members of the AEQUOR II team were not.

More profoundly, Vostrykaŭ's story seems to underscore several tropes in this long multi-generational story. Connections, both open and secret, were as important in the postwar period as they were decades before. Critical new sites and points of connection, such as England, the United States, and Belgium, brought these Belarusians together. Vostrykaŭ makes no mention of having similar values to Rahulia, but simply that some base of mutual interests was enough to warrant collaboration. Moreover, though the state appears to have the upper hand, this is not entirely the case. The fact that a man like Artsiusheŭski could have ended up in such a CIA-run operation and infiltrated it to the core is very revealing about the nature of western intelligence services. The question of who was using whom deserves some pause as well.

For these Belarusian nationalists, the postwar situation at the end of the 1950s was uncannily similar to 1921, as they failed to create an independent Belarusian state. An all too familiar sense of desperation was in the air, once again, with the international diplomatic mood moving away from the likelihood of a direct war between the Soviet Union and the West. Western powers were no longer in critical need of Belarusian nationalists for a direct conflict against the Soviet Union, just as after the First World War, and more powerful states did not have to lure smaller national groups to fight for them with promises of supporting postwar independence. This time, however, Belarusians found themselves not in neighbouring European states but spread out across continents and far removed from their Homeland. The diminishing reality of international conflict was juxtaposed with increasing divisions within the Belarusian émigré community that became not only politically and ideologically fractioned but also stratified by younger generations who were less willing to risk their comfortable lives for what was likely capture, incarceration, and decades of work in a labour camp in the Soviet Union.

Looking at the collective 1921 to 1956 period, there was no particular time during which these Belarusians were more successful in attaining their goal of independence. Heightened opportunities came with increased risks and participation in violence. Prior to the Second World War, they were successfully developing their networks, identity, and activism outside of Soviet Belarus. During the German occupation of Belarus, they had opportunities to create their armed units and actively engage with local Belarusians, whom they claimed to be fighting for. Yet this physical intimacy with Belarus, paired with their military capabilities, came with increasing separation between these nationalists and locals. Rather than garner public support, Belarusian nationalists participated in activities that antagonized and violently shaped local dynamics, which in turn provoked resentment and, even more frustrating, indifference toward their Belarusian cause. After the Second World War, they experienced the strongest period of foreign-backed support. Western intelligence services provided financial resources, the opportunity to publish émigré papers, and to train individuals in professional facilities. Yet this period came at a cost of being far removed from Belarus. With time, younger Belarusians became less inclined to fight for a country they had spent little time in and did not necessarily call their home. Among the older Belarusians, power struggles were fueled by geographic separation, which allowed them to garner support among émigrés in their separate corners of the world. Even after the 1950s, the feeling of displacement persisted and continues to persist. The Belarusian hubs that sprung up in New York, Toronto, London, and in other cities were meant to be temporary sites of refuge for Belarusians – both collaborators and others – until Belarus ceased to be under Soviet rule. Quite the opposite occurred throughout the years, and continues today, as small waves of Belarusians, who are able, continue to arrive in these hubs due to the ongoing situation in Belarus. The most prominent symbol of this perpetual state of displacement is the continued existence of the Belarusian People's Republic which has never returned to Belarus as a governing body since 1919 and continues to be the most significant European government-in-exile.

What about those individuals who were involved in the Holocaust and violence against Jews and other non-combatants? Does examining their lives prior and after the Second World War shed any light onto their roles and trajectories? Their earlier lives, though challenging, were certainly not unique to them and certainly gave no indication as to what they could be a part of later on during the war. In the aftermath of the war, far away from Belarus, many lived comfortably in cities or suburban neighbourhoods, taking up low key jobs or even pursuing their professional aspirations. To neighbours and friends, these could hardly be individuals who had been part of some of the worst crimes of the century. To intelligence services, the desire to get ahead in the espionage game far outweighed any moral responsibility to investigate, much less consider these Belarusians' previous activity.

By the end of this story, this multi-generational group of Belarusians were nationalists, though without a nation. What they had were shared sites, spaces, and experiences that bound them together, now preserved among themselves in small Belarusian hubs scattered around the world. In fact, one could even add another quality to their shared experience – that of permanent exile from their *Bats'kaŭshchyna.* In his interview in 1998, Vostrykaŭ recalled his time in the camps in the 1960s. He was far from the comforts that other Belarusian émigrés had in the West, and yet, he too lived in exile. Perhaps nothing better captures the final destination and fate of these actors than the following he describes:

> We had our own group where we talked about language, about history. We gathered and drank tea together. In 1962, a Belarusian library was established in the camps. I organized a sort of chain that allowed everyone to read all those things. Of the approximate 2000 prisoners, 60 or 70 gathered. There were more Belarusians by origin, but some would say "ia tozhe belorus," others "[ja] też jestem Białorusinem", and we had to say "ia taksama belarus".[2]

Selected Short Biographies

Mykola Abramchyk was born on 6 August 1903, close to Vilnius, in the former Russian Empire. Between 1922 and 1924 he served as representative of the Belarusian People's Republic (BNR) in the Vialeĭka area. In 1933, he became a member of the BNR's Rada, headquartered in Kaunas. Upon the death of Vasil′ Zakharka in 1943, he succeeded as president of the BNR. During the Second World War, he spent most of his time in the French Foreign Legion. He continued serving in this position in exile and maintaining contact with numerous Belarusian organizations in-exile from Australia where he died in 1970.

Fabian Akinchyts was born on 20 January 1886 around Stolbtsy. He studied law at a university in St. Petersburg and worked as a lawyer, while also being a member of the Socialist Revolutionaries starting in 1906. During the interwar period he lived in Wilno and took part in the BWRH in addition to the Society of Belarusian Schools. In 1933, his politics turned more toward the BNSP, which he eventually represented. Towards the end of the 1930s and into the early years of the Second World War, Akinchyts was active in Belarusian circles in Berlin and Warsaw, garnering a few enemies during this time. These conflicts continued during his time in Minsk from 1941 until 1943, when he was shot. Akinchyts was killed, allegedly, by the Soviet underground. Some attest that, in reality, he was murdered by Belarusian nationalists.

Mikhail Pavlovich Artsiusheŭski was born in 1925 in the Mahilieŭ region. In August 1943, he was sent to Germany, was liberated by American soldiers in March 1945, and worked as a mechanic for the US army. In 1946 he thought about returning to the BSSR, but was concerned that his work for the US army would put his life in danger. Between this time and 1951 he lived in Germany, the United States, and the UK until he was recruited in the beginning of 1952 as an agent by US intelligence services.

Radaslaŭ Astroŭski was born in a town in the Slutsk region in November 1887. He studied in different cities in the Russian Empire before returning to Slutsk and working as a teacher. Around the time of the revolutions of 1917, he became increasingly active in Belarusian organizations and movements. Years later during the German occupation of Belarus beginning in 1941, he collaborated and worked in the eastern regions of Briansk, Smalensk and Mahilieŭ. He is best known for being the leader of the Belarusian Central Rada in December 1943. The following year in July, he emigrated westward to Germany, later moving to England, Argentina, and eventually settling in the United States. He continued to be active among groups of Belarusian émigrés until his death in 1976.

Bronislav Konstantinovich Buko was born in 1924 in the Nieśwież region. He volunteered for the Polish army and was demobilized after the war. In 1948, an arrest warrant was submitted for him due to his activity with the Belarusian Home Guard, which prompted him to operate underground. He was captured and arrested by Soviet security forces in 1949 and was subsequently sentenced to 25 years in prison.

Nikolai Konstantinovich Demukh was born in 1920 in the Nieśwież region. From August 1944 to June 1945 he served in the Red Army, during which time he was injured. In May 1946, Soviet authorities discovered his moonshine production business. He was not immediately arrested but when he was to be taken in a few months later, the man who came to do the job allowed him the chance to leave and hide. It was after his wife's arrest that Demukh decided to join the partisan units led by Ivan Ramanchuk. In May 1949, he was involved in a skirmish with Soviet security forces, arrested, and sentenced to 25 years in a camp. After his release, he returned to Soviet Belarus but soon after passed away in a hospital whilst undergoing surgery.

Mikalaĭ Dziamidaŭ was born in the Belastok region in 1888 and was a great-nephew of Kastus′ Kalinoŭski, the famous Belarusian national hero of the 1863 uprising. He attended school in Warsaw and St. Petersburg. In 1918 he was in Vil′na organizing Belarusian armed formations to fight against the Bolsheviks. He served as a commander in Hrodna, as well as a representative of the BNR there. Together with Kushal′, he served on the committee of the Belarusian Military Commission until it was disbanded by Polish authorities. He was arrested by the Poles in the summer of 1919 and kept in captivity until the summer the following year. Afterward he joined Bułak-Bałachowicz's army, later forming his own unit, which was active until 1921. During the Second World War, he worked as part of the administration of German-occupied Belarus and assisted in the creation of the Belarusian Home Guard in Lida, a primarily Polish-populated town. After the war he moved to the United States and died in 1967.

Ivan Ermachênka was born on 13 May 1894 around Barysaŭ. He completed his primary studies in Moscow and later served as a volunteer in Tsarist army during the First World War. After 1917 he grew closer to the White Army and was eventually a colonel under General Wrangel. In the early 1920s he was more involved in Belarusian affairs and participated in the Belarusian People's Republic and was its representative in Istanbul. He eventually became the leader of the Belarusian People's Self-Help on 22 October 1941. During a conflict between the German SS and civil administration he was accused of being deceitful and for stealing and was sent to Prague under house arrest. In the spring of 1945, he left Prague for West Germany and eventually to the United States in 1947. He continued to be active in US-Belarusian affairs until his death on 25 February 1970 in Florida.

Kanstanty Ezavitaŭ was born on 5 November 1893 in Dvnisk (today Daugavpils, Latvia). During the First World War, he was active amongst Belarusian soldiers and became a member of the Central Belarusian Military Rada. He attended the First All-Belarusian Congress in December 1917. He became a representative of the Belarusian People's Republic and operated mainly in the Baltics, where he was arrested several times. During the Second World War he actively organized Belarusian schools and eventually joined the Belarusian Central Rada in June 1944. He attempted to organize a collective anti-Soviet block with Ukrainians and other national groups but to no avail. In April 1945 he was arrested by the NKVD and sent to Minsk. According to the official story, he died on 23 May 1946 from complications of tuberculosis and dystrophy. Other sources claim he was imprisoned and then shot.

Ianka Filistovich was born in 1926 in the town of Paniatsichy, in the Maladzechna district in the Minsk region today. In 1943, he was mobilized into the 13th Belarusian Auxiliary Police Battalion operating around Minsk and Vialeĭka. As the Red Army was taking back parts of Belarus, he escaped westward with the Germans. He was sent to Italy to fight against Allied forces in early 1945, after which he was captured by German forces, released, and later worked along the Polish-Czech border. He later moved to France and continued to be active in Belarusian émigré circles. In the early 1950s he was recruited and trained as a CIA agent to be infiltrated back into Soviet Belarus. One year after his infiltration he was found by Soviet security forces with the help of a local. He was tried in a military tribunal, found guilty, and allegedly shot.

Kurt von Gottberg was born on 11 February 1896 in East Prussia to an aristocratic family. He served in the First World War and afterwards returned to East Prussia to complete his education in agriculture. He joined the National Socialist Party in 1932. Despite some setbacks during his career, he was promoted as head of the SS and Belarusian police during the German occupation. In October 1943, he assumed the role of Generalkommissar, after Kube's untimely death. He was particularly known for his tenacity in anti-partisan operations, regardless of whether it targeted regular civilians. After evacuating Belarus, he was assigned various tasks in France, including organizing anti-partisan operations and monitoring the railroads. He was arrested by the Allies and took his own life on 31 May 1945, while under British captivity.

Father Vintsent Hadleŭski was born in Porazava (today in the Hrodna region), in November 1898. He completed his training in a Catholic seminary in Vil'na and often preached the liturgy in Belarusian. He was one of the attendees of the First Belarusian Congress in 1917 and a founding member of the Belarusian People's Republic. After the First World War, he was a prominent figure in Belarusian circles, especially in Wilno, where he served as editor of *Krynitsa* (The source). He also served as a Belarusian representative to the sejm, or Polish parliament. During the Second World War, Hadleŭski worked with the Germans and was also involved in the founding of the Belarusian Independence Party, together with Usevalad Rodz'ka. The Germans either discovered Hadleŭski's clandestine activity, or were tipped off by someone, and sent him to the Maly Trastsianets camp, just outside of Minsk. He was shot there on 24 December 1942.

Paul von Hindenburg was born in October 1847 in Posen (present-day Poznań in Poland) to a Prussian aristocratic family. He served in the Austro-Prussian War of 1866 and later in the Franco-Prussian War of 1870 to 1871. Hindenburg excelled in his military studies and advanced his military career thanks in part to his education as well as his family. In 1911 he retired from his military career, which had included fourteen years as a member of the General Staff. Upon the breakout of the First World War, he was selected to serve, by the German High Command and War Cabinet, under Erich Ludendorff. After the First World War, he was elected president of the German Reich in 1925. He died in August 1934.

Ėmanuil Iasiuk was born in 1906. He studied and completed his degree in Liège and later worked as an engineer. During the German occupation of Belarus, he was active in Belarusian Central Rada and attended the Second All-Belarusian Congress in June 1944. After the war, he moved to the United States and was active in Belarusian organizations. He died in 1977.

Mikhail Ivanovich Kal'nitski was born in November 1923 in the Polesie region of Belarus. During the Second World War, he served in the Belarusian auxiliary police. In October 1943 he left to Germany where he remained in a Displaced Person's camp until 1947 and then moved to Belgium. There he was very active in Belarusian circles, especially in Louvain. He was recruited by US intelligence services and was part of the AEQUOR II team. He was fatally wounded by Soviet security forces in September 1952.

Konstanty (Kastus') Kalinoŭski was born in 1838. He studied in St. Petersburg and Moscow and is credited with publishing the Belarusian newspaper, *Muzhyskaia praŭda* (The Peasants' Truth). He saw Belarusian peasants as being especially marginalized by not only Tsarist authorities but wealthier landlords. Together with Poles and Lithuanians he participated in the 1863 revolt. Tsarist authorities captured and imprisoned him. Kalinoŭski was tried by a court-martial and was convicted of inciting a revolt against the Russian Empire. On 22 March 1864, he was publicly executed in Vil'na at the age of twenty-seven. Belarusian nationalists would repeatedly use and re-appropriate Kalinoŭski's name in the twentieth century to refer to those who sacrificed their lives to the Belarusian cause.

Uladzimir Kachan was born in the town of Dokszyce in 1921. He served in the Polish Army and was later recruited by the Abwehr after the German invasion of Poland. He led the First Belarusian Assault Union, an anti-Soviet covert mission in the spring of 1941, just before the German invasion of the Soviet Union. He escaped to the West after the Second World War. Kachan finally settled in Australia where he died in 1982.

Aliaksandar Kalosha was born in 1905. After attending a Belarusian school, he moved to Prague in 1930 where he continued his studies. From 1940 onwards, he was active in Berlin as a member of the Belarusian Self-Help Committee in Germany. He was also a member of the Belarusian Central Rada. After the war, he moved back to Prague and became a Czechoslovak citizen, but his citizenship was revoked in 1948 and he was deported to the

USSR. There he was sentenced to twenty-five years of prison. In 1956 he was released and returned to Czechoslovakia. He died in 1985.

Dz'mitry Kasmovich was born in Nesvizh in 1909. He completed secondary school in a Belarusian school in Radoszkowice in 1927. He later studied in Belgium and came into contact with some Belarusians there. Between 1931 and 1934, he completed his military service in Poland. After the Soviet invasion of Poland in mid-September 1939, he moved back to his hometown to do some administrative work for the new occupying regime. During the German occupation of Belarus, he organized the auxiliary police in Minsk and worked in other transport and trade sectors. He later completed an officer's training course for the Belarusian Home Guard and worked as an inspector there. In the summer of 1944, he fled to Germany and continued to be active in Belarusian circles, albeit under a pseudonym. Between 1945 and 1952 he worked in the United Nations Relief and Rehabilitation Administration (later the International Refugee Organization). Kasmovich was also active in the World Anti-Communist League among other organizations. Through his writing and presence, he was well known among Belarusian émigré circles. He died in Stuttgart in 1991.

Genadiy Adamovich Kastsiuk was born on 19 June 1922 in the Navahrudak district. During the war he served in the Belarusian Home Guard in the Navahrudak battalion under the command of Rahulia, fighting against Soviet partisans. In the summer of 1944, he fled westward with retreating Germans, after which he was mobilized into the 30th Waffen Division. After the war until 1948, he was interned in a camp in Denmark. He later moved to France and organized a Belarusian youth organization along with Ianka Filistovich. In February 1952, Rahulia recruited Kastsiuk to participate in the covert mission as part of the AEQUOR II team.

Iakub Kolas was born in 1882 with the name of Kanstantsin Mitskevich, in the town of Stol'btsy. In 1898 he began his studies at the seminary in Nesvizh where he wrote poems and fairytales in Belarusian, drawing from folklore. During the First World War he served in the Russian Army. In 1921 he returned to Minsk, where he taught at the Belarusian State University. He was a member of the Belarusian Academy of Sciences and served as a member of the BSSR's Praesidium in 1929 and was active in Belarusian and Russian literature organizations. He died on 13 August 1956.

Aliaksandar Kryt was born in 1901 and became an orthodox priest. During the Second World War he worked in Germany together with the well-known National Socialist, Fabian Akinchyts. They worked together to bolster the party. At the end of the 1940s, he moved to Great Britain and took part in the organization of the Association of Belarusians in Great Britain. In 1961 he moved to the United States and eventually became the head of the Belarusian Autocephalous Orthodox Church. He died in 1983.

Wilhelm Kube was born on 13 November 1887 in Glogau, present-day Głogów, Poland. He was an early member of the National Socialist Party and joined the SS in 1934. In 1936, Kube was involved in a scandal that falsely accused a senior judge, and the latter's son, of being married to a Jewish woman. This false accusation caused his demotion from his posts and he was sent to work as a guard in Dachau. During the German occupation of Belarus, he was appointed Generalkommissar für Weißruthenien on 16 July 1941. By September 1941, he and the civilian administration officially took over the area from the German Army. He was, at times, in conflict with the SS over their activity that occurred without his knowledge or authority. This disagreement further strained relations between civil and SS authorities in occupied Belarus, as well as with higher-up authorities in Berlin. He was assassinated on 22 September 1943 by members of the Soviet underground.

Ianka Kupala was born in 1882 with the name of Ivan Daminikavich Lutsevich, around Molodechno. He wrote in both Polish and Belarusian, often contributing to the newspaper *Nasha niva.* He lived and wrote primarily in Vil'na and also translated Marxist writings into Belarusian. Suffering from ill health in the early 1940s, he moved to Tatarstan and continued to write. In 1942, he suffered a fatal accident when falling down a stairwell in Moscow.

Frantsishak Kushal' was born on 16 February 1895 in Pershai (today in the Minsk oblast). Between 1915 and 1917 he was conscripted into the Russian Army. From 1919 to 1920 he was a member of the Belarusian Military Commission, which strove to assemble a Belarusian military unit within the Polish army. Indeed, in the earlier part of his life he was involved in the military affairs of the Belarusian national movement, though played a less prominent role in politics at this time. Between 1924 and 1939 he was an officer of the Polish army, after which he was captured by the Red Army in L'viv. He spent some time in POW camps in Starobel'sk then elsewhere near Smolensk, and then was incarcerated in Lubianka, after which he was released, in June 1941. During the German occupation of Belarus, he organized training courses for the Belarusian police,

Belarusian Self-Defense, and Belarusian Home Guard. After the war, he lived some time in Munich with his wife and son, later emigrating to the United States in 1950. In New York he organized the Association for Belarusian Veterans and continued to be active in the Belarusian émigré community until his death in Rochester, New York on 25 May 1968.

Vatslaŭ Iustynavich Lastoŭski was born in November 1883. He is best known for being a Belarusian historian, literary critic, and politician. Along with the Lutskevich brothers, he was a proponent of reviving the former Grand Duchy of Lithuania. He has sometimes mistakenly been associated with the creation of the Belarusian People's Republic, yet he was not a participant of the declaration on 25 March 1918. Between 1909 and 1915 he was active in the publication of *Nasha niva*, and later for the journal *Homan* (Clamour). He was arrested by Polish authorities for being a proponent of Belarusian independence. After his release he continued to advocate for Belarusian independence in other countries through his diplomatic missions in Belgium, the Vatican, Italy, France, and Switzerland, among other places. In 1927 he returned to the BSSR, where he was one of the founders and members of the Belarusian Academy of Sciences during the interwar period. In 1937, Soviet authorities accused him of being part of the alleged Union for the Liberation of Belarus. After being imprisoned for six months, he was exiled to Saratov later that year and was shot on 23 January 1939.

Iazėp Mamon'ka was born in 1889 in the town of Zalesse in the Slutsk district. He served as a member of the Belarusian Socialist Revolutionary Party from 1907 until 1917. He spent a significant portion of his life incarcerated by the Russians, Poles, and Soviet authorities, primarily for his activity in Belarusian organizations in both the First All-Belarusian Congress and the Belarusian People's Republic. By the mid-1920s however, he broke ties with the BNR and upon his return to the BSSR was arrested and sent to Moscow, where he was sentenced to ten years of hard labour. In September 1937, he was sentenced to be shot by the NKVD. On 25 March 1993, he was rehabilitated by the prosecutor general of Russia. The famous Belarusian poet Ianka Kupala, referred to Mamon'ka as one of the heroes of the *tutėĭshy*, or locals.

Kanstantin Miarliak was born in a village in the Navahrudak district in December 1919. He claimed to have lived with his parents during the Second World War and to have worked as an interpreter for German and Belarusian armed groups stationed in Lida. Later he was captured and imprisoned by British forces, until he managed to escape to Italy. From there he moved to Argentina, where he served as the representative of the Belarusian People's Republic (BNR) and as the president of the "Association of the Byelorussians in Argentina". He later moved to the United States in 1954 where he was selected to be the chairman of the "Byelorussian-American Association" in New York.

Vitali Mikula was born in 1913 in the Nesvizh district. He attended a cadet school in the Polish army and served in Chełmo, under Kushal′. Later, Mikula completed artillery training in Grudziądz, after which he fought against the Germans with the Poles, until the latter was defeated. He returned to his home in 1942 when Kushal′ invited him to Minsk to lead officer training courses. Mikula continued organizing BKA formations, as well as other underground ones clandestinely behind the Germans. Any information pertaining to his life after the war remains unknown.

Iakub Novik (pseudonym Ataman Khareŭski) was born in 1900 in Pruzhany. He was active in anti-Polish partisan activity in the 1920s. He allegedly even proposed coordinating this anti-Polish fight along with Kiryl Arloŭski, a Bolshevik partisan active in the borderland region. Both Khareŭski and Ivan Perahud are said to have participated in the organization of an anti-Polish uprising for the creation of an independent West Belarusian state. During the war, he organized a partisan unit of about five thousand men in the Polesse region and allegedly coordinated with Ukrainian nationalist Taras Bul′ba in collective anti-German operations. After the war he engaged in anti-Soviet fighting but eventually escaped with his unit westward, eventually ending up in Brazil. He died in an automobile accident in 1968 in Porto Alegre, Rio Grande do Sul, Brazil. Some have speculated Soviet security forces were responsible for his death.

Ivan Perahud was born in 1898 in the Pinsk region. According to newspaper articles and published recollections, he participated in an anti-Polish partisan movement from 1922 to 1925 and continued to be active in Belarusian circles throughout the interwar period. His partisan group was active around the towns of Zhabinka and Drohichyn (both in the Brėst region), as well as northern areas of now Ukraine. By the end of 1945, he fled westwards through Poland, Czechoslovakia, and East Germany. From 1949 onwards, he lived in Brazil and continued to be active in émigré circles promoting Belarusian independence and meeting together with former veterans. He died in 1984 in Belo Horizonte, Brazil.

Józef Piłsudski was born in December 1867 in present-day Lithuania to a Polish family. He attended a Russian secondary school in Vil′na, later attending medical school at Kharkiv University. There he was active in the *Narodnaia volia* organization, a radical socialist party. He was arrested by Tsarist authorities for his brother's connection to a plot to assassinate Tsar Aleksandr III. As a result, Piłsudski was sentenced to five years in exile in Siberia, a tenure that was extended. After his release he returned home and joined the Polish Socialist Party. During the Russo-Japanese War of 1904 to 1905, he sought support from the Japanese in exchange for providing intelligence information. During the First World War he established the Polish Legions and the Polish Military Organization, both used to fight the Central powers. After the war, he was appointed Commander in Chief of the Polish forces and eventually Chief of State. Following a retirement of several years he returned to power in Poland in May 1926 via a coup-d'état. He remained in power until his death in 1935.

Panteleimon Kondratsevich Ponomarenko was born on 9 August 1902 in Krasnodar Krai, Russia. He served in the Red Army in 1918 and later was involved in the Komsomol. During the Second World War he led Soviet partisan units in German-occupied Belarus, serving as a member of the Soviet Belarusian Partisan Headquarters, later leading the organization. Between 1938 and 1947 he was First Secretary of the KP(b)B. Between 1948 and 1952, he was a candidate for the Politburo of the Communist Party of the Soviet Union, later becoming the Soviet ambassador to Poland from 1955 to 1957. He received numerous honours, including Order of the October Revolution and Order of the Patriotic War. He died in 1984.

Mikhail Puhachoŭ was born in 1903 in Minsk. He served as a captain in the Soviet Army but was later captured by the Germans. During the German occupation of Belarus, he worked in the Minsk city administration and was part of the head committee of the Belarusian Self-Defense Corps. Eventually he was the BKA leader in the Minsk region and worked closely with Kushal'. In the summer of 1944 he emigrated, living in Berlin and continuing his activity with the Belarusian Central Rada. In April 1945 he lived in the Sudeten region but eventually returned in the fall of that year to the BSSR, where he was captured and killed.

Barys Rahulia was born in the town of Turec in January 1920, where he also studied. During the Soviet occupation in 1939, he was arrested but managed to escape when the Germans invaded. During the Second World War, he initially worked as a translator in Navahrudak and also as a representative of the Belarusian Self-Help and Youth Union. Later he became a member of the Belarusian Central Rada and regional leader of the Belarusian Home Guard. He was also in charge of a special fighting unit in Navahrudak. After the war, he moved to Belgium where he completed his medical degree at the University of Louvain and recruited Belarusians for the CIA. In 1954, he moved to Canada and worked as a physician, until he died in 2005.

Symon Rak-Mikhaĭloŭski was born in April 1885 in the Vil′na district. He was a prominent Belarusian political and social activist. He participated in the First All-Belarusian Congress and was a member of the Belarusian People's Republic. Between 1922 and 1927 he served as a Belarusian ambassador to the *Sejm* of the Second Polish Republic. He later joined the Communist Party of Western Belarus in 1926 and was subsequently arrested by Polish authorities the following year. He later moved to the BSSR in 1930. In 1934 he was accused of being a counter-revolutionary member of the alleged Belarusian People's Centre, a German-sponsored Belarusian organization. He was subsequently exiled to the Solovetskie Islands. In August 1937 he was summoned to Minsk where the following year he was sentenced by the NKVD as being an agent of the Polish Army, for which he was shot in Minsk on 27 November 1938.

Viachaslaŭ Razumovich (pseudonym Ataman Khmara) was born in 1889 to the son of a priest in Brėst and former soldier in the Tsarist Army. Razumovich was active in Hrodno, working with the Bolsheviks to establish a military committee there. He later fled the area when the Polish army arrived. In late 1920, he was one of the main leaders of a Belarusian battalion in the Lithuanian Army. At another point he is rumoured to have worked together with Polish authorities. Indeed, his loyalty to various national armies remains questionable. In September 1924 he fled to Prague, where he is suspected to have died in 1937.

Usevalad Rodz′ka was born in 1920 in Chuchevichy, today in the Brėst Oblast, about 200 km southwest of Minsk. He attended a Belarusian school in Navahudrak, until it was closed by Polish authorities. He served in the Polish Army and in 1939 was captured by the Germans and recruited by them for some espionage work. He allegedly put together a few anti-Soviet underground groups. During the German occupation of Belarus, he led the 15th Battalion of the Belarusian Home Guard. In 1944, he fled Belarus and attempted to reorganize another covert group. He returned to Belastok and was captured in 1945, where he was presumably killed by Soviet authorities.

Alfred Rosenberg was born in January 1893 in Revel′ (present-day Tallinn) to a family of Baltic Germans. He later studied in Riga and Moscow, where he completed his doctoral studies in 1917. After the First World War he moved to Germany and joined the National Socialist Party fairly early. He became the interim leader of the Nazi Party during Hitler's incarceration. His work contributed ideologically to the party, and during the war he served as head of the Reich Ministry for the Occupied Eastern Territories (Reichministerium für die besetzten Ostgebiete). After the war, he was tried at Nuremberg, found guilty and executed in October 1946.

Iury Sabaleŭski was born in April 1889 in the city of Stolbtsy. He served as a member of the Polish Sejm and was active in the Belarusian Peasant-Worker's Hramada in Poland. During the German occupation of Belarus, he served as head of the Belarusian Self-Help and was a leading member of the Belarusian Central Rada. After the war, he moved to Germany where he continued to be active in Belarusian circles and also worked with Ukrainian émigrés as part of a larger anti-communist block. He died in Munich in 1957.

Nikalaĭ Shchors was born in 1913 in Novyi Sverzhen' (Minsk region). He completed his medical studies in Wilno, where he was involved in the Union of Belarusian Students. In 1939, he moved to Warsaw where he later became a member of the Belarusian committee there. In the fall of 1944, he went to Germany and was involved in the Belarusian Central Rada as well as the Belarusian Orthodox Union. From 1949 onward, he lived in the United States, participating in various émigré organizations and working as a physician. He died in December 1995.

Stsiapan Shnėk was born on 12 October 1900 in Liadnykh (now in the Slutsk district, Minsk region). From 1930 to 1936 he attended a military academy in Leningrad, later returning to Slutsk in 1939 to work as a teacher. During the German occupation, he led the Belarusian Auxiliary Police and eventually was the elected leader of the BKA in the Slutsk region. He was arrested by the Germans in the Spring of 1944 but released thanks to the help of Astroŭski. Along with many of the Belarusian leaders, he emigrated westwards and was mobilized as an officer of the German-organized, Belarusian brigade. He was active in some Belarusian émigré organizations and eventually moved to Australia in 1950, where he wrote some articles in the newspapers *Belaruskae slova* (The Belarusian word) and *Bats'kaŭshchyna* (The Homeland). He took his own life on 19 January 1952.

Viktar Sikora was born in 1925 in Malyia Alashki (Pastavy district). He completed his education in a Polish school after which he attended a teacher's seminary school in Pastavy. Sikora become one of the leaders of the Belarusian Youth Union in Pastavy and also the Belarusian Independence Party's representative there. He was mobilized into the Red Army but managed to desert in November 1944 and hid in various places. Sikora later formed a small partisan group but was arrested by Soviet authorities in December 1945 and was given a 10-year prison sentence. He worked as a forced labourer in a gold mine in Iakutia and later in Taishet for other work. Eventually he returned to his hometown in 1954.

Stanislaŭ Stankevich was born on 23 February 1907 around Ashmiany. He studied at the Slavic Department in Wilno University and later at university in Belgrade. During the Second World War, he briefly taught in the Vilnius district and Navahrudak, later served as an inspector in Baranavichi and wrote in the right-wing *Ranitsa* paper. For some time, he served as mayor of Barysaŭ and according to witnesses was connected to the mass murder of 6000 Jews there. After the war he continued to be active among Belarusian circles in Munich serving on the committee of various organizations. He later moved to the United States in 1958, though did not work closely with US intelligence services.

Anton Sokal-Kutyloŭski was born in Krasnaia Gorka, in the Pinsk region, in 1892. He completed his studies in St. Petersburg and later military training in Kazan. He fought in the First World War and later in the Slutsk Insurrection. He later lived in Poland and worked as an Orthodox Christian priest in Nowogródek and Słonim, until 1941 when he was arrested by Soviet security forces. During the German occupation of Belarus, he was a representative of numerous Belarusian groups in the Hantsevichi district. Toward the latter part of the war, he tried to help Belarusian soldiers escape to US zones of occupation. In 1947, US officials extradited him to the Soviet Union, where he was arrested and spent some time in different forced labour camps. After serving time, he went to Poland, where he died in 1983.

Lavrentii Fomich Tsanava (until 1938 his last name was Dzhandzhgava) was born in 1900 in the town of Nakhunavo, present-day Georgia. He served as the People's Commissar for Internal Affairs between 1938 and 1941, the People's Commissar for State Security of the BSSR from 1943 to 1946, and from 1946 to 1951 as the Minister for State Security of the BSSR. In April 1953 he was arrested largely because of his connection with Lavrenti Beria. He died in the Butyrka prison on 12 October 1955.

Vitaŭt Tumash was born in 1910. He attended medical school in Wilno and completed his studies in 1937. He also worked as a physician in

Germany and was an editor of the German-sponsored Belarusian right-wing paper, *Ranitsa.* During the Second World War, he was the mayor of Minsk and co-signed the order for the creation of the ghetto. In 1948 he emigrated to the United States where he continued to maintain contacts with Belarusian émigrés. He passed away in 1998.

Michal Vitushka was born in the town of Nesvizh in 1907. He initially attended a Belarusian school there until it was shut down by Polish authorities. He later studied in Kletsk and Wilno and eventually moved to Prague and Warsaw to complete his education at technical schools. Throughout the interwar period, he was active in Belarusian youth groups, leading the Union of Belarusian Student Organizations. He served in the Polish Army and was recruited by the Germans after the invasion of Poland in 1939. During the German occupation of Belarus, he organized police battalions and commanded numerous Belarusian armed groups. After his evacuation westward in the summer of 1944, he continued working with the Germans to organize anti-Soviet missions. In November 1944, he led a covert team into Soviet Belarus. The circumstances of his activity during this dispatch are not known. According to Soviet sources, he died in a scuffle between the Polish Home Army and Soviet security forces in January 1945. Over the years, witnesses claimed to have been in contact with him or to have even seen him.

Andrei Andreevich Vlasov was born in 1901 in Nizhny Novgorod. After leaving his studies at a Russian Orthodox Seminary he joined the Red Army in 1919. During the Second World War, he served as a Red Army General until he was captured by the Germans during the Siege of Leningrad. His motivation for defecting to the Germans is debated. Some claim his anti-Soviet sentiments were sincere, whereas others argue he was motivated by opportunism. After his defection, he led the Russian Liberation Army (*Russkaia osvoboditel'naia Armiia,* ROA), later turning again and participating in the anti-German Prague Uprising. While trying to escape westward, Soviet forces captured and imprisoned him in Lubianka. In the summer of 1946, he was tried and convicted of treason and executed on 1 August 1946.

Tsimafei Akimovich Vostrykaŭ was born in November 1922 in the Homel′ region. During the early part of the Second World War, he was mobilized into the Red Army but was captured by the enemy and interned. He managed to escape the POW camp he was in and returned home. Later during the war he was sent to Germany as a forced labourer. He decided to stay there rather than return to Soviet Belarus after the war. Until October 1946, he was interned in a camp for Poles around Marburg, in the American zone of occupation. Later he was transferred to a Belarusian camp until 1947 in Denmark. Along with other Belarusians, he moved to the UK and organized Belarusian goups, after which he was accepted as a student at the University of Louvain. He was recruited as an agent in January 1952 and participated in the AEQUOR II Mission.

Vasil′ Zakharka was born on 1 April 1877 around Hrodno. He worked as a school teacher until he was mobilized into the Russian Army. Zakharka was involved in several Belarusian organizations and attended the First All-Belarusian Congress in December 1917. He promoted Belarusian interests in Prague and in western Europe and became president of the BNR in 1928 after his predecessor's death. He also corresponded with the Germans, hoping to garner support for his cause. He died in Prague in 1943.

Aŭhen Zhykhar was born sometime around 1925 in the Pastavy region. During the Second World War he studied in the seminary and was a member of the Union of Belarusian Youth. He was active in an anti-Soviet partisan movement after 1944 and managed to survive in the forests until 1955, when he was ambushed.

Ryhor Zybaĭla was born in 1913, just outside of the city of Slonim. He served in the Polish Army and was on duty during the German invasion in 1939. He was captured by the Germans in September of that year and was likely recruited by the Abwehr. In the Spring of 1941, he participated in the Belarusian parachuting mission, led by Uladzimir Kachan, into the Soviet Union just prior to the German invasion. During the German occupation of Belarus, he served as the representative of the Belarusian People's Self-Help in Slonim and of the Belarusian Independence Party. When the Belarusian Home Guard was created, he also became its representative in Hlybokae. Towards the end of the war, he served in General Anders' Army. His exact whereabouts after this are not known.

Notes

A Note on Spelling, Language, and Terminology

1 Doris Bergen, "Collaboration – With Whom? German Presence and Absence in the East," (keynote address, Wiesenthal Institute for Holocaust Studies, Vienna, Austria, 5 December 2013).

2 "Collaboration (noun)", Oxford Learner's Dictionaries, Oxford University Press, 5 May 2021, https://www.oxfordlearnersdictionaries.com/us/definition/american_english/collaboration

3 Leonid Rein, *The Kings and the Pawns: Collaboration in Byelorussia during the World War II* (New York: Berghahn Books, 2011), 13.

4 I use Miroslav Hroch's understanding that "identification with a nation was thus a result of more or less spontaneous decisions, which were 'arbitrary' in the sense that they depended on a whole range of circumstances, influences and events specific to each individual." Hroch also argues that the pejorative connotation of nationalism also emerges once state-nations and nation-states became successful. Hroch, *European Nations: Explaining Their Formation,* 266.

5 See: Simon Lewis, *Belarus – Alternate Visions: Nation, Memory and Cosmopolitanism* (London: Routledge, 2019).

6 Juliette Cadiot, "Searching for Nationality: Statistics and National Categories at the End of the Russian Empire (1897–1917)," *Russian Review* 64, no. 3 (July 2005): 454.

7 Timothy Snyder, *The Reconstruction of Nations: Poland, Ukraine, Lithuania, Belarus, 1569–1999* (New Haven: Yale University Press, 2003), 52–53.

Introduction

1 The word *Bats'kaŭshchyna* can also refer to the Belarusian Fatherland or Motherland. *Bats'ka* is the word for "father" in Belarusian.

2 Those living on traditionally Belarusian lands also varied in religious affiliation and included Roman Catholics, Greek Catholics, Orthodox Christians, Jews, and, to a lesser extent, Muslims.
3 When talking about a "nation", I use Miroslav Hroch's definition which defines it as social group defined by series of different kinds of relations, be it territorial, linguistic, economic, political, cultural and any other. These relations are then used to define the connection between this group and specific territory and these relations are used to develop this group's consciousness. Miroslav Hroch, *Social Preconditions of National Revival in Europe: A Comparative Analysis of the Social Composition of Patriotic Groups among the Smaller European Nations,* trans. Ben Fowkes (New York: Columbia University Press, 2000), 5.
4 Though this book collectively examines and treats these individuals as one loose, multi-generational network, they may have not seen themselves in this way. There were also smaller pockets of individuals with shared values and ideologies within this network. However, when they are examined collectively, these individual offer historical and analytical value.
5 By "ideology" I mean motivations related to nationality, national or ethnic identity, or politics.
6 For existing scholarship, see for example: Jochen Böhler and Robert Gerwarth, *The Waffen-SS: A European History* (Oxford: Oxford University Press, 2017); Robert Gerwarth, *The Vanquished: Why the First World War Failed to End* (New York: Farrar, Straus and Giroux, 2016); Thomas Kühne, *Belonging and Genocide: Hitler's Community, 1918–1945* (New Haven: Yale University Press, 2010); Ben Shepherd, *War in the Wild East: the German Army and Soviet Partisans* (Cambridge: Harvard University Press, 2004); Peter Hart, *The I.R.A. and Its Enemies: Violence and Community in Cork 1916–1923* (Oxford: Clarendon Press, 1998); Christopher Browning, *Ordinary Men: Reserve Police Battalion 101 and the Final Solution in Poland* (New York: Harper Collins, 1992).
7 Aleksandr Feduta, Oleg Bogutskiĭ, and Viktor Martinovich, *Politicheskie partii Belrausi – neobkhodimaia chast' grazhdanskovo obshchestva: Materialy seminara* (Minsk: Fond imeni Fridrikha Ėberta, 2003), 10; "Programma Belorusskoĭ partii socialistov-revoliutsionerov [1919 g.]," *Biuletėn Zagranichnaĭ grupy Belaruskai partyi sotsyialistaŭ-revaliutsyianeraŭ, 1926,* p. 191–192.
8 Feduta, Bogutskiĭ, and Martinovich, *Politicheskie partii Belrausi,* p. 12.
9 Jerzy Grzybowski has written the most about Belarusian nationalists, focusing mainly on the period during the Second World War. Some of these works include: Jerzy Grzybowski, *Pogoń między Orłem Białym, swastika i czerwoną gwiazdą: białoruski ruch niepodległoś ci w latach 1939–1956* (Warszawa: BEL Studio, 2011); Jerzy Grzybowski, "An Outline History of the 13th (Belarusian) Battalion of the SD Auxiliary Police," (Schutzmannschafts

Bataillon der SD 13), *Journal of Slavic Military Studies 23* (2010): 461–476; Iury Hryboŭski, "Pershy belaruski shturmovy z'viaz," *Belaruski rėzystans* (February 2005): 1–27.

10 Lavrenti Tsanava, *Vsenarodnaia partizanskaia voina v Belorussii protiv fashistskikh zakhvachikov* (Minsk: Gosudarstvennoe Izdatel'stvo BSSR, 1951), 642–836; Vasil' Ramanoŭski, *Saŭdzel'niki ŭ zlachynstvakh,* (Minsk: Vydavetstva "Belarus'", 1964).

11 A. Khokhlov, *Krakh antisovetskoho banditizma v Belorussii v 1918–1925 godakh* (Minsk: Belarus', 1981), 14–20; A. Grintskevich, *Slutsk: istoriko-ekonomicheskii ocherk* (Minsk: Belarus', 1970), 51–63.

12 Siarheĭ Iorsh, *Viartan'ne BNP: Asoby i dakumenty Belaruskaĭ Nezalezhnickaĭ Partyi* (BHAKC: Mensk, 1998).

13 Igor Valakhanovich, *Antisovetskoe podpole na teritorii Belarusi v 1944–1953 gg.* (Minsk: BGU, 2002); and Ian Shumski, *Savetyzatsyia Zakhodniaĭ Belarusi (1944–1953): prapaganda i adukatsyia na sluzhbe idealohii* (Smalensk: Inbelkult, 2014); Alexander Statiev, *The Soviet Counterinsurgency in the Western Borderlands* (Cambridge: Cambridge University Press, 2010). There are also differences in scholarship within Belarus. Scholars in Minsk continue to be more traditional in their work than scholars in other cities. Those in Hrodna tend to test limits a bit more, yet their work focuses more on regional history. For a good sample of works and scholars there, see: *Zakhodni Rėhiion Belarusi Bachyma historykaŭ i kraiazyaŭtsaŭ: zbornik navukovykh artykulaŭ* (Hrodna: Ministėrstva Adukatsyi Hrodzenski Dziarzhaŭny Universitėt imia Ianki Kupaly, Kafedra Historyi Belarusi, 2006).

14 Documents from the Committee of State Security Archive (Kamitėt dziarzhaŭnaĭ biaspeki, KDB) are largely inaccessible and many documents from US and British intelligence services continue to be classified.

15 This name is a reference to the notorious leader of the Ukrainian Insurgent Army, Stepan Bandera. The reference to Bandera here is to designate his importance within the Belarusian national armed movement, just as Bandera is seen as such for the Organization of Ukrainian Nationalists. Such designations omit any discussion of racism or antisemitism."Tėlebachanne RF: Mikhal Vitushka-belaruski Bandėra", Belaruskae Radyio Ratsyia, 6 November 2017 <https://www.racyja.com/hramadstva/telebachanne-rf-mikhal-vitushka-belarus/ >

16 These include, for example: Aleh Dziarnovich, *Antysavetskiia rukhi ŭ Belarusi, 1944–1956 Davednik* (Minsk: Arkhiŭ Naĭnoŭshaee Historyi, 1999); Siarheĭ Iorsh, *Viartan'ne BNP: Asoby i dakumenty Belaruskaĭ Nezalezhnitskaĭ Partyi.* BHAKC: Mensk, 1998; Siarheĭ Iorsh, *Usevalad Rodz'ka: Pravadyr belaruskikh natsyianalistaŭ* (Mensk: Holas Kraiu, 2001).

17 Works on the involvement and role of women in the Ukrainian national movement, on the other hand, have increased tremendously, thanks in

part to the classification of documents and the rise in oral history that has preserved many of these women's voices and their experiences. See for example: Marta Havryshko "Illegitimate sexual practices in the OUN underground and UPA in Western Ukraine in the 1940s and 1950s," *Power Institutions in Post-Soviet Societies* 17, no. 17 (2016): 1–78; Marta Havryshko, "Love and Sex in Wartime: Controlling Women's Sexuaity in the Ukrainian Nationalist Underground," *Aspasia* 12 (2018): 35–67; Olena Petrenko, "Geschlecht, Gewalt, Nation: Die 'Organisation Ukrainischer Nationalisten' und die Frau," *Osteuropa* 66, no. 4 (2016): 83–93.

18 Jan Zaprudnik, *Historical Dictionary of Belarus* (Lanham: Scarecrow Press, 1998), 39.

19 Some of the more well-known Belarusian women during the Second World War are Masha Bruskina, a Jewish member of the underground resistance and Elena Mazanik, who worked in the home of the Generalkommissar of Belarus, whom she assassinated in 1943. Nechama Tec and Daniel Weiss, "A Historical Injustice: The Case of Masha Bruskina," *Holocaust and Genocide Studies* 11, no. 3 (Winter 1997): 366–377. Mikhas Shobka, "Nina Stuzhynskaia: 'U 20-ia hady zhanchyny vyĭshli z kushniaŭ i ŭznachal'vali paėstanskiia atrady,'" *Radyio svaboda,* 8 March 2011, https://www.svaboda.org/a/2331956.html

20 The term "state" is used broadly in this context. In this book, I use the terms "country, "state", and "government" relatively interchangeably. The reason for this is that, in particular contexts, as in the Soviet and German ones, both state and government were virtually inseparable. For purposes of consistency, these terms are used interchangeably when speaking about many different contexts, even though other cases do not follow this pattern.

21 Paul Hansbury, *Belarus in Crisis: From Domestic Unrest to the Russia-Ukraine War* (London: Hurst & Company, 2023), 16.

22 Aviel Roshwald, *Ethnic Nationalism and the Fall of Empires: Central Europe, Russia, and the Middle East, 1914–1923* (London: Routledge, 2001), 200; Peter Davies, *The Extreme Right in France, 1789 to the Present: From de Maistre to le Pen* (London: Routledge, 2002).

23 Though for both Belarusian and Ukrainian nationalists the unification of their territory with the Soviet annexation of their respective regions in 1939 was welcomed as a first step in unifying these lands, it was quickly followed up by envisioning this unification without Soviet rule.

24 John-Paul Himka, *Ukrainian Nationalists and the Holocaust: OUN and UPA's Participation in the Destruction of Ukrainian Jewry, 1941–1944* (Stuttgart: Ibidem Verlag, 2021), 122–130.

25 Grzegorz Rossoliński-Liebe, *Stepan Bandera: The Life and Afterlife of a Ukrainian Nationalist – Fascism, Genocide, and Cult* (Stuttgart: Ibidem-Verlag, 2014), 104–107.

26 Himka, *Ukrainian Nationalists and the Holocaust*, 14.
27 Jared McBride, "Peasants into Perpetrators: The OUN-UPA and the Ethnic Cleansing of Volhynia, 1943–1944," *Slavic Review* 75, no. 3 (Fall 2016): 631–632.
28 Joshua D. Zimmerman, "The Polish Underground Home Army (AK) and the Jews: What Postwar Jewish Testimonies and Wartime Documents Reveal," *East European Politics and Societies and Cultures* 34, no. 1 (Fall 2020): 196–197, 208. Abraham Melezin, interview 3382, Visual History Archive, USC Shoah Foundation Institute, accessed online at the United States Holocaust Memorial Museum on 21 October 2022, Segment 142.
29 Bernhard Chiari, "Der polnische Widerstand und die Juden: Anmerkungen zum Diskurs über den Zweiten Weltkrieg," *Osteuropa* 53, no. 12 (December 2003): 1849.
30 Zimmerman, "The Polish Underground Home Army (AK) and the Jews," 213; For a more comprehensive study by the same author, see: Joshua D. Zimmerman, *The Polish Underground and the Jews 1939–1945* (Cambridge: Cambridge University Press, 2015)
31 Justina Smalkyte, "Gender, Ethnicity, and Multidirectional Violence in the Last Months of the German Rule in Lithuania: A Case Study of Local Force Battalions," in *Reshaping the Nation: Collective Identities and Post-War Violence in Europe, 1944–48,* edited by Ota Konrád, Boris Barth, and Jaromír Mrňka (Cham: Palgrave, 2021), 36–37, 42.
32 Vykintas Vaitkevičius, "A History of the Lithuanian Partisan Underground State, 1944–1953," in *Violent Resistance from the Baltics to Central, Eastern and South Eastern Europe*, edited by Michael Gehler and David Schriffl (Paderborn: Verlag Ferdinand Schöningh, 2020), 55.
33 Franziska Exeler, *Ghosts of War: Nazi Occupation and its Aftermath in Soviet Belarus* (Ithaca: Cornell University Press, 2022), 10.
34 Alexander Statiev, *The Soviet Counterinsurgency in the Western Borderlands* (Cambridge: Cambridge University Press, 2010), 106, 111, 117–118.
35 Scholars have typically assessed Belarusian nationalism comparatively. They draw from sociologist Miroslav Hroch's three-phase model of nation building. Phase A represents initial efforts by activists to develop their nation's identity. The second B Phase denotes the continuation of such activism that reaches larger audiences beyond the initial nationalists. In the final phase C, there is large support for the nation building path and mass appeal beyond elites. According to such a model, the Belarusian nation-building effort plateaus at Phase A. Other scholars have discussed Belarusian nationalism as not as tied to the nation but more an expression of desired liberation from years of socio-economic repression. In their work on Belarusian nationalism, historian Per Anders Rudling convincingly shows the various expressions and attempts to create various Belarusian states. Ultimately, Soviet and Polish visions of the Belarusian nation won in

the end. Hroch, *Social Preconditions of National Revival in Europe*, 184; Nelly Bekus, *Struggle Over identity: The Official and the Alternative "Belarusianness"* (Budapest: Central University Press, 2010), 53–67; Nicholas P. Vakar, *Belorussia: The Making of a Nation* Cambridge: Harvard University Press, 1956), 87; Per Anders Rudling, *The Rise and Fall of Belarusian Nationalism* (Pittsburgh: University of Pittsburgh Press, 2015); Ian Shumski, *Savetyzatsyia Zakhodniaĭ Belarusi, 1944–1953: Prapaganda i adukatsyia na sluzhbe idealogii* (Smalensk: Inbelkul't, 2014), 53–54; Roger D. Petersen, Jon Elster, and Gudmund Hernes, eds., *Resistance and Rebellion: Lessons from Eastern Europe* (Cambridge: Cambridge University Press, 2001), 224–225.

36 The question of ideology, nevertheless, continues to be the basis of many public and academic conversations, especially when it comes to the legacies of these individuals and their beliefs today. See relevant cases in: *The Many Faces of the Far Right in the Post-Communist Space: A Comparative Study of Far-Right Movements and identity in the Region* (Stockholm: Centre for Baltic and East European Studies, 2022).

1 The Crumbs of a Nation in the Ruins of War

1 Frants Kushal', *Sproby stvaren'nia belaruskaha voiska* (Minsk: Belaruski Histarychny Ahliad, 1999), 141.

2 Alexander V. Prusin, *The Lands Between: Conflict in the East European Borderlands, 1870–1992* (New York: Oxford University Press, 2010), 72.

3 Simon Lewis, *Belarus – Alternative Visions: Nation, Memory and Cosmopolitanism* (New York: Routledge, 2019), 5.

4 Nelly Bekus, *Struggle Over Identity: The Official and Alternative "Belarusianness"* (Budapest: Central European University Press, 2010), 55.

5 Aliaksandr Laneŭski, "Da pytannia ab sialianskim supratsive ŭ Hrodzenskaĭ guberni padchas rėvaliutsyi 1905–1907 hadoŭ," *Białoruskie Zeszyty Historyczne* 48 (2017): 144.

6 The BSH was the successor party of the former Belarusian Revolutionary Party (Belaruskaia Rėvaliutsyĭnaia Partyia, BRP), founded in 1902, and of the Belarusian Revolutionary Hramada (Belaruskaia rėvaliutsyĭnaia hramada, BRH), created in 1903. The BSH changed its name in 1905.

7 The 1905 Revolution more pervasively affected relations between landlords and peasants, particularly in the Hrodna region. This disruption in social structure was politicized by some individuals although it was not an indication of peasant national awareness. Laneŭski, "Da pytannia ab sialianskim supratsive ŭ Hrodzenskaĭ guberni padchas rėvaliutsyi 1905–1907 hadoŭ," 165.

8 One member of the BSH, Ales' Burbis, organized peasant strikes in the Navahrudak district. The new Russian duma, or parliament, of 1906

included thirty-six Belarusian delegates. In 1906 another wave of protests occurred in the countryside. Zakhar Shybeka, *Narys Historyi Belarusi 1795–2002* (Minsk: Ėytsyklapedyks, 2003), 138–143.

9 Prusin, *The Lands Between,* 34–35.

10 Archiwum Akt Nowych (AAN), Sygn. 2/2015/0/7, p. 6.

11 *Nasha dolia*'s first issue included ten thousand copies but was eventually shut down by authorities, prompting the creation of *Nasha niva.* The latter was in operation until 1915 on a weekly basis. It was revived in 1991.

12 Shybeka, *Narys Historyi Belarusi,* 161.

13 Members of Socialist Revolutionary parties included primarily Belarusian elites who had studied in St. Petersburg. In 1902, a group of such Belarusian students broke away from the Polish Socialists to create the Belarusian Revolutionary Party, with Vatslaŭ Ivanoŭski as the leader. Their party paper, called *Svaboda,* or "Freedom", was published and distributed primarily in the Lida county. Centralne Archiwum Wojskowe (CAW), Sygn. VIII.804.17.32, p. 3.

14 Lizaveta Kasmach, *Belarusian Nation-Building in Times of War and Revolution* (Budapest: Central European University Press, 2023), 134, 139.

15 Dorota Michaluk and Per Anders Rudling, "From the Grand Duchy of Lithuania to the Belarusian Democratic Republic: The Idea of Belarusian Statehood during the German Occupation of Belarusian Lands 1915–1919," *The Journal of Belarusian Studies 7,* no. 2 (2014): 14.

16 Kasmach, *Belarusian Nation-Building in Times of War and Revolution,* 150.

17 Viachaslau Shved and Jerzy Grzybowski, *Historia Białorusi od Czasów Najdawniejszych do Roku 1991* (Warsaw: Wydawnictwa Uniwersytetu Warszawskiego, 2020), 115–166.

18 Lietuvos centrinis valstybės archyvas (LCVA), f. 361, ap. 2, b. 10, p. 9.

19 Valiantsin Mazets, "Hramadzianstva i mezhy BNR," *Białoruskie Zeszyty Historyczne* 15 (2001): 86; Vital′ Skalaban, "Usebelaruski z′ezd 1917 hoda: perspektyvy vyvuhėnnia," *Białoruskie Zeszyty Historyczne* 15 (2001): 75; Shved and Grzybowski, *Historia Białorusi od Czasów Najdawniejszych do Roku 1991,* 116.

20 Iurka Listapad, "Uz′bilisia na svoĭ shliakh, 1921 h.," in *Slutski zbroĭny chyn 1920- u dakumentakh i ŭspaminakh,* ed. U. Liakhoŭski, U. Mikhniuk and A. Hes′ (Minsk: Belaruski Histarychny Ahliad, 2006), 156.

21 Natsyianal′ny arkhiŭ Rėspubliki Belarus′ (NARB), f. 383, v. 1, s. 2, p. 64.

22 Destabilization of soldiers came with the declaration of Order no. 1, issued on 14 March 1917, by the Soviet of Workers' and Soldiers' Deputies. It called for soldiers to elect representatives and to keep possession of their weapons instead of turning them in to their superiors as well as to serve under the leadership of the Soviet of Workers' and Soldiers Deputies. It also eased restrictions on soldiers' civilian lives and abolished the requirement to address one's superiors formally or with any other titles of veneration. Jochen Böhler, "Generals and Warlords, Revolutionaries and

Nation State Builders," in *Legacies of Violence: Eastern Europe's First World War*, eds. Jochen Böhler, Włodzimierz Borodziej, and Joachim von Puttkamer (Münich: Oldenbourg Verlag, 2014), 55–56.

23 Kasmach, *Belarusian Nation-Building in Times of War and Revolution*, 168–169.

24 Oleg Łatyszonek, *Białoruskie formacje wojskowe 1917–1923* (Białystok: Białoruskie Towarzystwo Historyczne, 1995), 48.

25 M.M. Smol'ianinov, *Belarus' v pervoĭ mirovoĭ voĭne 1914–1918 gg* (Moscow: Fond "Istoricheskaia pamiat', 2017), 4–5.

26 Michaluk and Rudling, "From the Grand Duchy of Lithuania to the Belarusian Democratic Republic," 7.

The role of both the Orthodox Christian and Catholic churches in the mobilization and deportation process should be delineated. Whereas the former persuaded individuals to flee, the latter encouraged them to stay. Some scholars suggest that this disparity is reflected in the number of refugees from Belarusian territory, of which the majority were Orthodox Christian. Rudling, *The Rise and Fall of Belarusian Nationalism 1906–1931*, 68–70.

27 David R. Stone, *The Russian Army in the Great War: The Eastern Front, 1914–1917* (Lawrence: University Press of Kansas, 2015), 147.

28 Peter Gatrell, *A Whole Empire Walking – Refugees in Russia during World War I* (Bloomington: Indiana University Press, 2005), 210.

29 The majority of these locals who were uprooted left for the Tambov, Samara, Saratov, and Kaluga, provinces, the Ufimski district, and the present-day areas of Kazan and Ekaterinburg.

Historian Lizaveta Kasmach suggests this figure included 1.4 million people, whereas Oleg Łatyszonek offers a higher number of 2.3 million people. Zakhar Shybeka falls in the middle, with an estimated 2 million people. Lizaveta Kasmach, "Forgotten Occupation: Germans and Belarusians in the Lands of Ober Ost (1915–17)," *Canadian Slavonic Papers* 48, no. 4 (2016): 325; Łatyszonek, *Białoruskie formacje wojskowe 1917–1923*, 35; Shybeka, *Narys Historyi Belarusi 1795–2002*, 175.

30 Prusin, *The Lands Between*, 54.

31 Ibid., 54–55.

32 To execute this forced deportation, the state abolished the Pale of Settlement in 1915 – though legally not until 1917 the Provisional Government in 1917 – which included nearly all of Belarusian territory. The Pale of Settlement was a region of the western portion of Tsarist Russia enforcing a permanent residency for Jews and included present-day Lithuania, Belarus, Moldova and parts of Ukraine and Latvia. It was created by Catherine the Great in 1791. Movement out of the Pale was very limited with exceptions granted only to a few individuals who were privileged, due to financial or occupational status, or who were attending university.

33 Klaus Richter, "'Go with the Hare's Ticket' Mobility and Territorial Policies in Ober Ost (1915–1918)," *First World War Studies 6*, no. 2 (2015): 152.
34 Gatrell, *A Whole Empire Walking*, 149.
35 Some of these affected towns include Bobruisk, Begoml', Dokshitsy, Hlybokae, Kreva, Luninets, Postavy, and Smorgon'. Rudovich, "Belarus' u chas pershaĭ susvetnaĭ vaĭny: nekatoryia aspekty ėtnapalitychnaĭ historyi," 103.
36 Prusin, *The Lands Between*, 57.
37 Some of these towns on Belarusian territory where pogroms took place were also the homes of some of these Belarusians. They include Lida, Minsk, Pinsk, and Slutsk. See: Henry Morgenthau, Sr., "Mission of the United States to Poland: Henry Morgenthau, Sr. report," reprinted in *The New York Times,* 3 October 1919; William W. Hagen, *Anti-Jewish Violence in Poland, 1914–1920* (Cambridge: Cambridge University Press, 2018).
38 Per Anders Rudling, *The Rise and Fall of Belarusian Nationalism 1906–1931* (Pittsburgh: University of Pittsburgh Press, 2015), 116–117; Franziska Exeler, *Ghosts of War: Nazi Occupation and its Aftermath in Soviet Belarus* (Ithaca: Cornell University Press, 2022), 34.
39 LCVA, f. 361, ap. 1, b. 2, p. 1.
40 Richter understands "deterritorialization" as a process including demographic and mobility transformation enacted by military occupation policies in Eastern Europe. Richter, "'Go with the Hare's Ticket' mobility and territorial policies in Ober Ost (1915–1918)," 152–153.
41 Stanislaŭ Rudovich, "Belarus' u chas pershaĭ susvetnaĭ vaĭny: nekatoryia aspekty ėtnapalitychnaĭ historyi," in *Białoruś w XX Stuleciu*, ed. Dorota Michaluk (Toruń: Wydawnictwo Naukowe, 2007), 101.
42 For a large portion of 1918, German military occupation covered an additional eastern layer of Belarusian territory that included Minsk. Uladzimir Liakhoŭski, *Shkol'naia adukatsyia ŭ Belarusi padchas niametskaĭ akupatsyi 1915–1918* (Vilnius: Instytut balarusistyki, 2010), 75.
43 This policy was changed in the summer of 1917 when Ludendorff allowed the establishment of some self-governance in the region, primarily to garner local support.
44 Stephan Lehnstaedt, "Fluctuating between 'Utilization' and Exploitation: Occupied East Central Europe during the First World War," in *Legacies of Violence. Eastern Europe's First World War,* ed. Jochen Böhler, Włodzimierz Borodziej, and Joachim von Puttkamer (Münich: Oldenbourg Verlag, 2014), 98.
45 Christian Westerhoff, "'A Kind of Siberia': German Labour and Occupation Policies in Poland and Lithuania during the First World War," *First World War Studies 4*, no 1 (2013): 55.
46 Vejas Gabriel Liulevicius, *War Land on the Eastern Front: Culture, National Identity, and German Occupation in World War I* (Cambridge: Cambridge University Press, 2000), 64.

47 According to scholars, Jews represented a significant portion of those recruited. The reasons for this are still debated. Some historians posit that it resulted from antisemitism, while others attribute a larger unemployment rate among Jews. However, other scholars argue against this assumption and address other German policies toward Jews in *Ober Ost,* which included the abolishment of antisemitic laws and the recognition of Jewish organizations. Ibid., 56–57; Michaluk and Rudling, "From the Grand Duchy of Lithuania to the Belarusian Democratic Republic," 10.

48 Historian Christian Westerhoff cites this term from German-Jewish writer, Arnold Zweig, who worked as a press correspondent and depicted the conditions he witnessed. Westerhoff, "'A Kind of Siberia'," 56.

49 Richter, "'Go with the Hare's Ticket' Mobility and Territorial Policies in Ober Ost (1915–1918)," 155.

50 Liulevicius, *War Land on the Eastern Front,* 57.

51 A. Strazhas, *Deutsche Ostpolitik im Ersten Weltkrieg: Der Fall Ober Ost 1915–1917* (Weisbaden: Harrassowitz Verlag, 1993), 172–173. For more information on German policies of occupation and their interpretations during the First World War, see Jonathan E. Gumz, "Losing Control: The Norm of Occupation in Eastern Europe during the First World War," in *Legacies of Violence: Eastern Europe's First World War,* ed. Jochen Böhler, Włodzimierz Borodziej, and Jochim von Puttkamer (Münich: Oldenbourg Verlag, 2014), 83.

52 Population figures indicate that 34.4 percent of the area's inhabitants were Lithuanian, 20.8 percent Belarusian, 13.5 percent Jewish, 11.8 percent Polish, and 10.5 percent Latvian.

53 The first Belarusian school opened on 13 November 1915. The number of Lithuanian schools also saw a remarkable jump from 260 to 542, whereas Polish schools declined in number from 385 in 1916 to 291 the following year. Some scholars highlight the impact of German rule on Belarusian schools by comparing this period with the preceding Russian and following Polish regime's politics vis-à-vis Belarusian education. Jerzy Turonek, *Białoruś pod okupacją niemiecką* (Warsaw: "WERS", 1989), 21; Michaluk and Rudling, "From the Grand Duchy of Lithuania to the Belarusian Democratic Republic," 10–11; Marian Siemakowicz, "Polityka władz rosyjskich, niemieckich i polskich wobec szkolnictwa białoruskiego w latach 1903–1922," *Białoruskie Zeszyty Historyczne* 7 (1997), 48.

54 Liakhoŭski, Shkol'naia *adukatsyia ŭ Belarusi padchas niametskaĭ akupatsyi 1915–1918,* 77.

55 Kasmach, "Forgotten Occupation", 322–323.

56 Michaluk and Rudling, "From the Grand Duchy of Lithuania to the Belarusian Democratic Republic," 10.

57 The meeting took place on 21 February 1918 (or 3 February 1918 in the old, Gregorian style). "1-ia Ustavnaia Gramota k narodam Belorussii, 1918, 21 fevralia," in *Istoriia Belarusi v dokumentakh i materialakh*, edited by I.N. Kuznetsov and V.G Mazets (Minsk: Amalfeia, 2000), 301.
58 "2-ia Ustaŭnaia hramata da narodaŭ Belarusi, 1918, 9 sakavika," in *Istoriia Belarusi v dokumentakh i materialakh*, ed. I.N. Kuznetsov and V.G. Mazets (Minsk: Amalfeia, 2000), 302.
59 Shved and Grzybowski, *Historia Białorusi od Czasów Najdawniejszych do Roku 1991*, 117.
60 "2-ia Ustaŭnaia hramata da narodaŭ Belarusi, 1918, 9 sakavika," 302–303.
61 The official declaration of the BNR came during the third meeting of Belarusian delegates.
62 "3-ia Ustaŭnaia hramata Rady Belaruskae Narodnae Rėspubliki, 1918, 25 sakavika," in *Istoriia Belarusi v dokumentakh i materialakh*, ed. I.N. Kuznetsov and V.G Mazets (Minsk: Amalfeia, 2000), 303.
63 The BNR operated in Minsk until January 1919, after which the Bolsheviks took over control of the region. The BNR's council continues to operate abroad and continues to operate as a government-in-exile. The BNR is sometimes referred to as the Belarusian Democratic Republic. Michaluk and Rudling, "From the Grand Duchy of Lithuania to the Belarusian Democratic Republic," 17.
64 Kasmach, *Belarusian Nation-Building in Times of War and Revolution*, 207.
65 Łatyszonek, *Bialoruskie formacje wojskowe*, 192–195.
66 Iury Vesialkoŭski, *Bielarus' u piershaĭ sus'vetnaĭ vaĭne: histarychny narys* (London: Vesialkoŭski, 1996), 167.
67 Aleh Latyshonak, *Zhaŭnery BNR* (Smalensk: Inbelkul't, 2014), 110.
68 Vesialkoŭski, *Bielarus' u piershaĭ sus'vetnaĭ vaĭne: histarychny narys*, 168.
69 The BVK is also sometimes referred to as the Belarusian Military Committee. In spite of its creation, there was concern over the BVK stemming from fears that the individuals involved had Russian inclinations and would be internally dangerous. CAW, Sygn. VIII.800.73.2, p. 1–14.
70 Karpus, "Formowanie oddziałów wojskowych przez Białoruską Komisję Wojskową w Polsce w latach 1919–1920," in *Białoruś w XX Stuleciu*, edited by Dorota Michaluk (Toruń: Wydawnictwo Naukowe, 2007), 311.
71 Kushal′ recalls some tension during the organization of the Belarusian armed battalions, as the Poles originally envisioned the Belarusians to fight within a Lithuanian-Belarusian Division. On 22 October 1919, Piłsudski sanctioned the creation of two Belarusian battalions, separate from the Lithuanian-Belarusian division. Kushal′, *Sproby stvarėn′nia belaruskaha voĭska*, 26.
72 CAW, Sygn. I.300.7.32, p. 152–154.
73 Some prominent BVK members, aside from Kushal′, included Paval Aleksiuk, Hasan Kanapatski, Davyd Iakuboŭski, Szymon Rak-Mikhaĭloyski, Frantsishak Aliakhnovich, and Iustyn Murashka.

74 The limits and boundaries of what was meant by "Belarusian" territory were not made explicit. Latyshonak, *Zhaŭnery BNR*, 109–110.

75 Quoted in Uladzimir Ladyseŭ, *Shliakh da Svabody: Z historyi rėvaliutsyĭna-vyzvalenchaha rukhu ŭ Zakhodniaĭ Belarusi ŭ 1919–1939 hh.* (Minsk: Bibliatėchka hazety "Holas Radzimy", 1978), 6.

76 Jerzy Borzecki, *The Soviet-Polish Peace of 1921 and the Creation of Interwar Europe* (New Haven: Yale University Press, 2008), 70.

77 The Belarusians who sought an audience and place at the negotiating table included BNR members. Mikola Miazha, "Mizhnarodnapalitychny aspekt barats'by za belaruskuiu dziarzhaŭnasts' u pachatku 1920-kh hh.," *Białoruskie Zeszyty Historyczne 15* (2001): 126; AAN, Sygn. 2/390/0/6/47, p. 27.

78 The Lithuanian government wanted to attract Belarusian elites to join the *taryba*, or governing council, in order to show Lithuania's commitment to respect minorities in fulfillment of being a tolerant, democratic state. There was also a ministry for Belarusian affairs in existence between 1918 and 1923, led by Iazėp Varonka and Daminik Siamashka, to deal with some of these issues as well. Dorota Michaluk, *Białoruska Republika Ludowa 1918–1920: U Podstaw Białoruskiej Państwowości* (Toruń: Wydawnictwo Naukowe Uniwersytetu Mikołaja Kopernika, 2010), 349–357.

79 CAW, Sygn. I.301.8.471, p. 2–7.

80 CAW, Sygn. VIII.807.30.3, p. 1–3.

81 The first of these loans was in the amount of one million "Ost rubles" or German marks, with a yearly interest rate of 5 percent. CAW, Sygn. I.301.8.471, p. 8.

82 Ibid., 11.

83 In some literature, the Slutsk insurrection has been referred to as the "Slutsk Uprising". One scholar, Uladzimir Liakhoŭski, argues than an "uprising" occurs in reaction to an occupying regime and that at this point, the Bolsheviks had not yet fully settled in the Slutsk district. Another identificatory phrase used has been the Slutsk Front of the Belarusian People's Republic, also rejected by Liakhoŭski because the insurgents were operating in a neutral zone. Instead, he proposes the phrase "armed movement" (Slutski zbroĭny chyn). See: Uladzimir Liakhoŭski, "Sluchaki zmahalisia, a dzieiachy BNR siadzieli, iak myshy pad venikam," *Novy chas*, (28 November 2014), https://novychas.by/poviaz/uladzimier_ljachouski_slucaki.

84 The Slutsk district is in today's Minsk region, with the town of Slutsk as its capital. I use the term "Slutsk" as the county and city interchangeably. Edward Maliszewski's research of the Slutsk district in 1920 indicated that 71.1 percent of the population was Belarusian, 15.8 percent was Jewish, and 10.6 percent was Polish. AAN, Sygn. 2/515/0/4/160, p. 52.

85 Considering Poland's military advantage in September and October 1920 and based on how the discussions were going, the Polish delegation

was in a favorable position to press for more Belarusian territory. The decision not to absorb more Belarusian territory was largely due to a split in the delegation: between those who supported the creation of a federalist republic and those who wanted a more ethnically homogeneous Polish democratic state. The latter's proponents were also wary of incorporating significant Belarusian territory as they thought these would become hubs for expanding Belarusian nationalism. This inclusion would be dangerous for Poland, but in turn, could also be used against the Soviet state. Stanisław Dąbrowski, "The Peace Treaty of Riga," *The Polish Review* 5, no. 1 (Winter 1960): 10–12.

86 AAN, Sygn. 2/55/0/5/319 p. 12–13.

87 Ibid., 31–32.

88 NARB, f. 459, v. 1, s. 5, p. 12.

89 Nina Stuzhynskaia, *Belarus' miatsezhnaia: z historyi ŭzbroenaha antysavetskaha supratsivu ŭ 1920-ia hh.* (Minsk: Vydavets Varaksin A.M., 2012), 15.

90 Some noteworthy members of the leadership in charge of organizing the insurrection included Uladzimier Prakulevich, Vasil' Rusak, Pavel Zhaŭryd, Iul'ian Sasnoŭski, Iurka Listapad, and Siargeĭ Busel, and a few others, totaling seventeen. See: Aliakseĭ Kabychkin, "Slutskae paŭstan'ne", *Slutski zbroĭny chyn 1920- u dakumėntakh i ŭspaminakh,* 203; Łatyszonek, *Białoruskie formacje wojskowe,* 198–199.

91 Iurka Listapad, "Uz'bilisia na svoĭ shliakh, 1921 h.," 161.

92 Zbigniew Karpus and Waldemar Rezmer, "Powstanie słuckie 1920r w świetle polskich materiałów wojskowych," *Białoruskie Zeszyty Historyczne* 1(5) (1996): 75.

93 This request by the Slutsk Rada was made in an effort to stall the incoming Bolshevik troops, allowing extra time for preparation and organization. CAW, Sygn. I.311.4.238, p. 5, 15, 28.

94 Records from the beginning of February 1921 indicate that 1555 individuals had been captured and were being kept by the Poles. Karpus and Rezmer, "Powstanie słuckie 1920r w świetle polskich materiałów wojskowych", 79.

95 "Vytrymka z' neviadomaha artykula B. Rusaka," *Slutski zbroĭny chyn 1920- u dakumėntakh i ŭspaminakh,* 177; Anton Sokal-Kutyloŭski, "Mae ŭspaminy ab Slutskim zbroĭnym zmagan'ni z bal'shavikami ŭ 1920 hodze," *Slutski zbroĭny chyn 1920- u dakumėntakh i ŭspaminakh,*186–187.

96 NARB, f. 383, v. 1, s. 8, p. 1–6.

97 For a more detailed analysis on the Slutsk insurrection see: Aleksandra Pomiecko, "Slutsk in 1920: Entangled Fighters, Locals, and Conflicts," *Slavic Review* 80, no. 4 (Winter 2021): 749–768.

98 The border was not officially delineated until March 1921. Even after the signing of the Treaty of Riga, *Zialony dub* continued to operate on Soviet territory. CAW, Sygn. I.311.4.170, p. 98.

99 Stuzhynskaia, *Belarus' miatsezhnaia: z historyi ŭzbroenaha antysavetskaha supratsivu: 20-ia hh. XX stakhodzia*), 91–105; Nina Stużyńska, "Antysowiecka konspiracja i partyzantka Zielonego Dębu na terenie Białorusi w latach 1919–1925," in *Europa Nieprowincjonalna*, ed. R. Jasiewicz (Warsaw: Instytut Studiów Politycznych, PAN), 859–866.

100 These were men primarily from the Hrozaŭski regiment of the Slutsk battalion. Iurka Kharytonchyk, "Z uspaminaŭ slutskaha paŭstantsa, 1960 h," *Slutski zbroĭny chyn 1920- u dakumėntakh i ŭspaminakh*, 212.

101 CAW, Sygn. 1.311.4.193, p. 8–9.

102 Ales' Pashkevich, "Ataman Dziarhach: neviadomyia staronki biiahrafii, tsi da historyi palitychnaha avanturyzmu ŭ belaruskim natsyianal'nym rukhu," *Berastseŭski khranohraf* 4 (2004): 314–334.

103 NARB, f. 4p, v. 1, s. 16871, p. 32–36.

104 NARB, f. 4p, v. 1, s.16931, p. 85–87.

105 Ēriks Jēkabsons and Jerzy Grzybowski, "Łotewski 'ślad' w działalności atamanów białoruskich Wiaczesława Adamowicza 'Dziergacza' i Wiaczesława Razumowicza 'Chmary'," *Białoruskie Zeszyty Historyczne* 42 (2014): 82.

106 CAW, Sygn. I.375.3.185, p. 8; Eugeniusz Mironowicz, *Białorusini i Ukraińcy w polityce obozu piłsudczykowskiego* (Białystok: Wydawnictwo Uniwersyteckie, 2007), 29.

107 CAW, I.375.3.185, p. 12–13.

108 This Belarusian-Lithuanian point of cooperation came with the creation of a Belarusian battalion under the Lithuanian Army, as well as Razumovich's partisan group. This step toward cooperation, on behalf of the Belarusians, came largely at the disillusionment with the Germans' refusal to recognize the Belarusian People's Republic. Razumovich allegedly also negotiated to create a Lithuanian-Belarusian corridor around Kaunas, allowing for better Belarusian-Lithuanian coordination. Aušra Jurevičiūtė, "Belorusskie voennye formatsii v Litovskoi Armii 1918–1923 g.g.," *Białoruś w XX Stuleciu* (Toruń: Wydawnictwo Naukowe, 2007), 283; CAW, Sygn. VIII.804.21.64, p. 3–4.

109 CAW, Sygn. VIII.804.21.64, p. 12–15.

110 Piotr Cichoracki, *Stołpce-Łowcza-Leśna 1924: II Rzeczpospolita wobec najpoważniejszych incydentów zbrojnych w województwach połnocno-wschodnich* (Łomianki: Wydawnictwo LTW, 2012), 21.

111 CAW, Sygn. VIII.804.21.64, p. 17.

112 The last of such groups was disbanded on 28 July 1923. Jurevičiūtė, "Belorusskie voennye formatsii v Litovskoi Armii 1918–1923 gg", 306–307.

113 For more, see Ēriks Jēkabsons and Jerzy Grzybowski, "Łotewski 'ślad' w działalności atamanów białoruskich Wiaczesława Adamowicza 'Dziergacza' i Wiaczesława Razumowicza 'Chmary'," *Białoruskie Zeszyty Historyczne* 42 (2014): 80–96.

114 Dz'mitry Kasmovich, *Za vol'nuiu i suverennuiu Belarus'* (Vilnius: Gudas, 2006), 13.

115 NARB, f. 459, v. 1, s. 5, p. 14.
116 U.F. Ladyseŭ, "Stanaŭlenne natsyianal'na-vyzvalenchaha rukhu ŭ zakhodniaĭ Belarusi," in *Polska i Białoruś w XX wieku. Z dziejów Europy Środkowo-Wschodniej,* ed. Edward Czapiewski and Grzegorz Strauchold (Wrocław: Wydawnictwo GAJT, 2009), 87.

2 A Belarusian "Interwar" Period

1 In scholarship, these different battlefronts for developing Belarusian nationalism are separated geographically as well as politically. There are works, such as Aleksandra Bergman's, dedicated to Belarusian affairs in the Second Polish Republic that highlight repressive measures against minorities. Per Anders Rudling's work offers a look into both Poland and Soviet Belarus, including the policies enacted by these states. He also discusses these policies and ways in which they inhibited or encouraged the development of Belarusian nationalism. Other interpretations of Belarusian nationalism focus on particular groups of individuals. These include, for example, Belarusians who were in favor of autonomy or those who advocated complete independence. Collectively, this scholarship concludes the interwar period in 1939 and treats the 1939 to 1941 period separately. Aleksandra Bergman, *Sprawy Białoruskie w II Rzeczypospolitej* (Warszawa: Państwowe Wydawnictwo Naukowe, 1984); Per Anders Rudling, *The Rise and Fall of Belarusian Nationalism* (Pittsburgh: University of Pittsburgh Press, 2015).
2 Dz'mitry Kasmovich, *Za vol'nuiu i suverennuiu Belarus'* (Vilnius: Gudas, 2006), 15.
3 Kasmovich, *Za vol'nuiu i suverennuiu Belarus'*, 16–19.
4 Initially they went to Nowogródek. However, the boys were dissatisfied with the school there, citing Belarusian-Russian tensions. In Radoszkowice, Kasmovich recalled a much more welcoming environment. Ibid., 20.
5 Ibid., 21.
6 Inge Sanmiya, *Against the Current: The memoirs of Boris Ragula* (Montreal: McGill Queen's University Press, 2005), 16–17.
7 Janusz Żarnowski, *Społeczeństwo Drugiej Rzeczypospolitej 1918–1939* (Warszawa: Państwowe Wydawnictwo Naukowe, 1973), 374.
8 Some political parties, such as the Belarusian Peasant-Workers' Hramada, contested this figure, insisting that the number of those registered as Orthodox Christians (approximately 304,700) offered more indicative figures of the number of Belarusians living in the district. Another point of contestation by the Hramada was the fact that some individuals conducting the census were instructed to include any individuals calling themselves "tutejszy", or of local identity, within the Polish category. Archiwum Akt Nowych (AAN), Sygn. 172/II, p. 4; Centralne Archiwum Wojskowe (CAW), Sygn. VIII.804.17.4, p. 2.

9 AAN, Sygn. 172/II, 5.

10 Polonization was carried out by the Ministry of Military Affairs, Ministry of Internal Affairs, and Ministry of Foreign Affairs. Suggestions regarding ways to assimilate non-ethnic Poles also appeared outside of these institutions. One suggestion by the voivodship governor of Polesie, Stanisław Downarowicz, advised separating these national groups from each other, in order to better integrate them into Polish society. Eugeniusz Mironowicz, *Białorusini i Ukraińcy w polityce obozu piłsudczykowskiego* (Białystok: Wydawnictwo Uniwersyteckie, 2007), 36–37. For more information on the cultural and social elements of *Sanacja*, see: Eva Plach, *The Clash of Moral Nations: Cultural Politics in Piłsudski's Poland, 1926–1935* (Athens: Ohio University Press, 2006).

11 Eugeniusz Mironowicz, *Białoruś- Historia Państw Świata w XX Wieku* (Warszawa: Wydawnictwo Trio, 1999), 85; Marian Siemakowicz, "Szkoły z białoruskim językiem nauczania na tle polityki władz polskich wobec ludności białoruskiej w II Rzeczypospolitej," *Białoruskie Zeszyty Historyczne* 16 (2001): 105.

12 In the cities of Wilno, Nowogródek, Nieśwież, Radoszkowice, and Kleck, private schools existed during these periods respectively, 1919 to 1932, 1921 to 1932, 1921 to 1923, 1922 to 1928, and 1924 to 1931. Marian Siemakowicz, "Organizacja białoruskich gimnazjów i seminariów nauczycielskich w II Rzeczypospolitej," *Białoruskie Zeszyty Historyczne 11* (1999): 126.

13 Even the department of Belarusian studies at the University of Vilnius, prior to being shut down, taught courses in Polish. Lietuvos centrinis valstybės archyvas (LCVA), f. 361, ap. 1, b. 2, p. 3–5.

14 LCVA, f. 365, ap. 2, b. 17, p. 1.

15 Aside from restrictions on Belarusian schools, education in the countryside suffered. One report on the status of Belarusian students in Poland's rural areas shows that the 1935 to 1936 academic school year saw 605, 928 students entering the first class. However, students that managed to complete their fourth year of studies in 1936 reached only 125,088. If these numbers were consistent throughout the period of the Second Polish Republic, it would reveal that only 20 percent of Belarusians completed at least four years of schooling. AAN, Sygn. 172/II, p. 7–8.

16 Krystyna Gomółka, "Ruch białoruski w przededniu II wojny światowej," *Białoruskie Zeszyty Historyczne 13* (2000): 186.

17 In the Nowogródek province the Belarusian groups in operation, including *Zmahan'ne, Dobrobyt, Run', Sieŭba,* and *Sila,* were all liquidated. Dziarzhaŭny arkhiŭ Hrodzenskaĭ Voblastsi (DAHV), f. 200, v. 2, s. 13, p. 141; CAW, Sygn. I.301.8.471, p. 38.

18 DAHV, f. 200, v. 2 s. 23, p. 137.

19 Close monitoring of these organizations was carried out on multiple levels. For example, the Society of Belarusian Schools (*Tavarystva Belaruskaĭ Shkoly*, TBS) was closely monitored by Polish authorities who kept tabs on the students, the academics, and teachers, as well as the newspapers and known meetings of the organization. The TBS was officially headquartered in Vilnius but also had smaller regional centers around the eastern provinces of the Second Polish Republic. Surveillance also occurred in these smaller towns. A document from 1933 notes that Belarusian nationalists were allegedly organizing in Stołpce. DAHV, f. 200, v. 2, s. 13, p. 27 opp.

20 Land was also given to *osadnicy*, or Polish settlers, as compensation for their military service. Rudling, *The Rise and Fall of Belarusian Nationalism 1906–1931*, 170.

21 *Osadnicy* received as much as forty hectares of land, whereas a local family, if lucky, would receive between one and five hectares. CAW, Sygn. VIII.804.17.4, p. 2.

22 Ibid., p. 3.

23 These initiatives included increased taxation, the sale of state enterprises, and strict savings Piotr J. Wróbel, "The Rise and Fall of Parliamentary Democracy in Interwar Poland," in *The Origins of Modern Polish Democracy*, ed. M.B.B. Biskupski, James S. Pula, and Piotr J. Wróbel (Athens: Ohio University Press, 2010), 139.

24 Archiwum Wschodnie (AW), Sygn. I/617, p. 1–3.

25 These parties included, for example, the Belarusian Christian-Democratic Union (*Bialoruskie Zjednoczenie Chrześcijańsko-Demokratyczne*), the Belarusian Social-Democratic Party (*Białoruska Partia Socjal-Demokratyczna*), and the Belarusian Peasant Union (*Białoruski Związek Włościański*). Eugeniusz Mironowicz, "Białorusini wobec państwa polskiego w latach 1918–1925," *Białoruskie Zeszyty Historyczne 1* (1994): 27; Jerzy Holzer, *Mozaika polityczna Drugiej Rzeczypospolitej* (Warszawa: Książka i Wiedza, 1974), 253–260; Bergman, *Sprawy Białoruskie w II Rzeczypospolitej*, 115–116.

26 Wiesław Choruży, "Działalność Białoruskiej Włościańsko-Robotniczej Hromady w powiecie białostockim, bielskim i sokólskim w latach 1925–1927," *Białoruskie Zeszyty Historyczne* 1 (1994): 44, 62; AAN, Sygn. 172/II, p. 17, 19–20; Jerzy Grzybowski, "Grupa białoruskich narodowych socjalistów w Polsce w przededniu II wojny światowej," *Politeja – Pismo Wydziału Studiów Międzynarodowych i Politycznych Uniwersytetu Jagiellońskiego 22,* no. 3/21 (2012), 5; Sylwia Szyc, "Działalność Białoruskiej Włościańsko-Robotniczej Hromady w latach 1925–1927," *Studia Białorutenistyczne* 7 (2013): 50.

Despite its repeated efforts to serve as a distinct party from the Polish Communist Party, this status was not granted by the Comintern. In the early 1930s, the Białystok voivodship estimates that between the Polish Communist Party, KPZB, and their respective youth communist organizations, there were approximately 3842 members. It was disbanded on orders from the Comintern in 1938, followed by a purge of many of its members. AAN, Sygn. 266/II/1, p. 46–47; U.F. Ladyseŭ, "Stanaŭlenne natsyianal'na-vyzvalenchaha rukhu ŭ zakhodniaĭ Belarusi," in *Polska i Białoruś w XX wieku. Z dziejów Europy Środkowo-Wschodniej,* ed. Edward Czapiewski and Grzegorz Strauchold (Wrocław: Wydawnictwo GAJT, 2009), 900.

27 Bergman, *Sprawy Białoruskie w II Rzeczypospolitej,* 103.

28 Dziarzhaŭny arkhiŭ Brėstskaĭ voblastsi (DABV), f. 67, v. 1, s. 874, p. 2–3; AAN, Sygn. 266/II.5, p. 359.

29 DAHV, f. 679, v. 1, s. 10, p. 172; Natsyianal'ny arkhiŭ Rėspubliki Belarus' (NARB), f. 242p, v. 2, s. 399, p. 74.

30 AAN, Sygn. 2/2015/0/2, p. 3.

31 Kasmovich, *Za vol'nuiu i suverennuiu Belarus',* 22.

32 DABV, f. 98, v. 1, s. 2059, p. 1–6.

33 Bereza Kartuska was a penal camp located in today's Biaroza, Belarus (Polesie province in the Second Polish Republic). The opening of the camp was largely motivated by the assassination of the Minister of Internal Affairs, Bronisław Pieracki, on 15 June 1934. Pieracki was assassinated by individuals from the Organization of Ukrainian Nationalists. The camp detained people perceived to be enemies of the state, which included communists and minorities but also far-right Polish nationalists. Polish authorities arrested and incarcerated individuals and were not required to issue a formal charge or organize a trial. Throughout its existence, there was a tremendous amount of secrecy surrounding the camp, as locals were strictly prohibited from taking pictures or contacting prisoners, while journalists were denied access. The camp continued operating until it was taken by Soviet authorities in September 1939. Wojciech Śleszyński, *Obóz odosobnienia w Berezie Kartuskiej, 1934–1939* (Białystok: Dom Wydawniczy Benkowski, 2003), 14–16. DABV, f. 98, v. 1, s. 2060, p. 1–2.

34 Sakovich was not the only former Communist turned to the right. Fabian Akinchyts, a former member of both the Communist Party of Western Belarus and Belarusian Peasant-Workers' Hramada, had a change of heart after he was incarcerated by the Poles in 1927. He severed all contacts with the communist party and the Hramada and was later one of the leaders of the Belarusian National Socialist Party. Other Belarusian elites also became disillusioned with any socialist or communist project during the mass terror. Grzybowski, "Grupa białoruskich narodowych socjalistów w Polsce w przededniu II wojny światowej," 5.

35 CAW Akta Personalne (AP) 4916, p. 3–25.

36 He continued in this position in the Chełmno Cadet Corps in 1926 and later in 11th Infantry Regiment in Pułtusk.

37 CAW Akta Personalne (AP) 317, 1–90.

38 CAW Kolekcja Krzyża Zasługi (KZ) 11–564, p. 4.

39 For example, Kushal′ was part of a committee composed to investigate the Klaipėda Coup of 1923. Despite Lithuanian participation in the takeover, in his statement Kushal′ suggested that the Poles might be behind the coup because of a Polish newspaper publication announcing the coup the day before. LCVA, f. 671, ap. 1, 43, p. 10 opp.

40 According to historian Krystyna Gomółka, between 1921 and 1939 Belarusians accounted for 10 percent of the Polish armed forces. On the other hand, figures from Jerzy Grzybowski's research indicates that in 1922, 188,250 served in the army. Out of this number 147,442, or 78.3 percent, were Polish and 40,808, or 21.7 percent, were of non-Polish background. Out of the non-Polish demographic, 12,521, or 30.7 percent, were Belarusian, which estimates to approximately 6.7 percent out of the total number that year. Gomółka, "Ruch białoruski w przededniu II wojny światowej," 189; Grzybowski, *Białorusini w polskich regularnych formacjach wojskowych w latach 1918–1945*, 71–73.

41 Grzybowski, *Białorusini w polskich regularnych formacjach wojskowych w latach 1918–1945*, 72, 75.

42 Some scholars, however, suggest otherwise. Marek Wierzbicki notes that, based on Polish sources, on the eve of the German invasion of Poland, overall morale in the army was high, including that of Belarusians. Marek Wierzbicki, "Białorusini w Wojsku Polskim w czasie kampanii wrześniowej 1939r," *Białoruskie Zeszyty Historyczne* 2 (6) (1996): 67.

43 Grzybowski, *Białorusini w polskich regularnych formacjach wojskowych w latach 1918–1945*, 175.

44 When the BSSR was created in 1921, it was composed of six districts in the Minsk province, with a population of over one and a half million inhabitants. In March 1924, the regions of Mahilieŭ, as well as parts of Vitsebsk, Homel, and Smalensk, were incorporated into the BSSR. This process not only doubled the BSSR's territorial size but also increased its population from 1.5 to 4.2 million, out of which 70.4 percent were ethnic Belarusian. Again, in December 1926, the BSSR incorporated more territory, adding an additional 649,000 people to the existing population. A 1926 census ascribing nationality based on language showed that the majority of the population was Belarusian, followed by Jewish, Russian, and Polish. The majority of Belarusians were peasants, whereas cities were largely composed of Jews. Of the total number of Belarusians, 89 percent resided in the countryside. Jews accounted for 8.2 percent of the total population and 40 percent of urban dwellers. Russians accounted for approximately 7.7 percent of the BSSR's population and 15.6 percent of urban residents. Lastly, Poles comprised 1.96 percent of the total population split nearly evenly between the countryside and cities. The russification of

some regions prior to their annexation to Soviet Belarus may have affected these figures especially when comparing nationality to language spoken.

Helena Głogowska, *Białoruś 1914–1929: Kultura pod presją polityki* (Białystok: Białoruskie Towarzystwo Historyczne, 1996), 76, 95–96; T.C. Prot'ko, *Stanovlene sovetskoi totalitarnoi sistemy v Belarusi* 1917–1941 (Minsk: Tesei, 2002), 324, 330.

45 Aleksandra Bergman notes that Belarusian peasants certainly thought they would live better in the BSSR. Ivan Lubachko even refers to the 1920s in the BSSR as the "Golden Age of Belorussian Culture", referring to the effects of the New Economic Policy and nationality politics. Ivan Lubachko, *Belorussia under Soviet Rule 1917–1957* (Lexington: The University Press of Kentucky, 1972), 80–92.

46 Initial allowances for the development of Belarusian identity were largely due to Soviet nationality politics from the top, stemming from the 10th Party Congress in 1921. The policies implemented in the BSSR were strongly intertwined with policies enacted in the USSR.

47 However, until 1921, Moscow's policy toward a Belarusian socialist state were primarily driven by a desire to create a buffer zone against "capitalist encroachment" from the West. The area was not in the plans to become a driving contributor to a developing communist state. Anatol' Trafimchyk, "Da prablemy stanaŭlennia dziarzhaŭnastsi Belarusi (1917–1921): palityka Kramlia," *Białoruskie Zeszyty Historyczne* 31 (2009): 113.

48 For more on nationality policies in the Soviet Union, see: Terry Martin, *The Affirmative Action Empire: Nations and Nationalism in the Soviet Union, 1923–1939* (Ithaca: Cornell University Press, 2001).

49 Prot'ko, *Stanovlene sovetskoi totalitarnoi sistemy v Belarusi 1917–1941*, 321.

50 This Soviet policy slogan intended to instill the Soviet regime's values in a language that was understood by non-Russian ethnic and national groups.

51 *Belarusization* was paired with policies of *yiddishization* and *polonization* in order to prevent the dominance of one that would foster national opposition. In February 1921, the BSSR's Central Executive Committee formally adopted four official languages in the republic: Belarusian, Russian, Yiddish, and Polish. Rudling, *Rise and Fall of Belarusian Nationalism*, 134–141.

52 Głogowska, *Białoruś 1914–1929*, 107

53 Rudling, *Rise and Fall of Belarusian Nationalism*, 148.

54 Bergman, *Sprawy Białoruskie w II*, 17.

55 For a comprehensive study on the *belarusization* policies of the 1920s, see: Alena Marková, *The Path to a Soviet Nation: The Policy of Belarusization* (Paderborn: Brill Schöningh, 2022).

56 NARB, f. 1450, v. 2, s. 51, p. 30–31.

57 The term has two connotations. It refers to the Slutsk insurrection, which occurred in November 1920. November in Belarusian is "listapad". The term

ironically also refers to Iurka Listapad, whose last name mimics the month of the uprising. *Listapadaŭtsy* was also spelled in the Polish way in some texts (*listopadowcy*) giving it an air of something supported by foreign agents.

58 "Pratsės listapadautsau," *Zvezda,* no. 52, 4 March 1926, p. 3; "Delo listopadovtsev v okruzhnom sude," *Zvezda,* no. 56, 9 March 1926, p. 4. Accessed through AAN Sygn. 2/322/0/6703, p. 360, 362.

59 Uladzimir Adamushka, *Palitychnyia rėprėsii 20–50 hadoŭ na Belarusi* (Minsk: "Belarus'", 2004), 30.

60 There is some debate among scholars as to whether or not there were significant numbers of wealthy peasants in Belarus at this time. This discussion, however, has little impact on the "dekulakization" process in Belarus, as this term was used for many reasons beyond that of repressing only wealthy, capitalist peasants. Adamushka, *Palitychnyia rėprėsii 20–50 hadoŭ na Belarusi,* 36.

61 Prot'ko, *Stanovlene sovetskoi totalitarnoi sistemy v Belarusi,* 337.

62 NARB, f. 242p, v. 2, s. 399, p. 78.

63 There continues to be a significant lacuna in our knowledge of Soviet Belarusian experiences during the mass terror, mass operations, and repression. This research gap, however, can be ameliorated by examining works conducted on the experience of the terror and mass operations in other Soviet republics. This scholarship offers not only a general understanding of the nature of repression during the 1930s but also its pervasiveness beyond upper-ranking party members. A few Belarusian scholars were able to gather archival information during the brief research thaw period in Minsk in the early 1990s. Although still far from complete, their work allows us to at least construct some sort of picture of Soviet Belarus during the 1930s. Works by Belarusian scholars include: Uladzimir Adamushka, *Palitychnyia rėprėsii 20–50 hadoŭ na Belarusi* (Minsk: "Belarus'", 2004) and Tatiana Prot'ko, *Stanovlene sovetskoi totalitarnoi sistemy v Belarusi (1917–1941).* Minsk: Tesei, 2002. Works discussing repression, the purges, and mass operations involving Soviet Belarus's neighbors and national minorities include: Kate Brown, *A Biography of No Place: From Ethnic Borderland to Soviet Heartland* (Cambridge: Harvard University Press, 2013); Mikołaj Iwanów, *Pierwszy Naród Ukarany – stalinizm wobec polskiej ludności kresowej 1921–1938* (Warsaw: Państwowe Wydawnictwo Naukowe, 1991); Lynne Viola, *Stalinist Perpetrators on Trial: Scenes from the Great Terror in Soviet Ukraine* (New York: Oxford University Press, 2017). Other works give us a picture of the ubiquitous nature of the purges and repression at various political, center, and peripheral levels. See J. Arch Getty, *Origins of the Purges* (New York: Cambridge University Press, 1985) and William Chase, *Enemies within the Gates? The Comintern and the Stalinist Repression, 1934–1939* (New Haven: Yale University Press, 2001).

64 This figure is a very rough estimate, and the figures may not necessarily reflect those repressed from the annexed eastern regions of interwar Poland in 1939. Adamushka, *Palitychnyia rėprėsii 20–50 hadoŭ na Belarusi,* 43–44; Franziska Exeler posits that the number of victims of the mass terror included around 60,000 individuals, of which 30,000 were murdered. Franziska Exeler, *Ghosts of War: Nazi Occupation and Its Aftermath in Soviet Belarus* (Ithaca: Cornell University Press, 2022), p. 43.

65 Exeler, *Ghosts of War,* 44.

66 Some Belarusian activists continue to remember the Kurapaty killings with candlelight vigils held once a month, as well as with protests against the government's plans to build a new highway and casino in the area. For a recent interpretation of the memory and recognition of the Kurapaty killings in Belarus, see: David R. Marples and Veranika Laputska, "Kurapaty: Belarus' Continuing Debates," *Slavic Review* 79, no. 3 (Fall 2020): 521–543.

67 The authors of the report faced a lot of pressure from the Central Committee of the KP(b)B prior to its official publication. The article includes accounts noting that individuals were shot from the side to maximize the bullets' efficacy. These testimonies also alleged that bodies were buried in pre-dug holes and later pine trees were planted on top.

68 The Central Committee demanded that the number of victims be deleted and that chronological adjustments be made to end the execution time period in 1939. This would omit any notion that the citizens of the re-absorbed eastern provinces of Poland in western Belarus had also been victims of these mass killings. A more fantastical story from the state indicated "that access by the press about information concerning Kuropaty can be treated as a camouflage for 'dirty work' of Byelorussian nationalists. Here Byelorussians were not murdered [...] rather 38,000 German officers were shot after the war." Even after the fall of the Soviet Union, this line of argumentation persisted and even adopted new explanations. Mironchikova, "Kuropaty: fal'sifikatsiia veka? Pora skazat' pravdu (Zaiavlenie obshchestvennoi komissii po rassledovaniu v Kuropatakh)," *My i vremia,* 12 avgusta 1994; Mikolaj Iwanow, "The Politics of Perestroika in the USSR and Byelorussian Nationalism," *The Ukrainian Quarterly* XLVIII, no. 2 (Summer 1992): 190; Alexandra Goujon, "Memorial Narratives of WWII Partisans and Genocide in Belarus," *East European Politics and Societies* 24, no. 1 (Winter 2010): 15; Ihar Kuzniatsoŭ, "Palitychnyia rėprėsii ŭ Belarusi ŭ 1939–1941 hadakh," *Białoruskie Zeszyty Historyczne* 13 (2000): 57–70.

69 David R. Marples, "Kuropaty: The Investigation of a Stalinist Historical Controversy," *Slavic Review 53,* no. 2 (Summer 1994): 513–514.

70 Bergman, *Sprawy Białoruskie w II Rzeczypospolitej,* 102.

71 Uladzimir Liakhoŭski, "Chėkhiia i belaruski vyzvol'ny rukh u pershaĭ trėtsi XX stahoddzia," in *Białoruś w XX stuleciu w kręgu kultury i polityki,* ed. Dorota

Michaluk (Toruń: Wydawnictwo Naukowe Uniwersitety Mikolaja Kopernika, 2007), 492.

72 Czechoslovakia was even willing to support the Belarusian cause at the League of Nations. DABV, "Komandovanie okruga korpusa no. 9 Ministerstva voennykh del/dok-1kh, gor. Brest," f. 67, v. 1, s. 326, p. 1–4.

73 Daniela Kolenovská, "Heros and Anti-Heros of the Belarusian Independence Project in Chechoslovakia," *The Journal of Belarusian Studies* 8, no, 3 (2018): 70.

74 Národni archiv České republiky (NAČR), Signatura 225-1204-3, p. 243.

75 NAČR, "Policejní ředitelství Praha II= všeobecná spisovna," Sig. Zacharko Vasil, Z 197/4.

76 NAČR, " Sig. Abramčuk Mikova 1903, A16/29.

77 Liakhoŭski, "Chėkhiia i belaruski vyzvol'ny rukh u pershaĭ trėtsi XX stahoddzia," 507–508.

78 One of the main sources of funding came from the Czech-Ukrainian Assistance Committee for Ukrainian and Belarusian Students, created in November 1921. This Committee was not supported with state funds.

79 Liakhoŭski, "Chėkhiia i belaruski vyzvol'ny rukh u pershaĭ trėtsi XX stahoddzia," 503–504.

80 The first Belarusian university did not appear until October 1921, with the opening of the Belarusian State University (*Belaruski Dziarzhŭny Ŭniversitėt*).

81 NAČR, Sig. Vituško Alexander, V 1992/7; NAČR, Sig. 225-1204-3, p. 241

82 NAČR, Sig. Vituško Michail, V 2992/4.

83 Grzybowski, "Grupa białoruskich narodowych socjalistów w Polsce w przededniu II wojny światowej," 4–5.

84 Jerzy Grzybowski, "Białoruski ruch narodowy a III Rzesza (wrzesień 1939-czerwiec 1941)," *Przegląd Historyczny,* 101, no. 1 (2010): 53.

85 NARB, f. 4p, v. 1, s. 16871, p. 176–177; Grzybowski, "Białoruski ruch narodowy a III Rzesza (wrzesień 1939-czerwiec 1941)," 69.

86 Sakaloŭski and Liakhoŭski, "Niamechchyna ĭ belaruski natsyianal'ny rukh napiarėdadni ĭ u pershyia hady Druhoe Sus'vetnae Vaĭny," 6.

87 Jerzy Turonek, *Białoruś pod Okupacją Niemiecką* (Warszawa: Książka i Wiedza, 1993), 29.

88 Grzybowski, "Grupa białoruskich narodowych socjalistów w Polsce w przededniu II wojny światowej," 9–10.

89 Grzybowski, "Grupa białoruskich," 9–10.

90 S. Bulat, "Zhydy i sus'vetnaia palityka," *Ranitsa,* no. 3, 17 December 1939, p. 1.

91 S. Bulat, "Zhydy u Belarusi," *Ranitsa* no. 3, 17 December 1939, p. 2.

92 Iazep Maletski, *Pad znakam Pahoni: Uspaminy* (Toronto: Vydavetstva "Pahonia", 1976), 48.

93 Grzybowski, "Grupa białoruskich narodowych socjalistów w Polsce w przededniu II wojny światowej", 21.

94 AAN, Sygn. 2/2431/0/9, p. 157.

95 AW, II/530, p. 8.

96 Marek Wierzbicki, “Ludność białoruska i polska wobec Armii Czerwonej po 17 września 1939 r,” *Białoruskie Zeszyty Historyczne* 11, (1999): 157.

97 Document no. 8, “1939, wrzesień 17, miejsce postoju- Odezwa dowódcy Frontu Białoruskiego M. Kowalowa do ludności ‘Zachodniej Białorusi’”, NARB f. 4, v. 21, s. 1742, p. 1, in Władimir Adamuszko, ed., “Zachodnia Białoruś” 17 IX 1939–22VI 1941: Wydarzenia i losy ludzkie, *Źródła do historii Polski XX wieku ze zbiorów Narodowego Archiwum Republiki Białoruś* (Warsaw: Oficyna Wydawnicza RYTM, 1998), 93.

98 Talochka, “‘Pakhod’ Chyrvonaĭ Armii ŭ zakhodniuiu Belarus′ u verasni 1939 hoda va ŭspryniatstsi nasel′nitstva BSSR,” 395.

99 Bogdan Musial, “Jewish Resistance in Poland’s Eastern Borderlands during the Second World War, 1939–41,” *Patterns of Prejudice* 38, no. 4 (2004): 374.

100 Ciesielski, Materski, and Paczkowski, *Represje sowieckie wobec Polaków i obywateli polskich* (Warsaw: Ośrodek KARTA, 2002), 12.

101 Joanna Michlic, “The Soviet Occupation of Poland, 1939–41 and the Stereotype of the Anti-Polish and Pro-Soviet Jew,” *Jewish Social Studies* 13, no. 3 (Spring/Summer 2007): 143.

102 Jan T. Gross, *Revolution from Abroad: The Soviet Conquest of Poland’s Western Ukraine and Western Belorussia* (Princeton: Princeton University Press, 1988), 19.

103 Ciesielski, Materski, and Paczkowski, *Represje sowieckie wobec Polaków i obywateli polskich,* 13; Piotr J. Wróbel, “Class War or Ethnic Cleansing?” 20–28; Stanislaŭ Sil′vanovich, *Antysavetskae* padpol′e *ŭ zakhodnikh ablastiakh Belarusi (verasen′ 1939h – chėrven′ 1941h.*) Aŭtarėferat dysertatsyi na saiskanne vuchonaĭ stupeni kandydata histarychnykh navuk (Minsk: Natsyianal′naia Akadėmiia Navuk Belarusi Instytut historyi, 2000), 10.

104 A.E. Gur′ianov, ed. *Repressii protiv poliakov i pol′skikh grazhdan* (Moscow: Zven’ia, 1997), 103, 101–111.

105 Zmitser Talochka, “‘Pakhod′ Chyrvonaĭ Armii ŭ zakhodniuiu Belarus’ u verasni 1939 hoda va spryniatstsi nasel′nitstva BSSR,” in *Białoruś w XX Stuleciu,* ed. Dorota Michaluk (Toruń: Wydawnictwo Naukowe, 2007), 387.

106 Iury Hryboŭski, “Palitychnaia chynnasts′ starshyni Rady BNR Vasilia Zakharki napiarėdadni i ŭ hady Druhoĭ susvetnaĭ vaĭny (1938–1943),” *Histarychny al′manakh 15* (2009): 120.

107 Iury Hryboŭski, “Pershy belaruski shturmovy z′viaz,” *Belaruski Rėzystans* (February 2005), 5; Olga Baranova, *Nationalism, Anti-Bolshevism or the Will to Survive: Forms of Belarusian Interaction with the German Occupation Authorities, 1941–1944* (Saarbrücken: Lap Lambert, 2010), 73.

108 Jerzy Turonek, "Działalność grupy Fabiana Akinczyca (1939–1943)," *in Białoruś w XX Stuleciu w Kręgu Kultury i Polityki,* ed. Dorota Michaluk (Toruń: Wydawnictwo Naukowe, 2007), 406–410.

109 "78 Befehl des Chefs des Generalstabes der Heeresgruppe B zum Einsatz von Diversanten beim Überfall auf die Sowjetunion, 20. Mai 1941", in *Fall Barbarossa- Dokumente zur Vorbereitung der faschistischen Wehrmacht auf die Aggression gegen die Sowjetunion (1940/41),* selected and ed. Erhard Moritz (Berlin: Deutscher Militärverlag, 1970), 260; Grzybowski, *Białorusini w polskich regularnych formacjach wojskowych w latach 1918–1945*, 189.

110 Igor Valakhanovich, *Antisovetskoe podpol'e na territorii Belarusi v 1944–1953gg* (Minsk: BGU, 2002), 25.

111 AAN, Sygn. 172/II, p. 19.

112 Daniela Kolenovská, "Heros and Anti-Heros of the Belarusian Independence Project in Chechoslovakia," *The Journal of Belarusian Studies* 8, no, 3 (2018): 76–77.

113 While Zakharka communicated with the Germans, his goal for the Belarusian situation was to garner autonomy within a Polish state. Zakharka believed that because Poland, in 1939, had found itself in a difficult situation, the state would be more open to a future Polish state with an autonomous Belarus, if the latter assisted the Poles in reinstating their independence. Iury Hryboŭski, "Belaruski rukh i Niamechchyna napiarėdadni i ŭ pachatku Drugoĭ sus'vetnaĭ vaĭny," *ARCHE 5*, (May 2009), 145.

114 Instytut Pamięci Narodowej (IPN), BU 003172/33/4, p. 112–114.

115 In September 1941, the leader of the BSP became Ermachėnka, at the request of Alfred Rosenberg. Turonek, "Działalność grupy Fabiana Akinczyca (1939–1943)", 405.

116 There were also Belarusian groups that were created and strengthened in Latvia and in Prague. Sakaloŭski and Liakhoŭski, "Niamechchyna ĭ belaruski natsyianal'ny rukh napiarėdadni ĭ u pershyia hady Druhoe Sus'vetnae Vaĭny", 13–14.

117 Lietuvos ypatingasis archyvas (LYA), F. K-1, ap. 58, d. 46997/3, baudžiamoji byla, p. 64.

118 Kasmovich, *Za vol'nuiu i suverennuiu* Belarus', 94–95.

119 After the war, Soviet security forces captured and sentenced to death in late summer 1945.

120 Hryboŭski, "Pershy belaruski shturmovy z'viaz," 5.

121 "AEQUOR/Reports on Belorussian Émigré Groups, 6 October 1952"; Ostrowski, Radislaw; Second Release of Name Files under the Nazi War Crimes and Japanese Imperial government Disclosure Acts; Records of the Central Intelligence Agency, Record Group 263; National Archives and Records Administration (NARA); p. 6.

122 IPN BU 003172/33/2, p. 117.

123 According to a Soviet report, the school was opened between May 10th and 13th, while Grzybowski notes the May 6th date. Grzybowski also settles on a more exact number of fifty-four participants in the program. NARB, "Tsentral'nyi Komitet Kommunisticheskoi Partii Belorussii," f. 4p, v. 1, s. 18372, p. 170; Grzybowski, *Białorusini w polskich regularnych formacjach wojskowych w latach 1918–1945*, 188; Grzybowski, "Białoruski Ruch Narodowy a III Rzesza," 88.

124 The Prypiatskiia Marshes are also known as the Pinsk Marshes. This report stressed the need to protect critical areas from "Asiatic Russia". "32 Operationsstudie des Gruppenleiters Heer in der Abteilung Landesverteidigung im OKW für die Aggression gegen die Sowjetunion (Loßberg-Studie), 15 September 1940," in *Fall Barbarossa*, 126.

125 Belaruskaia Bibliatėka imia Frantsishka Skaryny (BBiFS), "Dzion'nik unutranykh zagadaŭ 1-ha Belaruskaha shturmovaha z'viazu," p. 1.

126 IPN BU 003172/33/2, p. 59

127 Ibid., 60.

128 German-language courses were also offered by another Belarusian Assault Union member. Ibid., 3–4.

129 Ibid., 10–11.

130 "78 Befehl des Chefs des Generalstabes der Heeresgruppe B zum Einsatz von Diversanten beim Überfall auf die Sowjetunion, 20. Mai 1941," in *Fall Barbarossa*, 260

131 NARB, f. 4p, v. 1, s. 18372, p. 171.

132 The report even mentions the names of individuals who were tasked with blowing up the lines. NARB, f. 4p, v. 1, s. 18372, p. 170; BBiFS, "Dzion'nik unutranykh zagadaŭ 1-ha Belaruskaha shturmovaha z'viazu," p. 1–36; Hryboŭski, "Pershy belaruski shturmovy z'viaz," 8.

133 The names of these seven men match seven names coming from the document pertaining to the First Belarusian Assault Union. Using the spelling of the actual document, they included Levon Khranovitć, Albin Iakimovitć, Albert Assŭski, Teodor Sabila, Francić Vajnoŭski, Mikałaj Branisheŭski, and Kastuś Habinski. BBiFS, "Dzion'nik unutranykh zagadaŭ 1-ha Belaruskaha shturmovaha z'viazu," p. 1–39.

134 NARB, f. 4p, v. 1, s. 18372, p. 200.

135 IPN BU 003172/33/2, p. 60.

136 Hryboŭski, "Pershy belaruski shturmovy z'viaz," 9.

137 IPN BU 003172/33/2, p. 180

138 In fact, the report specifically mentions the Lamsdorf school. *Pogranichnye voiska SSSR 1939–1941: sbornik dokumentov i materialov* (Moscow: Izdatel'stvo "Nauka", 1970), 353, 357, 400.

139 NARB, f. 4p, v. 1, s. 16871, p. 12.

3 Opportunities and Limitations in German-occupied Belarus

1 Instytut Pamięci Narodowej (IPN), BU 003172/33/ 3, p. 5.
2 "Chamu z nemtsami?" *Za praŭdu*, 6 April 1944, p. 1.
3 Bernhard Chiari, *Shtodzionnasts' za liniiaĭ frontu: akupatsyia, kalabaratsyia i supratsiŭ u Belarusi 1941–1944h.* (Minsk: Bibliiatėka chasopisa "Belaruski Histarychny Ahliad, 2008), 176.
4 IPN BU 003172/33/4, p. 77.
5 Ibid., p. 74–75.
6 Ibid., p. 80–84.
7 Waitman Wade Beorn, *Marching into Darkness: The Wehrmacht and the Holocaust in Belarus* (Cambridge: Harvard University Press, 2014), 6–10, 64.
8 Alfred Rosenberg was placed in charge of the Reich Ministry for the Occupied Eastern Territories (Reichsministerium für die besetzten Ostgebiete, RMfdbO) and under him, Hinrich Lohse served as Reichskomissar of Reichskommissariat Ostland. The Generalbezirk Weißruthenien was officially under administrative control of Reichskommissariat Ostland.
9 Later, on 1 April 1944, Generalkommissariat Weißruthenien was separated from Reichkommissariat Ostland, as a small concession to Belarusian nationalists as well as for administrative purposes. The Germans used the term "Weißruthenien" to refer to Belarus, as suggested by Eugen von Engelhardt, the author of a book dedicated to the history of Belarus. Another proposed name was Kryvia, in reference to one of the Slavic groups in the early middle ages, where some Belarusians claimed to originate from. The intention was to ethnographically delineate Belarus from Russia. Alexander Dallin, *German Rule in Russia, 1941–1945: A Study of Occupation Policies.* Second Edition (Boulder: Westview Press, 1981), 223.
10 Christian Gerlach, *Kalkulierte Morde: die deutsche Wirtschafts und Vernichtungspolitik in Weißrußland 1941 bis 1944* (Hamburg: Hamburger Edition, 1999), 159, 195.
11 The least researched region of occupied Belarusian territory during the Second World War remains to be the military one in the east Belarusian region, encompassing the areas of today's Homel', Mahilieŭ, and parts of Vitsebsk. Gerlach, *Kalkulierte Morde,* 134.
12 The GK Weißruthenien territory was organized into eleven districts, or Gebiets: Lida, Slonim, Navahrudak, Baranavichi, Hantsevichi, Vialeĭka, Hlybokae, Minsk (region), Minsk (city), Barysaŭ, and Slutsk.
13 Dallin, *German Rule in Russia 1941–1945,* 86; Ernst Piper, "Alfred Rosenberg," translated by Olivier Mannoni, *Revue d'Histoire de la Shoah* 208, no. 1 (2018): 221–238.
14 Each Reichskommissariat had both an administrative and an SS representative. The latter, officially called the *Höhere SS und Polizei Führer,*

received direct orders from Himmler and not the administration, which led to significant friction between these spheres.

15 Rein, *The Kings and the Pawns*, 88–89.

16 For a more comprehensive study on Germans stationed in the East and their attitudes toward Slavs, see: Michaela Kipp, *"Grossreinemachen im Osten": Feindbilder in deutschen Feldpostbriefen im Zweiten Weltkrieg*, thesis, Frankfurt am Main, 2014.

17 Quoted in Timm C. Richter, "Belarusian Partisans and German Reprisals," in *Stalin and Europe: Imitation and Domination, 1928–1953*, ed. Timothy Snyder and Ray Brandon (Oxford: Oxford University Press, 2014), 210.

18 Bundesarchiv (BA) Berlin-Lichterfelde, "Reichskommissar für das Ostland," R90/126, p. 463–464.

19 The word *papyrossi* is not a German word. If borrowed from Russian, it refers to stronger cigarettes made with darker tobacco. Alternatively, it could refer to a tobacco shortage more generally. BA Berlin-Lichterfelde, R90/126, p. 473.

20 Jerzy Turonek, *Białoruś pod okupacją niemiecką* (Warszawa: Książka i Wiedza, 1993), 87–94.

21 Dallin, *German Rule in Russia, 1941–1945*, 204.

22 Ibid., 208–209.

23 Richter, "Belarusian Partisans and German Reprisals", 224.

24 Other scholars have referred to him as "the more enlightened of the German administrators." See: David Littlejohn, *The Patriotic Traitors: A History of Collaboration in German-Occupied Europe, 1940–1945* (London: Heinemann, 1972), 297; "Heneral'ny Kamisar Haŭliaĭtar Vil'hėl'm Kubė zaginuŭ ad podlae zaboĭskae ruki," *Hazeta Sluchchyny*, no. 36, 3 October 1943, p. 1.

25 Gerlach, *Kalkulierte Morde*, 162.

26 Jerzy Grzybowski, "Białoruski ruch niepodległościowy wobec Polski i Polaków na ziemiach północno-wschodnich II Rzeczypospolitej pod okupacją niemiecką (1941–1944)," *Dzieje najnowsze* 1 (2011): 78.

27 Natsyianal'ny arkhiŭ Rėspubliki Belarus' (NARB), f. 1450, o. 4, d. 53, p. 475.

28 Ul. Kazloŭski, "Belaruskiia Afitsėry," *Belaruskaia hazėta*, 9 August 1942, p. 1. For more information on such functions of newspapers in occupied Belarus see: Aleksandra Pomiecko, "Belarusian Nationalists and Nation-Building Efforts in the Twilight of World War II," in *Collective Identities and Post-War Violence in Europe, 1944–48: Reshaping the Nation*, edited by Ota Konrád, Boris Barth, and Jaromir Mrňka (Basingstoke: Palgrave Macmillan, 2022): 65–90.

29 Gerlach, *Kalkulierte Morde*, 209.

30 Centralne Archiwum Wojskowe (CAW), Sygn. VIII.804.45.1 p. 2–4; Tomasz Strzembosz, *NKWD o Polskim Podziemiu 1944–1948: Konspiracja polska na Nowogródczyźnie i Grodzieńszczyźnie* (Warszawa: Instytut Studiów Politycznych Polskiej Akademii Nauk, 1997), 24; Grzybowski, "Białoruski

ruch niepodległościowy wobec Polski i Polaków na ziemiach północno-wschodnich II Rzeczypospolitej pod okupacją niemiecką (1941–1944)," 78.

31 The Germans later exiled Ermachėnka to Prague for his alleged shady activity and replaced him with Iuri Sabaleŭski, another notable Belarusian. Ermachėnka was accused of stealing money from the Germans. According to Soviet intelligence, this sum amounted to 1.5 million rubles. NARB, f. 1450, o. 4, d. 53, p. 478; Dallin, *German Rule in Russia,* 217; NARB, f. 1450, o. 4, d. 53, p. 476–477; Antonio J. Munoz and Oleg V. Romanko, *Hitler's White Russians: Collaboration, Extermination, and Anti-Partisan Warfare in Byelorussia, 1941–1944* (Bayside, NY: Europa Books, 2003), 29.

32 Other groups created in occupied Belarus during the German occupation, included the Belarusian Academic Society (under Edvard Shyperka), the Belarusian Society for Culture (led by Evgeniĭ Kolubovich), the Belarusian Youth Union (under Mikhail Han'ko), and the United Fight against Bolshevism (under Mikhaĭl Oktan).

33 In 1942 similar language was used to ascribe symbolic roles to Belarusians. In August 1942, for example, the Germans called Ermachėnka the "honorary president" of the Belarusian Self-Help Organization. BA, Berlin-Lichterfelde, R90/110, p. 278; NARB, f. 1450, v.4, s. 53, p. 479–480; NARB, f. 1450, v. 2, s. 46, p. 258.

34 NARB, f. 1450, o. 4, d. 53, p, 494.

35 "Pieršaje pasiedżańnie Biełaruskaje Centralnaje Rady," *Pahonia,* 26 January 1944, p. 1.

36 NARB, f. 1450, o. 4, d. 53, p. 472.

37 Ibid., 473.

38 Frants Kushal', *Sproby stvaren'nia belaruskaha voiska* (Minsk: Belaruski Histaryćny Ahliad, 1999), 38.

39 Rein, *The Kings and the Pawns,* 326–327.

40 The auxiliary police, or Schutzmannschaft, was officially subordinate to the German Ordnungspolizei, or "order police". The 1st and 2nd battalions included Estonians, while the 3rd and 4th involved Latvians. The 13th Battalion was Belarusian. It is unknown if there were battalions between the 5th and 12th numeration, though it is unlikely they did not exist. Grzybowski, "An Outline History of the 13th (Belarusian) Battalion of the SD Auxiliary Police (Szhutzmannschafts Bataillon der SD 13)," *Journal of Slavic Military Studies,* 23 (2010): 463; Jerzy Grzybowski, *Białoruski ruch niepodległościowy w czasie II wojny światowej* (Warsaw: Instytut Pamięci Narodowej, 2021), 170.

41 This post was later assigned to Mikhail Puhachoŭ, who had more experience in military affairs.

42 Martin Dean, *Collaboration in the Holocaust: Crimes of Local Police in Belorussia and Ukraine, 1941–1944* (Washington: USHMM, 2000), 60; NARB, f. 1450, o. 4, d. 53, p. 473.

43 Dz'mitry Kasmovich, *Za vol'nuiu i suverennuiu Belarus'* (Vilnius: Gudas, 2006), 106.

44 Elizaveta Ainzendorf, interview 7691, Visual History Archive, USC Shoah Foundation Institute, accessed online at the United States Holocaust Memorial Museum on 24 March 2021, Segment 22.

45 Vladimir Apatskii, interview 48054, Visual History Archive, USC Shoah Foundation Institute, accessed online at the United States Holocaust Memorial Museum on 24 March 2021, segment 73; Naum Bratkovskii, interview 24546, Visual History Archive, USC Shoah Foundation Institute, accessed online at the United States Holocaust Memorial Museum on 29 March 2021, segment 41.

46 Mikhail Grushkin, interview 19913, Visual History Archive, USC Shoah Foundation Institute, accessed online at the United States Holocaust Memorial Museum on 26 March 2021, segment 50.

47 Grigorii Aizenberg, interview 36087, Visual History Archive, USC Shoah Foundation Institute, accessed online at the United States Holocaust Memorial Museum on 24 March 2021, Segment 39–40.

48 Chiari, *Shtodzionnasts' za liniiaĭ frontu,* 179.

49 NARB, f. 1450, v. 2, s. 51, p. 236–237.

50 Chiari, *Shtodzionnasts' za liniiaĭ frontu,* 179.

51 Ibid., 182.

52 Mikhail Barshai, interview 38470, Visual History Archive, USC Shoah Foundation Institute, accessed online at the United States Holocaust Memorial Museum on 24 March 2021, Segment 44.

53 Dean, *Collaboration in the Holocaust,* 61.

54 Kushal', *Sproby stvarėn'nia belaruskaha voĭska,* 39.

55 For more information on these non-Belarusian groups, see Rudling, "Terror and Local Collaboration in Occupied Belarus: The Case of the Schutzmannschaft Battalion 118," *Historical Yearbook,* 2011 and "Unichtozhit'kak mozhno bol'she: Latviiskie kollaboratsionistskie formirovaniia na territorii Belorussii, 1942–1944," *Sbornik dokumentov,* 2009.

56 Richard Breitman, *Himmler's Police Auxiliaries in the Occupied Soviet Territories,* Annual 7, Chapter 2, paper presented at meeting of the American Historical Association, San Francisco, 30 December 1989.

57 BA Berlin-Lichterfelde, "Reichskommissar für das Ostland,“ R 90/126, p. 471–472.

58 Efraim Zuroff, *Occupation: Nazi – Hunter. The Continuing Search for the Perpetrators of the Holocaust* (Hoboken: KTAV Publishing House, Inc in association with the Simon Wiesenthal Center, 1994), 45; Dean, *Collaboration in the Holocaust,* 44.

59 Per Anders Rudling, "Rehearsal for Volhynia: Schutzmannschaft Battalion 201 and Hauptmann Roman Shukhevych in Occupied Belorussia, 1942," *East European Politics and Societies and Cultures* 34, no. 1 (February 2020): 163.

60 According to some leaders of the Self-Defense Corps, the number of fighters came to include around 15,000. Grzybowski, *Białoruski ruch niepodległościowy w czasie II wojny światowej*, 191; Munoz and Romanko, *Hitler's White Russians*, 35.
61 NARB, f. 384, v. 1, s. 28, p. 34.
62 Grzybowski, *Białoruski ruch niepodległościowy w czasie II wojny światowej*, 186.
63 The First Division operated in the regions of Minsk and Slutsk, the Second Division in Baranavichi, and the Fourth in Vialeĭka.
64 Munoz and Romanko, *Hitler's White Russians*, 36; NARB, f. 1450, v. 3, s. 189, p. 7.
65 The majority of recruits were of Orthodox Christian faith. Battalions were typically made up of three rifle companies and one cavalry squadron and retained a dual Belarusian-German command structure. NARB, f. 465, v. 1, s. 3, p. 20–32; NARB, f. 465, v. 1, s. 6, p. 1–25; NARB, f. 1450, v. 2, s. 46, p. 193.
66 NARB, f. 1450, v. 2, s. 48, p. 68.
67 Ibid., 91.
68 Ibid., 195–196.
69 Ibid., 200–203.
70 Other noteworthy regional representatives included Sokol-Kutyloŭski, stationed in Hantsevichi, and Cheslav Naĭdiuk, in Vialeĭka. Other individuals appointed to the Head Belarusian Leadership of the Self-Defense Corps included Uladzimir Val′kovich, Ihar Aŭchyn′nikaŭ, Ivan Asyk, Iulian Sakovich, Frants Kushal′, Uladzimir Kazloŭski, and Viktar Chabatarevich. NARB, f. 1450, v. 2, s. 46, p. 198.
71 NARB, f. 1450, v. 2, s. 48, p. 88.
72 NARB, f. 1450, v. 2, s. 46, p. 193; NARB, f. 384, v. 1, s. 69, p. 3.
73 NARB, f. 1450, v. 3, s. 189, p. 7.
74 NARB, f. 1450, v. 2, s. 46, p. 193.
75 NARB, f. 1450, v. 2, s. 48, p. 91.
76 Turonek, *Białoruś pod okupacją niemiecką*, 100.
77 Archiwum Wschodnie (AW), I/25, p. 2.
78 Kushal′, *Sproby stvaren′nia belaruskaha voiska*, 56–58.
79 NARB, f. 1450, v. 2, s. 48, p. 100; NARB, f. 384, v. 1, s. 69, p. 1.
80 Turonek, *Białoruś pod okupacją niemiecką*, 101.
81 NARB, f. 1450, v. 2, s. 46, p. 193.
82 Jack Shepsman, interview 21079, Visual History Archive, USC Shoah Foundation Institute, accessed online at the United States Holocaust Memorial Museum on 27 March 2021, segment 110.
83 Archiwum Akt Nowych (AAN), Sygn. 2/2431/0/20, p. 2.
84 NARB, f. 1450, v. 2, s. 48, p. 82.
85 Ibid., 84.
86 Inge Sanmiya, *Against the Current: The Memoirs of Boris Ragula* (Montreal: McGill-Queen's University Press, 2005), 75.

87 Some members of the Eskadron saw it as the first step towards gaining national independence, as doing so would elevate their importance to the Germans who were now struggling to battle Soviet partisans. Others feared that if the Germans retreated from the area, Soviet forces would react with repressive measures, because of the Eskadron's activities. There is also some dispute as to whether or not there was overlap between Rahulia's squadron and other Belarusian armed groups in Navahrudak. Iury Hryboŭski, "Navahradski eskadron Barysa Rahuli – viadomae i neviadomae," *Białoruskie Zeszyty Historyczne* nr 30 (2008): 108–114

88 When a CIA case officer later asked Miarliak about his involvement in crimes against locals, as part of the 68th battalion's anti-partisan operations, Miarliak denied any direct involvement. "Assessment of Constantine Mierlak, 8–12 July 1957"; Mierlak, Constantine; Second Release CIA; Record Group 263; National Archives and Records Administration (NARA); p. 12.

89 AAN, Sygn. 2/2431/0/59, p. 68.

90 Leonid Nikhamkin, interview 44465, Visual History Archive, USC Shoah Foundation Institute, accessed online at the United States Holocaust Memorial Museum on 27 March 2021, segment 48; Sergei Shpringer, interview 20090, Visual History Archive, USC Shoah Foundation Institute, accessed online at the United States Holocaust Memorial Museum on 27 March 2021, segment 24.

91 Basia Liubkina, interview 38878, Visual History Archive, USC Shoah Foundation Institute, accessed online at the United States Holocaust Memorial Museum on 26 March 2021, segment 44–45; Asia Kotova, interview 32023, Visual History Archive, USC Shoah Foundation Institute, accessed online at the United States Holocaust Memorial Museum on 26 March 2021, segment 12; Grigorii Kaz, interview 43212, Visual History Archive, USC Shoah Foundation Institute, accessed online at the United States Holocaust Memorial Museum on 27 March 2021, segment 79; Elena Ioffe, interview 24950, Visual History Archive, USC Shoah Foundation Institute, accessed online at the United States Holocaust Memorial Museum on 26 March 2021, segment 15; Iosif Mirkin, interview 44835, Visual History Archive, USC Shoah Foundation Institute, accessed online at the United States Holocaust Memorial Museum on 26 March 2021, segment 52; Raisa Soloveva, interview 45575, Visual History Archive, USC Shoah Foundation Institute, accessed online at the United States Holocaust Memorial Museum on 27 March 2021, segment 155.

92 Samuel Palec, interview 12549, Visual History Archive, USC Shoah Foundation Institute, accessed online at the United States Holocaust Memorial Museum on 27 March 2021, segment 80; Mikhail Piernik, interview 25693, Visual History Archive, USC Shoah Foundation Institute,

accessed online at the United States Holocaust Memorial Museum on 28 March 2021, segment 49; Peter Silverman, interview 54319, Visual History Archive, USC Shoah Foundation Institute, accessed online at the United States Holocaust Memorial Museum on 27 March 2021, segment 48; Deborah Sufrin, interview 2385, Visual History Archive, USC Shoah Foundation Institute, accessed online at the United States Holocaust Memorial Museum on 27 March 2021, segment 103.

93 Noakh Mel'nik, interview 8765, Visual History Archive, USC Shoah Foundation Institute, accessed online at the United States Holocaust Memorial Museum on 27 March 2021, segment 94.

94 Martin Small, interview 29975, Visual History Archive, USC Shoah Foundation Institute, accessed online at the United States Holocaust Memorial Museum on 27 March 2021, segment 15.

95 Irina Godes, interview 30248, Visual History Archive, USC Shoah Foundation Institute, accessed online at the United States Holocaust Memorial Museum on 27 March 2021, segment 84; Samuil Kaplan, interview 49150, Visual History Archive, USC Shoah Foundation Institute, accessed online at the United States Holocaust Memorial Museum on 28 March 2021, segment 84; Galina Morgunova, interview 26772, Visual History Archive, USC Shoah Foundation Institute, accessed online at the United States Holocaust Memorial Museum on 27 March 2021, segment 86; David Nalibotskii, interview 14529, Visual History Archive, USC Shoah Foundation Institute, accessed online at the United States Holocaust Memorial Museum on 27 March 2021, segment 85; Vladimir Rudkevich, interview 2436, Visual History Archive, USC Shoah Foundation Institute, accessed online at the United States Holocaust Memorial Museum on 27 March 2021, segment 14; Anna Tolochinskaia, interview 27078, Visual History Archive, USC Shoah Foundation Institute, accessed online at the United States Holocaust Memorial Museum on 27 March 2021, segment 40, 62.

96 Gerlach, *Kalkulierte Morde,* 214.

97 Dallin, *German Rule in Russia,* 333.

98 Although the Germans established delivery quotas, individuals could maintain their individual plots of land and were exempt from taxation of that property. These personal plots could also be enlarged, so long as they did not interfere with delivering the quota demands. There was a tentative plan to eventually de-centralize the kolkhoz system completely. The Germans decided, however, that doing so would be a slow and tedious process. It would be better not to disrupt the existing structure and potentially decrease productivity. Furthermore, requisitioning supplies from existing centralized kolkhozes was easier than from individual farms. Ibid., 335.

99 Ibid., 46–49.

100 One of Rosenberg's plans even included extending the borders of Belarus as close as 250 kilometers from Moscow and resettling Poles from Belarus to the Smolensk area, in order to create a separation between Belarusians and Russians. Because Polish national sentiments were strong, Rosenberg hoped that it would prove to be a powerful buffer.

101 Kasmovich, *Za vol'nuiu i suverennuiu Belarus'*, 104.

102 AAN, Sygn. 2/2431/0/6/ p. 24.

103 It should be noted, however, that Soviet policy between 1939 and 1941 also attempted to elevate Belarusians to higher positions of power over Poles. Archiwum Wschodnie, Sygn. AW I/115, p. 4.

104 Grzybowski, "Białoruski ruch niepodległościowy wobec Polski i Polaków na ziemiach północno-wschodnich II Rzeczypospolitej pod okupacją niemiecką (1941–1944)," 86; Dean, *Collaboration in the Holocaust,* 42.

105 NARB, f. 384, v. 1, s. 5, p. 7.

106 AW, Sygn. ZS 366, p. 4.

107 CAW, Sygn. VIII.804.39.2 p. 54.

108 AW, Sygn. AW I/617, p. 2.

109 This term was referencing Władysław Sikorski, a very prominent individual in Polish military history. After the dual invasion of Poland in 1939, Sikorski became the Prime Minister of the Polish Government-in-exile and Commander-in-Chief of the Polish Armed Forces.

Grzybowski, "Białoruski ruch niepodległościowy wobec Polski i Polaków na ziemiach północno-wschodnich II Rzeczypospolitej pod okupacją niemiecką (1941–1944)," 84.

110 Iury Hryboŭski, "Pol'ska-belaruski-belaruski kanflikt u Heneral'naĭ akruze Belarus'," *Białoruskie Zeszyty Historyczne* 25 (2006): 120.

111 These include the collective testimonies of Dz'mitry Kasmovich, Ian Koloshcha, and Vladimir San'ko, "Results of Confidential Informant T-1's Report Dated September 19, 1950"; Jasiuk, Emanuel; Second Release of Name Files under the Nazi War Crimes and Japanese Imperial government Disclosure Acts; Records of the Central Intelligence Agency, Record Group 263, NARA; 3.

112 AAN, Sygn. 2/2431/0/59 p. 13.

113 The document alleges that Father Hadleŭski provoke many of these anti-Polish attacks on priests and that he has belarusified religious services. "Document no 113: Położenie Kościoła w Polsce w Początku 1943 r.," A.44 Ambasada Rzeczypospolitej przy Watykanie, 1921–1970; RG-59.042 United States Holocaust Memorial Museum (USHMM), p. 8.

114 Other Polish-dominated areas included Shchuchyna, Volozhyn, and Stoŭptsy. The city that suffered the least from Polish-Belarusian tension was Minsk.

115 The National Armed Forces, from 1942 to 1947, fought both Soviet partisans and Nazi German forces, but occasionally also had skirmishes with the Polish Home Army.

116 Out of the entire Navahrudak region, Lida had the highest concentration of AK soldiers. The AK was divided into two sections: those centered in the town of Lida and those in the Lida county. One of the most infamous AK groups in the area was the "Krysia" group, led by Jan Borysewicz. AAN, Sygn. 2/2431/0/58 p. 29, 44–49. Grzybowski, "Białoruski ruch niepodległościowy wobec Polski i Polaków na ziemiach północno-wschodnich II Rzeczypospolitej pod okupacją niemiecką (1941–1944)," 84.

117 Nathan Dimitry, Interview 53975, Visual History Archive, USC Shoah Foundation Institute, accessed online at the United States Holocaust Memorial Museum on 24 March 2021, Segment 74.

118 Zygmunt Boradyn, *Niemen rzeka niezgody: Polsko-sowiecka wojna partyzancka na Nowogródczyźnie 1943–1944* (Warsawa: Oficyna Wydawnicza Rytm,1999), 33.

119 Another major leader in the cultural Belarusian sphere was Frantsishak Aliakhnovich, who was murdered in Vilnius on 3 March 1944. Some suspect it was the Polish Home Army that killed him. Iorsh, *Viartan'e BNP: Asoby i dakumenty Belaruskaĭ Nezalezhnitskaĭ Partyi* (Minsk: Arkhiŭ Naĭnoŭshae Historyi, 1998), 63; Iuri Turonak, "Zahadka z'mertsi Frantsishka Aliakhnovicha," *ARCHE* (2008), 688–691.

120 Kushal', *Sproby stvarėn'nia belaruskaha voĭska,* 98.

121 AAN, Sygn. 2/2431/0/59, p. 11.

122 Ibid., 15.

123 AAN, Sygn. 2/2431/0/20, p. 13.

124 Ibid., 16.

125 AAN, Sygn. 2/2431/0/58 p. 41.

126 AAN, Sygn. 2/2431/0/23 p. 70.

127 Esfir' Charnaia, interview 9782, Visual History Archive, USC Shoah Foundation Institute, accessed online at the United States Holocaust Memorial Museum on 27 March 2021, segment 37.

128 Dean, *Collaboration in the Holocaust,* 45–48.

129 Eta Chernova, interview 12134, Visual History Archive, USC Shoah Foundation Institute, accessed online at the United States Holocaust Memorial Museum on 30 March 2021, segment 48; Riveka Charno, interview 15651, Visual History Archive, USC Shoah Foundation Institute, accessed online at the United States Holocaust Memorial Museum on 30 March 2021, segment 129; Eduard Fridman, interview 7085, Visual History Archive, USC Shoah Foundation Institute, accessed online at the United States Holocaust Memorial Museum on 29 March 2021, segments 23, 40.

130 Eta Chernova, Interview 12134, Visual History Archive, USC Shoah Foundation Institute, accessed online at the United States Holocaust Memorial Museum on 26 March 2021, segment 48–49; Elżbieta Dolega-Wrzosek, interview 39086, Visual History Archive, USC Shoah Foundation Institute, accessed online at the United States Holocaust Memorial Museum on 27 March 2021, segment 44–45; Eugene Katz, interview 54165, Visual History Archive, USC Shoah Foundation Institute, accessed online at the United States Holocaust Memorial Museum on 27 March 2021, segment 71; Anna Kavalerchik, interview 50760, Visual History Archive, USC Shoah Foundation Institute, accessed online at the United States Holocaust Memorial Museum on 29 March 2021, segment 53–54; Michael Kutz, interview 55274, Visual History Archive, USC Shoah Foundation Institute, accessed online at the United States Holocaust Memorial Museum on 26 March 2021, segment 115; Mikhail Novodvorski, interview 30143, Visual History Archive, USC Shoah Foundation Institute, accessed online at the United States Holocaust Memorial Museum on 27 March 2021, segment 36.

131 Grigorii El'per, interview 20833, Visual History Archive, USC Shoah Foundation Institute, accessed online at the United States Holocaust Memorial Museum on 30 March 2021, segment 46.

132 Zuroff, *Occupation: Nazi – Hunter*, 52.

133 Olga Baranova, *Nationalism, Anti-Bolshevism or the Will to Survive? Forms of Belarusian Interaction with the German Occupation Authorities, 1941–1944* (Saarbrücken, Germany: Lambert Academic Publishing, 2010), 140.

134 John Loftus and Mark Aarons, *The Secret War Against the Jews: How Western Espionage Betrayed the Jewish People* (New York: St. Martin's Press, 1994), 507.

135 Dean, *Collaboration in the Holocaust*, 81.

136 Ibid., 84–97.

137 Etia Buslovich, interview 40367, Visual History Archive, USC Shoah Foundation Institute, accessed online at the United States Holocaust Memorial Museum on 30 March 2021, segment 82.

138 Alexander Brakel, "The Relationship Between Soviet Partisans and the Civilian Population in Belorussia under German Occupation, 1941–4," in *War in a Twilight World: Partisan and Anti-Partisan Warfare in Eastern Europe, 1939–1945*, ed. Ben Shepherd and Juliette Pattinson (New York: Palgrave Macmillan, 2010), 80.

139 Turonek, *Białoruś pod okupacją niemiecką*, 83.

140 During the interwar period, the Red Army chief of staff debated using partisans as a defensive plan to prevent future foreign invasion. This idea was never pushed forward because of fears that partisan activity would not be controlled would lead to their spread and a lack of control. By

the conclusion of 1941, however, the idea of using partisans was revisited and agreed on. Richter, "Belarusian Partisans and German Reprisals," 210–211.

141 The most important access point for Soviet partisans into Belarusian territory until 1942 was the so called "Vitsebsk Gate", a forty-kilometer-wide corridor in the region of Vitsebsk, specifically between the towns of Velizh and Usviaty (both in present-day Russia). The opening connected the Red Army with partisans in the Vitsebsk region. It is estimated that about twenty thousand soldiers were sent through this region to fight, in addition to food and supplies. In an effort to continue communication and transportation of supplies between Moscow and occupied Belarus, Soviet authorities built nearly fifty partisan airports that allowed partisans to receive radio sets, ammunition, and medical treatment. For more information on Soviet partisan activity, see: Kenneth Slepyan, *Stalin's Guerrillas: Soviet Partisans in World War II* (Lawrence: University Press of Kansas, 2006).

142 Gerhard L. Weinberg, *A World at Arms: A Global History of World War II* (New York: Cambridge University Press, 2005), 428–429.

143 Beorn, *Marching into Darkness*, 95–96.

144 Ibid., 97–104.

145 Himmler was especially fixated on the correct usage of terms, refusing to use the word "partisans" as it was a term of veneration by the Soviets. Instead, he opted for words such as "bandits", "franc-tireurs", and "outlaws".

This series of meetings precipitated in Directive 46, which presented six tenets for combatting partisans. These stipulations included resorting to extreme measures in anti-partisan warfare, if necessary, and fostering good relations with civilians in an effort to cut off local support for the partisans.

146 "Land", *Encyclopedia Britannica*, accessed 6 May 2017. https://www.britannica.com/place/Europe/Land#ref309389

147 BA Berlin-Lichterfelde, R 19/304, p. 211.

148 Philip W. Blood, *Hitler's Bandit Hunters: the SS and the Nazi Occupation of Europe* (Washington D.C.: Potomac Books, 2006), 187; for a more comprehensive analysis of these efforts to drain these swamps see: Diana Siebert, *Herrschaftstechniken im Sumpf und ihre Reichweiten. Landschaftsinterventionen und Social Engineering in Polesien von 1914 bis 1941* (Weisbaden: Harrassowitz Verlag, 2019).

149 Blood, *Hitler's Bandit Hunters,* 167–169.

150 Some scholars have posited that the role of Belarusian collaborators was less impactful as that of collaborators from neighboring nations. Zuroff, *Occupation: Nazi-Hunter,* 52.

151 Grzybowski, "An Outline History of the 13th (Belarusian) Battalion of the SD Auxiliary Police (Szhutzmannschafts Bataillon der SD 13)," 463.

152 CAW, Sygn. VIII.804.39.2 p. 47–50.
153 AAN, Sygn. 2/2431/0/20 p. 4.
154 Kushal′, *Sproby stvarėn′nia belaruskaha voĭska*, 62.
155 Grzybowski, "An Outline History of the 13th (Belarusian) Battalion of the SD Auxiliary Police (Szhutzmannschafts Bataillon der SD 13)," 464.
156 Ibid., 465.
157 Kushal′, *Sproby stvarėn′nia belaruskaha voĭska*, 62.
158 As was the case with Lieutenant Mazur whom Kushal′ refused to replace and was subsequently sent to Berlin for work by the German SD. Kushal′, *Sproby stvarėn′nia belaruskaha voĭska*, 64.
159 *Trial of the Major War Criminals Before the International Military Tribunal.* 14 November 1945–1 October 1946. Volume IV, 220.
160 Approximately 33 out of the 1024 victims came from the Slonim Belarusian Self-Defense Corps. Turonek, *Białoruś pod okupacją niemiecką*, 81.
161 BA Berlin-Lichterfelde, R 58/219, p.68.
162 NARB, f. 370, v. 6, s. 98, p. 3.
163 Other scholarship has similarly underscored the fact that many more non-combatants were victims of anti-partisan operations than partisans themselves. Roger D. Petersen, Jon Elster, and Gudmund Hernes, eds., *Resistance and Rebellion: Lessons from Eastern Europe* (Cambridge: Cambridge University Press, 2001), 218.
164 Richter, "Belarusian Partisans and German Reprisals," 224.
165 CAW, Sygn. VIII.804.39.2, p. 33.
166 NARB, f. 384, v. 1, s. 28, p. 72.
167 Czesław Madajczyk, *Faszyzm i Okupacje: Wykonywanie okupacji przez państwa Osi w Europie, 1938–1945.* Vol. 1. (Poznań: Wydawnictwo Poznańskie, 1983), 608.
168 Aliaksandar Lukashuk, *Filistovich: viartan′ne natsyianalista* (Minsk: Nasha Niva, 1997), 11.
169 Grzybowski, Białoruski ruch niepodległościowy w czasie II wojny światowej, 173.
170 Kushal′, *Sproby stvarėn′nia belaruskaha voĭska*, 34.
171 Soviet Belarusian narratives assert that Mazanik was a loyal Soviet partisan who received orders from Moscow and then sought employment in the Kube household in order to engage in subversive activity. Other accounts, including later interviews and confessions of former organizers of the assassination, reveal that she was coerced to participate in the assassination by Soviet underground. She died in 1996. "V teni u Mazanik," *Belarus′ sevodnia*, 4 August 2007, accessed 17 September 2022 < https://www.sb.by/articles/v-teni-u-mazanik.html>

4 In the Twilight of War

1 There has been speculation that the 23 of February was intentionally chosen for the official creation of the BKA to replace the existing 23 February 1918 anniversary of the creation of the Red Army. However, no concrete evidence of such intent has been found. Aleh Hardzienka, *Belaruskaia Tsentral'naia Rada BTsR: stvaren'ne, dzieĭnasts', zaniapad, 1943–1995* (Minsk: "Knihazbor", 2016), 109.

2 Frants Kushal', *Sproby stvaren'nia belaruskaha voiska* (Minsk: Belaruski Histarychny Ahliad, 1999), 36.

3 Ibid., 34.

4 File M41/112, Reel 11, RG-68.116M, "Holocaust Related Records from European Archives Collected by Yad Vashem," United States Holocaust Memorial Museum (USHMM), 17.

5 Kushal', *Sproby stvarėn'nia belaruskaha voĭska,* 72.

6 "Za zbroiu, za voliu! Adozva Belaruskaĭ Tsėntral'naĭ Rady," *Belaruskaia hazeta,* no. 20 (238), 11 March 1944.

7 "Ab pryznachen'ni akruhovykh nachal'nikaŭ Belaruskai Kraevaĭ Abarony," in *Za Dziarzhaŭnuiu Nezalezhnasts Belarusi: Dakumenty i matar'ialy sabranyia i padrykhtavanyia dlia publikatsyi I. Kasiakom, pragledzhanyia i aprabavanyia dlia druku kamisiiaĭ Belaruskai Tsentral'nai Rady pad kiraŭnitsvam praf. R. Astroŭskaha* (London: Vydan'ne Belaruskai Tsentral'naĭ Rady, 1960), 86.

8 These kinds of slogans were also published in newspapers in an effort to recruit people and spread positive propaganda about the Belarusian Central Rada. For example, "Zmagatstsa za Bats'kaŭshchynu nikoli nia pozna," *Pahonia,* 29 January 1944: 2; Natsyianal'ny arkhiŭ Rėspubliki Belarus' (NARB), f. 383, v. 1, s. 11, p. 3.

9 For example, Usevalad Rodz'ka was head of the propaganda department, Mikhail Pugachoŭ was commander of the BKA in the Minsk district, and Rahulia commanded in Navahrudak. Jerzy Grzybowski, "The Belarusian National Defence: The History of its Establishment and Activity (1944–1945)," *Latvijas Vēstures Institūta Žurnāls,* no. 3(92), (2013): 98.

10 Aleksandr Gelogaev, "Belaruskie vooruzhennye formirovania v General'nom okruge "Belarus'" v 1941–1944gg," in *Dedy: daidzhest publikatsii o belaruskoi istorii,* ed. Anatolii Taras, volume 7 (Minsk: Kharvest, 2011), 140

11 Mobilization orders indicate that individuals born between 1908 to 1918 and 1921 to 1924 were pushed to sign up. NARB f. 1450, v. 2, s. 51, p. 290.

12 Hardzienka, *Belaruskaia Tsentral'naia Rada BTsR,* 110

13 "Shchyl'nymi radami u Belaruskuiu Kraiovuiu Abaronu," *Belaruskaia hazeta,* no. 22 (240), 18 March 1944. "Matchynyia pravodziny synoŭ u Kraiovuiu Abaronu," *Belaruskaia hazeta,* no. 32 (250), 22 April 1944.

14 Hardzienka, *Belaruskaia Tsėntral'naia Rada BTsR,* 107.

15 Some generous figures from postwar accounts of Belarusian nationalists indicate that in the entire Belarusian region there were approximately 100,000 volunteers for the BKA. Motyka, Wnuk, Stryjek, and Baran *Wojna po wojnie: antysowieckie podziemie w Europie Środkowo-Wschodniej w latach 1944–1953,* 120; Iazep Maletski, *Pad znakam pahoni: Uspaminy* (Toronto: Vydavetstva "Pahonia", 1976), 135.
16 NARB, f. 383, v. 1, s. 2, p. 13, 25; "Memorandum for the Record, Subject: Frantisek Kushal, 14 October 1952'; Kushel, Francis; National Archives and Records Administration (NARA), p. 3.
NARB, f. 382, v. 1, s. 20, p. 11.
17 Hardzienka, *Belaruskaia Tsėntral'naia Rada BTsR,* 110–111.
18 Dziarzhaŭny arkhiŭ Minskaĭ voblastsi (DAMV), f. 1039, v. 1, s. 165, p. 1–7; Jerzy Grzybowski, "Białoruski ruch niepodległościowy wobec Polski i Polaków na ziemiach północno-wschodnich II Rzeczypospolitej pod okupacją niemiecką (1941–1944)," *Dzieje najnowsze* 1 (2011): 103.
19 Ibid., 58.
20 NARB, f. 382, v. 1, s. 4, p. 23–37.
21 NARB, f. 382, v. 1, s. 3, p. 40.
22 Ibid.
23 DAMV, f. 1039, v. 1, s. 34, p. 1.
24 Ibid.
25 NARB, f. 383, v. 1, s. 2, p. 16.
26 NARB, f. 382, v. 1, s. 4, p. 134.
27 Ibid., p. 6.
28 Kushal', *Sproby stvarėn'nia belaruskaha voĭska,* 40.
29 Jerzy Turonek, *Białoruś pod okupacją niemiecką* (Warsaw: "WERS", 1989), 98.
30 NARB, f. 1450, v. 2, s, 46, p. 195.
31 Kushal', *Sproby stvarėn'nia belaruskaha voĭska,* 83.
32 For more on the training and molding of Belarusian soldiers, see: Aleksandra Pomiecko, "'It's never too late to fight for one's family and nation': Attempts at 'Belarusifying' Soldiers in German-sponsored Armed Formations, 1941–1944," *Journal of Slavic Military Studies* 33, no. 2 (2020): 259–276.
33 NARB, f. 382, v. 1, s. 19, p. 27.
34 NARB f. 382, v. 1, s. 14, p. 39.
35 DAMV, f. 1039, v. 1, s. 126, p. 155.
36 Another holiday established was that of the 22nd of June, commemorating the day when the Germans "halted the Soviet push towards Europe". Portraits of Adolf Hitler were hung in the banquet halls and there were lectures on the importance of Belarusian-German work. NARB, f. 382, o. 1, d. 14, p. 48; NARB, f. 382, v. 1, s. 4, p. 31; "Prėzydėnt BTsR da zhaŭneraŭ BKA," *Belaruskaia hazeta,* no. 45 (263), 7 June 1944.

37 "Slutskae Paŭstan'ne," *Holas vioski* no. 3 (109), 21 January 1944.
38 NARB, f. 383, v. 1, s. 11, p. 1–3.
39 Ibid., p. 3.
40 Iury Hryboŭski, "Abmundziravanne belaruskikh vaĭskovykh farmavanniaĭ na niametskaĭ sluzhbe padchas druhoĭ susvetnaĭ vaĭny," *ARCHE 5* (2010): 479.
41 Dz'mitry Kasmovich, *Za vol'nuiu i suverennuiu Belarus'* (Vilnius: Gudas, 2006), 206.
42 "Pahonia" is a historic coat of arms picturing an armed horseman. Adopted from the coat of arms of the Grand Duchy of Lithuania, the Pahonia was revived with the creation of the Belarusian People's Republic in March 1918. It continues to be controversial due it its association with Belarusian collaboration with the Germans. Gelogaev, "Belaruskie vooruzhennye formirovania v General'nom okruge "Belarus'" v 1941–1944gg," 143.
43 Antonio J. Munoz and Oleg V. Romanko, *Hitler's White Russians: Collaboration, Extermination, and Anti-partisan Warfare in Byelorussia, 1941–1944* (Bayside, NY: Europa Books, 2003), 56.
44 Lietuvos ypatingasis archyvas (LYA), F. K-1, ap. 58, bylo, P-11132, p. 138–139.
45 NARB, f. 382, v. 1, s. 3, p. 236.
46 The arms problem was not one particular to only the Belarusian case. Other studies have demonstrated that it was a consistant problem in other arenas, such as as the Baltic states. See: Heinrihs Strods, "The Latvian Partisan War between 1944 and 1956," in *The Anti-Soviet Resistance in the Baltic States,* ed. Arvydas Anušauskas (Vilnius: Du Ka, 1999), 150–159.
47 Leonid Rein, *The Kings and the Pawns: Collaboration in Byelorussia during the World War II* (New York: Berghahn Books, 2011), 326.
48 Maletski, *Pad znakam pahoni,* 137.
49 File M41/110, Reel 11, RG-68.116M, Holocaust Related Records from European Archives Collected by Yad Vashem, United States Holocaust Memorial Museum Archives, Washington, DC (USHMM), p. 1.
50 NARB, f. 1450, v. 2, s. 51, p. 288.
51 DAMV, f. 1039, v. 1, s. 34, p. 1.
52 Ibid., s. 158, p. 3
53 Ibid., s. 159, p. 1–3.
54 Ibid., s. 164, p. 19–70.
55 Gelogaev, "Belaruskie vooruzhennye formirovania v General'nom okruge "Belarus'" v 1941–1944gg," 141; DAMV, f. 1039, v. 1, s. 171, p. 1–14.
56 NARB, f. 382, v. 1, s. 14, p. 27.
57 Grzybowski, "Białoruski ruch niepodległościowy wobec Polski i Polaków na ziemiach północno-wschodnich II Rzeczypospolitej pod okupacją niemiecką (1941–1944)," 103.

58 NARB, f. 382, v. 1, s. 14, p. 35–36.
59 File M41/107, Reel 11, RG-68.116M, Holocaust Related Records from European Archives Collected by Yad Vashem, (USHMM), p. 1.
60 NARB, f. 1450, v. 2, s. 51, p. 291.
61 Leonid Rein, "Local Collaboration in the Execution of the 'Final Solution' in Nazi-occupied Belorussia," *Holocaust and Genocide Studies* 20, no. 3 (Winter 2006): 395.
62 Ibid., 382.
63 Kushal', *Sproby stvaren'nia belaruskaha voiska,* 39.
64 Munoz and Romanko, *Hitler's White Russians,* 33–34.
65 Memorandum for the Record, Subject: Byelorussia, 17 October 1952; Kushel, Francis; Second Release of Name Files under the Nazi War Crimes and Japanese Imperial government Disclosure Acts; Records of the Central Intelligence Agency, Record Group 263; National Archives and Records Administration (NARA); 3.
66 NARB, f. 1450, v. 2, s. 51, p. 40–44; However, others opt for a later foundation date. Aleh Dziarnovich, *Antysavetskiia rukhi ŭ Belarusi, 1944–1956 Davednik* (Mensk: Arkhiŭ Naĭnoŭshae Historyi, 1999), 120–121.
67 According to Kasmovich's memoir, the BNP's main representatives met in secret on 29 July 1942 (in the Rūdninkai forests) and later on 10 October 1942 in Minsk. Kasmovich, *Za vol'nuiu i suverennuiu Belarus'*, 149–152.
68 Rodz'ka's influence increased in 1944 and he allegedly attempted to organize an anti-German uprising in Minsk with the support of clandestine Belarusian armed forces. Siarheĭ Iorsh, *Usevalad Rodz'ka: Pravadyr belaruskikh natsyianalistaŭ* (Mensk: Holas Kraiu, 2001), 3–6.
69 Kasmovich, *Za vol'nuiu i suverennuiu Belarus'*, 95–99.
70 NARB, f. 1450, o. 4, d. 53, p. 495.
71 Motyka, Wnuk, Stryjek, and Baran, *Wojna po wojnie,* 118.
72 Liavon *Iurėvich, Zhyts'tsio pad Ahniom-Partrėt belaruskaha voenachal'nika i palitychnaha dzeiacha Barysa Rahuli na fone iaho epokhi* (Minsk: Arche, 1999), 239–240.
73 Instytut Pamięci Narodowej (IPN) BU 003172/22/1, p. 154.
74 Iurėvich, *Zhyts'tsio pad Ahniom,* 235.
75 Iorsh, *Viartan'ne BNP,* 46–49.
76 Ibid., 26.
77 Dziarnovich, *Antysavetskiia rukhi ŭ Belarusi,* 119.
78 Kasmovich, *Za vol'nuiu i suverennuiu Belarus'*, 184; NARB, "Glavnoe upravlenie voiskovykh del BTsR, g. Berlin, 1942–1943," f. 383, v. 1, s. 6, p. 3.
79 Igor Valakhanovich, *Antisovetskoe podpol'e, 1944–1953* (Minsk: BGU, 2002), 25–26.
80 Ataman Khareŭski, along with Ataman Suvory, was the leader of a group called the Belarusian People's Partisans, consisting of allegedly 3000

members. It was mainly anti-German, although some accounts allege that various armed formations also fought Poles and Soviets. See Ia. Taŭpeka, "25-tyia uhodki Belaruskaha zbroĭnaha antyhitliaroŭskaha rezystantsu, 1942–1947," *Belaruski holas*, November 1967; Ia. Khareŭski, "Ab belaruskaĭ partyzantsy ŭ aposhniuiu vaĭny," *Belaruski holas*, January 1968.

81 Bul'ba-Borovets' asserted that there was a Polissian Sich delegation sent at some point to meet the Belarusians, with Pietr Dovmatiuk-Nalivajk as the main representative. Both the Ukrainians and Belarusians were aligned ideologically and apparently got along very well. However, there is no specific mention of Bul'ba-Borovets' personally meeting either Vitushka or Rodz'ka. See Taras Bul'ba-Borovets', *Armiia bez derzhavy*, (Winnipeg, 1981), 126–127. Manuscript accessed from the Archive of Wiktor Poliszczuk, AAN, "Archiwum Wiktora Poliszczuka," Sygn. 2/2394/0/246.

82 Jerzy Grzybowski, "Białoruskie zbrojne podziemie antysowieckie w latach 1944–1956," *Przegląd Historyczno-Wojskowy* R. 10, nr 1(2009): 122.

83 Jared McBride, "Olevsk", in *The United States Holocaust Memorial Museum Encyclopedia of Camps and Ghettos, 1933–1945*, edited by Geoffrey P. Megargee, vol.2, part b (2012): p. 1553.

84 The term *kalinoŭshiki* was used in honor of the 1863 revered revolutionary hero Kastus' Kalinoŭski. Valakhanovich, *Antisovetskoe podpol'e, 1944–1953*, 21

85 "Spravazdacha Prėzydėnta BtsR praf. R. Astrouskaha," in Druhi Usebelaruski Kanhrės: matar'ialy sabranyia i apratsavanyia na padstave pratakol'nykh zapisau kamisiiaĭ Belaruskaĭ Tsėntral'naĭ Rady pad rėdaktsyiaĭ praf. R. Astrouskaha (Munich: Druckerei Cicero, 1954), 16–25.

86 Historian Igor Valakhanovich estimates that, collectively, between 500,000 and 700,000 people were evacuated from Belarus. This number includes 390,000 civilians, 60,000 Belarusians fighting in the Polish Army, 50,000 Belarusians fighting in the Soviet Army, as well as 10,000 Belarusian youths; "Memorandum for the Record, Subject: Byelorussia (Litsva), 17 October 1952"; Kushel, Francis; Second Release of Name Files under the Nazi War Crimes and Japanese Imperial government Disclosure Acts; Records of the Central Intelligence Agency, Record Group 263; NARA; p. 3.

87 Historian Jerzy Grzybowski asserts that only the 23rd and 34th BKA battalions made it to Germany, in addition to some individuals training in the school. Individuals from the sapper battalions were placed directly under Wehrmacht control. Grzybowski, "The Belarusian National Defence: The History of its Establishment and Activity (1944–1945), 124.

88 NARB, f. 383, v. 1, s. 2, p. 18–19.

89 Iury Hryboŭski, "Monte-Kasina: neviadomyia staronki belaruskaĭ historyi," *Białoruskie Zeszyty Historyczne* 17 (2002): 181.

90 Ibid., 182.

91 "Mierlak, Kanstantyn, January 1957"; Mierlak, Constantine; Second Release of Name Files under the Nazi War Crimes and Japanese Imperial government Disclosure Acts; Records of the Central Intelligence Agency, Record Group 263; NARA; p. 1.

92 "Interrogation Research Division – 25 July 1957"; Mierlak, Constantine; NARA; p. 5.

93 IPN BU 003172/33/1, p. 113.

94 As far as more inclusive numbers of Belarusians living in Greater Germany, including combatants and non-combatants, a debatable number of 700,000 exists according to reports from the Belarusian Central Rada. Greater Germany encompassed territories within the Third Reich, including Austria, Czechoslovakia, and Poland. According to this source, of the 700,000 Belarusians living within these confines: 500,000 were laborers, 60,000 were in the Polish Army, 50,000 in the Soviet Army, 10,000 were youths, and around 80,000 were deserters and evacuees. NARB f. 383, v. 1, s. 2, p. 11. The numer range attributed to the numer of Belarusian combatants comes from: Grzybowski, *Białoruski ruch niepodległościowy w czasie II wojny światowej*, 221.

95 NARB, f. 383, v. 1, s. 2, p. 23.

96 Ibid., p. 25; NARB f. 383, v. 1, s. 9, p. 17.

97 NARB, f. 383, v. 1, s. 2, p. 37.

98 Ibid.

99 The creation of the Head Leadership for Military Affairs of the Belarusian Central Rada (Haloŭnae Kiraŭnitstva Vaĭskovykh Spraŭ, HKVS) was officially announced on 13 September 1944, in Berlin. Its predecessor was the Head Department for Military Affairs of the Rada. It began with a staff of approximately twelve people in the following sectors: General Office, Mobilization Department, Regulatory Commission, and Personal Department, later including more. Kanstanty Ezavitaŭ was in charge of the HKVS. In October 1944 the Regulatory Commission was expanded to fourteen people, including Frantsishek Kushal', Ŭladzimer Guts'ka, Ŭsevalad Rodz'ka, and Barys Rahulia.

100 NARB, f. 383, v. 1, s. 11a, p. 72.

101 NARB, f. 383, v. 1, s. 2, p. 27, 32; s. 11a, p. 36–39; s. 2, p. 25.

102 Hryboŭski, "Monte-Kasina: neviadomyia staronki belaruskaĭ historyi," 187.

103 Leonid Rein, "Untermenschen in SS Uniforms: 30th Waffen-Grenadier Division of Waffen SS," *Journal of Slavic Military Studies* 20, no. 2 (2007): 333–343.

104 "Memorandum for the Record, Subject: Byelorussia (Litsva), 17 October 1952"; Kushel, Francis; NARA; p. 4.

105 In some literature, this unit is also referred to as the First Belarusian Division. There were approximately one thousand soldiers in this division.

There were plans for the creation of another regiment, in case of more volunteers. Iury Hryboŭski, "Belaruski kambatantski rukh na zakhadze pas'lia druhoŭ sus'vetnaĭ vaĭny," *Zapisy* 32 (2009), 404; NARB, f. 383, v. 1, s. 11a, p. 44–44opp.

106 It is worth pointing out that this Belarusian Division did not participate in any actual fighting, and instead, operated as a training space for Belarusian soldiers. Iury Hryboŭski, "Belaruski lehiion SS: mify i rėchaisnasts'," *Belaruski Histarychny Ahliad* 14 (2007): 135.

107 NARB, f. 383, v. 1, s. 11a, p. 50.

108 NARB, f. 382, v. 1, s. 20, p. 7.

109 NARB, f. 383, v. 1, s. 11a, p. 52.

110 Leonid Rein, *The Kings and the Pawns: Collaboration in Byelorussia during the World War II* (New York: Berghahn Books, 2011), 338–339.

111 Historian Jerzy Grzybowski also notes that Ziegling was openly hostile toward the Belarusians and favored the Russians. This tension was paired with the Germans demoting Belarusians in leadership positions upon joining the brigade. Grzybowski, "The Belarusian National Defence", 125.

112 For a background on formulating figures for wartime losses see: Franziska Exeler, *Ghosts of War: Nazi Occupation and Its Aftermath in Soviet Belarus* (Ithaca: Cornell University Press, 2022), 245–251.

113 The SS-Jagdverbände project was divided into geographic units: Jagdverbände Ost, Jagdverbände Süd Ost, Jagdverbände Süd West, and Jagdverbände Nord West, in addition to two German battalions – Jagdverbände Mitte and Fallschirm Jäger Battalion 600. The Belarusians would have been mobilized into Jagdverbände Ost, although they are typically labeled as "Russians". For a comprehensive study on German military intelligence services during the Second World War, see Katrin Paehler, *The Third Reich's Intelligence Services: The Career of Walter Schellenberg* (New York: Cambridge University Press, 2017).

114 The other school was the "Kampf-Schule" that focused more on standard military training. The "Agenten-Schulen" also trained students to fend for themselves if left alone or in small groups behind enemy lines. Preparation also included intensive terrain and intelligence training. Parachuting missions took up 20 to 30 percent of this program.

115 "Headquarters US Forces European Center Interrogation Center, Individual Operations, The German Sabotage Services, 23 July 1945, Operations Freischuetz I-IV"; Rudl, Karl; First Release of Name Files Under the Nazi War Crimes and Japanese Imperial Government Disclosure Acts, ca 9/18/1947–1999; Records of the Central Intelligence Agency, Record Group 263; NARA; p. 6.

116 IPN BU 003172/33/1, p. 117.

117 Valakhanovich, *Antisovetskoe podpol'e*, 1944–1953, 21.

118 The Youth Union had developed its own training camps in the spring of 1944, under the oversight of the Home Guard and Rada. What became known as the Albertino and Florianov training camps for youth involved similar pedagogical training as the BKA. NARB, f. 385, v.1, s. 18.
119 IPN BU 0003172/33/2, p. 214–224.
120 Valakhanovich, *Antisovetskoe podpol'e*, 1944–1953, 22.
121 IPN BU 003172/33/2, p. 223.
122 Grzybowski, "Białoruskie Zbrojne Podziemie Antysowieckie w Latach 1944–1956," 117.
123 One researcher has allegedly claimed that through contact with Vitushka's own son, he found out that the former died at the old age of 99 in a nursing home facility in the Alps, on 27 April 2006. See Siarheĭ Iorsh, "Mikhal Vitushka pamior dvoĭchy", *Nasha niva,* 29 June 2006. The latter date is also mentioned in Kasmovich, *Za vol'nuiu i suverennuiu Belarus'*, 12.
124 Ibid., 6–7; Centralne Archiwum Wojskowe (CAW), Sygn. VIII.800.38.3, p. 27.
125 Although the Polish document does not list Vitushka as one of the victims of this attack, it is possible he would not have been included in the list for at least two reasons. The first is that he may have joined the group unofficially. Another reason for his omission in the victim list may have been because he was not an official member of the Polish Home Army.
126 Those that remained with Vitushka from the original dispatched members and joined the Polish "Komar" group included Gleb Viacheslavovich Bogdanovich, Mikhail Shunko, Ivan Grigartsevich, and Tamara Cheremchagina or Cheremshchagina or Cheremchapina. LYA, "Vituško Michail Afanasjević, gim. 1907 m," F. K-1, ap. 45, b. 285, p. 7, 12.
127 "Report on the Byelorussian underground movement, 27 August 1952"; Ostrowski, Radoslaw; NARA; p. 1.
128 "Bajatstsa uspaminy 'chornaha kata'," *Belaruski holas,* May 1967, p. 4.
129 Valakhanovich, *Antisovetskoe podpol'e, 1944–1953,* 22; AEQUOR/ RG 263, ZZ-18, box Reports on Belorussian Émigré Groups- 6 October 1952"; Ostrowski, Radislaw; NARA, p. 13–14.
130 IPN BU 003172/33/1, p. 128–129.
131 "Headquarters US Forces European Theatre Interrogation Center: Final Disposition of the Jagd Verbaende, The German Sabotage Services, 23 July 1945"; Rudl, Karl; NARA; p. 2; IPN BU 003172/33/1, p. 148.
132 IPN BU 003172/33/1, p. 62.
133 Valakhanovich, *Antisovetskoe podpol'e, 1944–1953,* 34.

5 Belarusian Émigrés and Covert Activity after the War

1 Monitch's real name was Antoni Duda. "Colonel Kushal' (Kuszal) – 6 July 1950"; Kushel, Francis; Second Release of Name Files under the Nazi War Crimes and Japanese Imperial government Disclosure Acts, ca. 1981-ca. 2002; Records of the Central Intelligence Agency, Record Group 263; National Archives and Records Administration (NARA); p. 3.

2 Ibid., 3–4.

3 Jerzy Grzybowski, "Białoruskie Zbrojne Podziemie Antysowieckie w Latach 1944–1956," *Przegląd Historyczno-Wojskowy* 10, no. 1 (2009): 125.

4 This chapter benefits from the 2007 declassification of CIA documents. The reason for declassification of CIA documents stems from the CIA's more laxed understanding following the 1998 Nazi War Crimes Disclosure Act. The CIA declassified and passed on these documents to the National Archives and Records Administration (NARA). These amounted to several thousand previously unseen pages of documents. Richard Breitman and Norman J.W. Goda, *Hitler's Shadow: Nazi War Criminals, US intelligence, and the Cold War* (Washington DC: National Archives and Records Administration, 2010), 2.

5 Aleksei Litvin, "Voina posle osvobozhdenia: sobitiia 1945 goda na territorii Belarusi v dokumentakh vnutrennikh voisk NKVD SSSR," *Belaruskaia dumka*, no. 2 (July 2015): 34–61.

6 After March 1946 People's Commissariat for Internal Affairs (*Narodnyi komissariat vnutrennikh del*, NKVD), or *Narodny kamisaryiat unutranykh spravaŭ* (NKUS) in Belarusian, was renamed the Ministry of Internal Affairs (*Ministėrstvo ŭnutranykh spraŭ*, MUS). Alexander Statiev, *The Soviet Counterinsurgency in the Western Borderlands* (Cambridge: Cambridge University Press, 2010), 7.

7 Natalia Rybak, "Metady i srodki likvidatsyi akaŭskikh i postakaŭskikh farmiravanniaŭ u zakhodnikh ablastsiakh Belarusi ŭ 1944–1954 hh," *Białoruski Zeszyty Historyczne* 14 (2000): 168.

8 Statiev, *The Soviet Counterinsurgency in the Western Borderlands*, 98.

9 Statiev, *The Soviet Counterinsurgency in the Western Borderlands*, 113.

10 According to Alexander Statiev, the root of peasant discontentment with the Soviet regime was a dislike of collectivization. Ibid., 104.

11 Grzegorz Motyka, Rafał Wnuk, Tomasz Stryjek, and Adam F. Baran, *Wojna po wojnie: antysowieckie podziemie w Europie Środkowo-Wschodniej w latach 1944–1953* (Warszawa: Wydawnictwo Naukowe Scholar, Instytut Studiów Politycznych, Muzeum II Wojny Światowej, 2012), 627.

12 For more information on the Polish AK activity on Belarusian territory, see: Sitkevich S.A., Sil'vanovich, C.A., Barabash V.V., and N.A. Rybak, *Pol'skoe podpol'e na territorii zapadnykh oblastei Belarusi 1939–1954gg* (Grodno: GGAU, 2004).

13 Statiev, *The Soviet Counterinsurgency in the Western Borderlands*, 118.
14 Ibid., 117.
15 Evidence for this claim comes from Valakhanovich's work on the issue, gathered from the KDB archive in Belarus. Material is also drawn from Soviet historian V. Ramanoŭski's *Saŭdzel'niki ŭ zlachynstvakh* (Minsk: Instytut Historyi Akademii Navuk BSSR, 1964). Despite the latter's state-driven analysis, Ramanoŭski had access to internal security records and drew from them in his work.
16 Iurka Stasevich, "(adkaz na zapytan'ni chytachoŭ) Belaruskaia Partyzanka na II Vaĭne," *Belaruski holas*, April 1981.
17 Ibid.
18 Aleh Dziarnovich, *Antysavetskiia rukhi ŭ Belarusi, 1944–1956 Davednik* (Minsk: Arkhiŭ Naĭnoŭshaee Historyi, 1999), 78.
19 Igor Valakhanovich, *Antisovetskoe podpol'e, 1944–1953* (Minsk: BGU, 2002), 38–40.
20 There are numerous towns in Belarus by the name of "Karpavichy." Zhykhar was likely active and caught in the Karpavichy located in the Pastavy district, Vitsebsk region.
21 Valakhanovich, *Antisovetskoe podpol'e na territorii Belarusi v 1944–1953*, 40–41.
22 Uladzimir Skrabatun, "Zhykhar byŭ vialikim prakhadzimtsam- iashchė i sionnia na Hlybochchyne i Pastaŭshchyne pamiataiuts' antysavetskaha partyzana Iaŭhena Zhykhara. Pisha Uladzimir Skrabatun," *Nasha niva*, 6 May 2012. <https://nn.by/?c=ar&i=72444>
23 Siarheĭ Iorsh, *Viartan'ne BNP: Asoby i dakumenty Belaruskaĭ Nezalezhnitskaĭ Partyi* (BHAKC: Mensk, 1998), 21.
24 The same version of the story appeared as recently as 2017. This article stated that by the time of Zhykhar's death, many of the members of his group had been either caught by Soviet security forces or had fled to Poland. See: "11 studzienia 1955 hodu zaginuŭ kamandzir antysavetskaha rukhu", *Pol'skae Radyio*, 11 January 2017. <http://www.radyjo.net/4/88/Artykul/288365>
25 Jan Szumski, *Sowietyzacja Zachodniej Białorusi 1944–1953: Propaganda i edukacja w służbie ideologii* (Kraków: ARCANA, 2010), 41.
26 Kushal' Franz, 0.1/29655422/ITS Digital Archive, United States Holocaust Memorial Museum Archives (USHMM), Washington DC; "List of all allied Nationals and all other foreigners, German Jews and stateless etc, who were temporarily or permanently stationed in the community, but are no longer in residence, Amberg, Ordner 25, seite 35," 2.1.1.1/69795030/ITS Digital Archive, USHMM; Kushel Franzishak, 0.1/29655421/ITS Digital Archive, United States Holocaust Memorial Museum (USHMM).
27 CM 1-584708, Application for Assistance, 3.2.1.1/79637595/ITS, USHMM.

28 The Rada dissolved itself during its Sixth Party Plenum, on the 23 to 24 September 1945. Astroŭski insisted that it was a temporary measure, in order to protect the party's members from Soviet repression. He cited concern that the Rada's members would be tracked and arrested for collaborating with the Germans. Many of the party's members changed their names and went into hiding. The party was later revived at the Seventh Party Plenum, on the 8 to 9 May 1948. Jerzy Grzybowski, "Białoruska Centralna Rada w latach 1943–1956: próba podsumowania problemu w świetle dotychczasowych badań i najnowszych źródeł," *Białoruskie Zeszyty Historyczne 32* (2009), 191–199; Nicholas P. Vakar, *Belorussia: The Making of a Nation* (Cambridge: Harvard University Press, 1956), 220.

29 Members of the Belarusian People's Republic group were known as *krivichi,* in reference to Belarusian Krievan origins. Those in the Rada were referred to as *zarubezhniki* (foreigners). Valakhanovich, *Antisovetskoe podpol'e, 1944–1953,* 32–33.

30 "Chapter Five: The Long Experience in the Anti-Soviet Game"; CIA and Nazi War Criminals and Collaborators; RG 263; NARA; p. 1; Norman J.W. Goda, "Nazi Collaborators in the United States: What the FBI Knew," in *U.S. Intelligence and the Nazis* (New York: Cambridge University Press, 2005), 227; Benjamin Tromly, *Cold War Exiles and the CIA: Plotting to Free Russia* (Oxford University Press, 2019), 4–5.

31 One such example is Operation Sunrise, which was a series of negotiations between Dulles and the high-ranking SS leader in Italy, Karl Wolff. These talks occurred without Soviet presence, giving the British and Americans insight and advantages into the region. For a more detailed account of Operation Sunrise, see: Kerstin von Lingen, *Allen Dulles, the OSS, and Nazi War Criminals: The Dynamics of Selective Prosecution.* Translated by Dona Geyer. New York: Cambridge University Press, 2013; Mark Stout, "World War I and the birth of American intelligence culture," *Intelligence and National Security* 32, no. 1 (2017), 383.

32 Richard Rashke, *Useful Enemies: John Demjanjuk and America's Open-Door Policy for Nazi War Criminals* (New York: Delphinium Books, 2013), 327.

33 Ibid.

34 See, for example: Annie Jacobsen, *Operation Paperclip: The Secret Intelligence Program to Bring Nazi Scientists to America* (New York: Little, Brown and Company, 2014).

35 Roger Daniels, *Guarding the Golden Door: American Immigration Policy and Immigrants Since 1882* (New York: Hill and Wang, 2004), 98.

36 Jerzy Grzybowski, *Pogoń między Orłem Białym, Swastyką i Czerwoną Gwiazdą: Białoruski ruch niepodległościowy w latach 1939–1956* (Warsaw: BEL Studio, 2011), 575–576.

37 Ibid., 107.

38 Rashke, *Useful Enemies*, 334.

39 Christoph Schiessl, *Alleged Nazi Collaborators in the United States after World War II* (Lanham: Lexington Books, 2016), 94.

40 Ibid., 57.

41 Ibid., 74.

42 Based on a sample of investigated individuals, the majority of those entering the USA came during the existence of the Displaced Persons' Act as well as the 1953 Refugee Relief Act (also referred to as the Nazi Relief Act by scholars). See Schliessl, *Alleged Nazi Collaborators*, 61; Rashke, *Useful Enemies*, 318.

43 Ibid., 3.

44 The first CIA-sponsored airdrop mission took place in September 1949 with two Ukrainians dispatched to L'viv. Both were apprehended by Soviet authorities. "Chapter 6: Common Ground with New Partners"; CIA and Nazi War Criminals and Collaborators; RG 263; NARA; p. 14.

Aside from the collective Cold War attitude driving much of these operations, allowing such individuals to reside in the United States also emanated from a lack of interest by the American public to consider Holocaust victims, as well as the reluctance of the latter to testify as eyewitnesses. Interest and focus on the Holocaust and Nazi collaborators came more attentively only with the trial of Adolf Eichmann in 1961. Schliessl, *Alleged Nazi Collaborators*, 101, 103–104.

45 "Basis for Operational Collaboration Proposed by Belorussian National Council, 15 February 1951"; Rogula, Boris, Vol. 1; NARA; p. 2.

46 "List of all allied Nationals and all other foreigners, German Jews and stateless etc, who were temporarily or permanently stationed in the community, but are no longer in residence," Amberg, Ordner 25, seite 35, 2.1.1.1/69795030/ITS Digital Archive, United States Holocaust Memorial Museum Archives, Washington, DC (USHMM); List of political, social security and labour employment office records, Bereich des BKA Regensburg, Ordner 1467, seite 109, 2.1.1.1/70196802/ITS, USHMM.

47 "Extract from HICOG Despatch 2617, 17 March 53,"; Stankiewicz, Stanislaw; Second Release of Name Files under the Nazi War Crimes and Japanese Imperial government Disclosure Acts, ca. 1981-ca. 2002; Records of the Central Intelligence Agency, Record Group 263; National Archives and Records Administration (NARA), p. 45.

48 His residence in Marburg is mentioned in his memoirs. CM 1-584708, Application for Assistance, 3.2.1.1/79637595/ITS, USHMM.

49 The Office of Strategic Services (OSS) was a US intelligence agency founded by the Joint Chiefs of Staff to organize espionage activity during the Second World War. It was disbanded and replaced with the Central Intelligence Agency. "Chapter Five: The Long Experience in the Anti-Soviet Game"; CIA and Nazi War Criminals and Collaborators; RG 263; NARA; p. 2–4.

50 Quoted in "Chapter Five: The Long Experience in the Anti-Soviet Game"; CIA and Nazi War Criminals and Collaborators; RG 263; NARA; p. 8, from "Translation of Aide Memoire Prepared by Kedia," 28 April 1945 [no declassification listed]; DO Records.
51 A report from the US Army installation in Karlsruhe communicated that it found Monitch's story unreliable and that he mostly likely did not even leave Poland. The reason for this distrust was because of Monitch's insistence on communicating only and directly to Kushal′. Other reasons for concern included Monitch's request to obtain a visa to the United States and his frequent bouts of intoxication and "considerable weakness for women" in Germany. The same report also indicated that Kushal′ had political aspirations and that having direct ties with partisans in Belarus would boost his image. "General – Operational, Specific- Antoniĭ Duda, 30 October 1950"; Kushel, Francis; NARA; p. 1–2.
52 "Byelorussia (Litsva), 17 October 1952"; Kushel, Francis; NARA; p. 1–5; "Meeting with Kuszal, 11 October 1952"; Kushel, Francis; NARA; p. 1.
53 "CSOB/Bi-Weekly Report #1- dated 9 July 1951", AEQUOR vol. 1; RG 263; NARA; p. 1–2.
54 "Progress Report from CSOB Semi-Monthly Report No. 8, dated 28 January 1952, 830-CMGWU (TS 59661); AEQUOR I; NARA; p. 2.
55 "DTDORIC/QKACTIVE/OPERATIONS," Stankiewicz, Stanislaw; NARA, p. 9–11, 64.
56 "Basis for Operational Collaboration Proposed by Belorussian National Council, 15 February 1951"; Rogula, Boris, Vol. 1; NARA; p. 2.
57 Belaruskaia Bibliatėka imia Frantsishka Skaryny (BBiFS), "Letter to Lt. Gen. M. Ridgway, Supreme Commander of N.A.T.O. Forces in Europe, 5 December 1952," Box 9P – Belarusian coordinating committee UK, Belarusian Liberation Front, Belarusian Publishing Front, p. 2.
58 Ibid., p. 6.
59 "Conference with Mikola Abramchik, 7 November 1951"; Abramtchik, Mikola; NARA; p. 4.
60 There was another project entitled AEPRIMER with the purpose creating and infiltrating assets into the BSSR. It lasted from 1957 to 1959. AEQUOR. AEPRIMER; Second Release of Name Files Under the Nazi War Crimes and Japanese Imperial Government Disclosure Acts, ca. 1981-ca. 2002; Record group 263: Records of the Central Intelligence Agency, 1894–2002; NARA; "Project Outline: AEQUOR 8 August 1951," AEQUOR I; NARA; p. 6.
61 "AEQUOR Progress Report, 20 September 1951"; Rogula, Boris, Vol. 1; NARA; p. 6.
62 "Contact Report with Cambista 2, 15 July 1952"; Rogula, Boris, Vol. 1; NARA; p. 7.
63 "Project AEQUOR, 30 August 1951"; AEQUOR I; NARA; p. 2.

64 "AEQUOR/Transmittal of 'CAMBISTA II: New Proposals, 6 July 1951"; AEQUOR Vol. 1; NARA; p. 1.
65 "Contact Report with Cambista 2, 15 July 1952"; Rogula, Boris, Vol. 1; NARA; p. 1.
66 Ibid.
67 Latin America may have been another area for recruitment. There was an individual with the cryptonym AECULTIVATE 1 who was approved to be sent from Poland to Argentina to train and later return to the Belarusian-Polish area to merge "anti-communist elements." It is possible that Astroŭski may have participated in similar activity when he was in Argentina, but there is no concrete information about this. "A Review of the Byelorussian National Council (BNR), 17 March 1958"; AEQUOR, Vol III; NARA; p. 12.
68 "Basis for Operational Collaboration Proposed by Belorussian National Council, 15 February 1951"; Rogula, Boris, Vol. 1; NARA; p. 3.
69 "Conference with Cambista 2 Regarding Agent Prospects, 4 June 1951"; Rogula, Boris, Vol. 1; NARA; p. 3.
70 "Report to Chief, SR/3 regarding Meeting with Cambista 4, 26 May 1953"; Abramtchik, Mykola; NARA; p. 3.
71 "REDBIRD/Operational- Mission Outline- CAMPOSANTO 1"; AEQUOR vol. 1; RG 263, ZZ-19, box 6 dated 2 July 1951, p. 1–3.
72 There were some exceptions. In one case, two individuals who did not meet the requirements were dispatched with orders to observe and monitor two airfields that were thought to store atomic bomb carriers and were sites were atomic installation may have been occurring.
73 "Contact Report with Cambista 2, 15 July 1952"; Rogula, Boris, Vol. 1; NARA; p. 8.
74 Ibid.
75 Motyka, Wnuk, Stryjek, and Baran, *Wojna po wojnie: antysowieckie podziemie w Europie Środkowo-Wschodniej w latach 1944–1953,* 74.
76 Aliaksandar Lukashuk, *Filistovich: viartan'ne natsyianalista* (Minsk: Nasha Niva, 1997), 11.
77 His name appears in a roster of the police battalion stationed in Vialeĭka between April and September 1943. Dziarzhaŭny arkhiŭ Minskaĭ voblastsi (DAMV), f. 1039, v. 1, s. 116, p. 8.
78 He also founded the newspaper *Moladz'* ("Youth"). Halina Filistovich, "Za kozhnaĭ khvoiaĭ ja bachyla brata," *Belaruski rėzystans: chasopis naĭnoŭshaĭ historii Belarusi,* no. 1 (2004), 21.
79 Lukasuk, *Filistovich: viartan'ne natsyianalista,* 42.
80 Filistovich was recruited along with another individual CAMPOSANTO 2. Reports claim that CAMPOSANTO 2 was a Belarusian living in England, interested in journalism, and although "brighter" than Filistovich, he lacked the latter's physicality. He did not go on the mission. Both were trained

at some point in Germany and the other individual was to train and be dispatched with other people – members of the AEQUOR II team – at a later date. "Conference with Cambista 2 Regarding Agent Prospects, 4 June 1951"; Rogula, Boris, Vol. 1; NARA; p. 1, and "Project AEQUOR, from Field Station in Munich, no date"; Ragula, Boris, volume 1; NARA; p. 2.

81 "Conference with Cambista 2 Regarding Agent Prospects, 4 June 1951"; Rogula, Boris, Vol. 1; NARA; p. 1.

82 "REDBIRD/Operational, Mission Outline- CAMPOSANTO 1, 2 July 1951"; AEQUOR I; NARA; p. 1–2. Additional tasks also included intelligence gathering.

83 Ibid., p. 3.

84 "Ibid., 4.

85 An alternative meeting between Abramchyk and Filistovich was arranged in Strasbourg on 6 September 1951. "AEQUOR PROGRESS REPORT, 20 September 1951"; AEQUOR I; NARA; p. 1–2.

86 "Project AEQUOR, from Field Station in Munich, no date"; Ragula, Boris, volume 1; NARA; p. 2.

87 "Progress Report from CSOB Semi-Monthly Report No. 8, dated 28 January 1952, 830-CMGWU (TS 59661); AEQUOR I; NARA; p. 1.

88 "Contact Report on Mikola Abramchik, 31 January 1952"; Abramtchik, Mykola; NARA; p. 1.

89 "REDSOX/Operational, AEQUOR/Commitments to CAMPOSANTO 1, 5 June 1953"; AEQUOR II; NARA; p. 1.

90 Much of what we know about these missions from Belarusian sources were published in the early 1990s, during an archival thaw in the KDB Archive in Belarus. Valakhanovich, *Antisovetskoe podpol'e,* 14.

91 One was a pamphlet called *Zhyve Belarus'* ("Long" Live Belarus).

92 Vera Filistovich, "Ianka Skazaŭ, shto zmagaetstsa za svaikh liudzieĭ," *Belaruski rėzystans,* no. 1 (2011): 11.

93 Valakhanovich, *Antisovetskoe podpol'e, 1944–1953,* 42–43.

94 Filistovich, "Za kozhnaĭ khvoiaĭ ia bachyla brata," 27.

95 Lukashuk visited the towns where Filistovich was active and met with individuals who knew him and had helped him. According to Lukashuk, their stories pertaining to the apprehension and arrest of Filistovich matched up. Lukashuk, *Viartanne natsyianalista: dakumental'nyia tvory,* 254–255.

96 There have been, however, other accounts of his betrayer. The CIA received information from Lashuk, a friend of Filistovich's, claiming that it was the latter's brother-in-law who informed on his whereabouts. This information was presented to the CIA from some of Filistovich's family that later resided in Poland. However, Filistovich's sister, Vera, does not mention her estranged husband's actions in her interview in 2001. "REDWOOD/AEQUOR/AEACRE/Operations, Operational Contact with AECAMBISTA-4, 18 June 1959"; AEQUOR III; NARA; p. 2. See interview: Filistovich, "Ianka Skazaŭ, shto zmagaetstsa za svaikh liudzieĭ," *Belaruski rėzystans* no. 1 (2011).

97 Ibid., 55.

98 When asked by her interviewer if she personally believed he was dead, Halina, Filistovich's older sister, replied that she did not feel like he was. His other sister, Vera, also doubted his execution and believed he was still living under a different name.

99 Filistovich, "Za kozhnaĭ khvoiaĭ ia bachyla brata," 30–31.

100 "Operational/REDWOOD/AEQUOR/KUCAGE, Minutes of Meeting with AECAMBISTA-4, 7 February 1957,"; AEQUOR III; NARA; p. 3.

101 "Capture of AECAMPOSANTO-1 by Soviet Authorities, 9 September 1957"; AEQUOR III; NARA; p. 1–12.

102 This comment was made by Aliaksandar Lashuk, an aquaintance of Kushal's whom he kept in contact with during the postwar era. In his contribution to a series of comments on Filistovich, Lashuk notes that Filistovich's "Heroism was great. But that, what he planned to do, was not possible." From Lukashuk, *Viartan'ne natsyianalista: dakumental'nyia tvory*, 248.

103 Ibid., 251.

104 Lukashuk, *Filistovich: viartan'ne natsyianalista*, 32.

105 "Transmittal of Outline of AEQUOR Operation Plan, 26 February 1952"; AEQUOR, Vol. I; NARA; p. 2.

106 Ibid., 3.

107 Ibid.

108 Some of these instructors even had personal experiences living "black" in Siberia. Other aspects of training included unarmed defense, field topography, scouting, patrolling, guerilla warfare techniques, field photography, clandestine communications, and lessons on Soviet controls. "Transmittal of AEQUOR/CAMPOSANTO Progress Report covering period 11 February to 16 March 1952, 20 March 1952"; AEQUOR, Vol. I; NARA; p. 1–5.

109 "Transmittal of AEQUOR/CAMPOSANTO Progress Report, 1 March 1952"; AEQUOR, Vol. I; NARA; p. 1.

110 "AEQUOR Progress Report covering 15 Oct. 1951–16 Feb. 1952, 16 February 1952"; AEQUOR, vol. I; NARA; p. 2.

111 Due to the sensitivity of the mission and the potential instability of Camposanto 7, it was decided that the best approach would be to keep him in the Louvain complex, where his whereabouts would be more closely monitored. However, visa issues inhibited this plan, after which a trusted principal agent (PA) was sent to London with Camposanto 7 as his custodian. "AEQUOR Progress Report covering 15 Oct. 1951–16 Feb. 1952, 16 February 1952"; AEQUOR, vol. I; NARA; p. 3.

112 "AEQUOR Progress Report covering 15 Oct. 1951–16 Feb. 1952, 16 February 1952"; AEQUOR, vol. I; NARA; p. 3–4.

113 "Transmittal of AEQUOR/CAMPOSANTO Progress Report, 1 March 1952"; AEQUOR, Vol. I; NARA; p. 3.
114 Ibid., 1.
115 "Agent Evaluation Reports, 21 March 1952"; AEQUOR, Vol. I; NARA; p. 1.
116 "Agent Evaluation Reports, 21 March 1952"; AEQUOR, Vol. I; NARA; p. 1.
117 "REDSOX/AEQUOR/CAMPOSANTO 2, Case Officers' Evaluation, 21 March 1952"; AEQUOR, Vol. I; NARA; p. 1–2.
118 "CAMPOSANTO 5: Case Officer's Evaluation, 21 March 1952"; AEQUOR, Vol. 1; NARA; p. 1.
119 "Transmittal of AEQUOR/CAMPOSANTO Progress Report covering period 11 February to 16 March 1952, 20 March 1952"; AEQUOR, Vol. I; NARA; p. 3.
120 "Transmittal of AEQUOR/CAMPOSANTO Progress Report, 1 March 1952"; AEQUOR, Vol. I; NARA; p. 2.
121 His position in the mission was especially important as he was the only qualified w/t operator, and Camposanto 4 still had not had enough training to completely replace the former. "Transmittal of AEQUOR/CAMPOSANTO Progress Report, 1 March 1952"; AEQUOR, Vol. I; NARA; p. 2–3.
122 "Annex to AEQUOR I Final Report: Events Leading up to the Cancellation of the Mission"; AEQUOR, Vol. 1; NARA; p. 1.
123 "Final Report on AEQUOR I, 10 June 1952"; AEQUOR, Vol. I; NARA; p. 1.
124 Ibid., 2.
125 "AEQUOR II Progress Report 1 May-1 July, 14 July 1952"; AEQUOR, Vol. I; NARA; p. 2.
126 "AEQUOR II Operational plan"; AEQUOR, Vol. 1; NARA; p. 1.
127 List of political, social security and labour employment office records, 1947 Höchstadt/Aisch, 2.1.1.1/69944514/ITS Digital Archive, USHMM; Artuszewski, Michael, 1949, 0.1/13499080/ITS Digital Archive, USHMM.
128 A.E.F. Assembly Center Registration Card, 1947, 0.1/26911874/ITS Digital Archive, USHMM.
129 A.E.F. Assembly Center Registration Card, 3.1.1.7/101081984/ITS Digital Archive, USHMM.
130 BBiFS, Box 22P – Belarusians in France, no. 71, 129, p. 1–2.
131 AEF. Assembly Center Registration Card, .1/50362178/ITS Digital Archive, USHMM.
132 "AEQUOR II Progress Report: 1 July–1 September, 21 September 1952"; AEQUOR, Vol. 2; NARA; p. 12
133 These were their cover names: Mikhail Semenovich Baran (Camposanto 4), Mikhail Akimovich Bobrovnichi (Camposanto 6), Viktor Petrovich Kaminskii (Camposanto 8), and Mikhail Vasil'evich Dubrovskii (Camposanto 9).

134 “Summary Review of AEQUOR II Operation: 26 August–10 December 1952”; AEQUOR, Vol. II; NARA; p. 1.
135 “AEQUOR II- Progress Report 1 September–1 November 1952”; AEQUOR, Vol. I; NARA; p. 1.
136 During this time at the safe house, their cover involved being Icelandic citizens who were training with the United States for NATO purposes. “AEQUOR II Progress Report: 1 July–1 September, 21 September 1952”; AEQUOR, Vol. 2; NARA; p. 14.
137 “AEQUOR II Progress Report: 1 July–1 September, 21 September 1952”; AEQUOR, Vol. 2; NARA; p. 13.
138 Valakhanovich, *Antisovetskoe podpol'e na territorii Belarusi 1944–1953*, 46.
139 “AEQUOR II- Progress Report 1 September–1 November 1952”; AEQUOR, Vol. I; NARA; p. 1–2.
140 Valakhanovich, *Antisovetskoe podpol'e na territorii Belarusi 1944–1953*, 47–48.
141 Ibid., 48.
142 “Summary Review of AEQUOR II Operation: 26 August-10 December 1952”; AEQUOR, Vol. II; NARA; p. 3–4.
143 “Expansion and Exploitation of Existing operational facilities, 2 November 1953”; AEQUOR, Vol. II; NARA; p. 2.
144 Ibid., 4.
145 Ibid., 3.
146 “AEQUOR/FI, Extension of, 27 September 1955”; AEQUOR, Vol. II; NARA; p. 2.
147 “AEQUOR Team II, Report of Surfacing, 2 January 1957”; AEQUOR, Vol. II; NARA; p. 1–2.
148 “Iznoŭ ab ‘parashutystykh’,” *Belaruski holas*, March 1957: 2.
149 Iurka Stasevich, “Belaruskaia Partyzanka, 1944–1952hh.,” *Belaruski holas*, April 1975: 2–3.
150 In 1997 Vostrykaŭ and Kastsiuk’s cases were reviewed by a court that concluded that neither men were eligible for rehabilitation as victims of political repression from the 1920s to 1980s.
151 Valakhanovich, *Antisovetskoe podpol'e na territorii Belarusi 1944–1953*, 48–49.
152 “Informants-Pullach, 6 November 1950”; Rogula, Boris vol. 1; NARA; p. 4.
153 “Review of AEQUOR KUFIRE collaboration with AECAMBISTA 1, 15 February 1954”; AEQUOR, Vol. II; NARA; p. 2.
154 “Progress Report covering period 15 Oct. 1951–16 Feb. 1952, 21 February 1952”; AEQUOR vol. I; NARA; p. 1.
155 “AEQUOR/Spotting and Recruitment in U.S. and Canada, 24 July 1952”; AEQUOR, Vol. 1; NARA; p. 3.
156 Ibid.
157 “Planning for AEQUOR KUFIRE FY 1955, 26 March 1954”; AEQUOR, Vol. II; NARA; p. 9.

158 "Belarusian-Ukrainian Section: Progress Report for January 1953–16 February 1953"; AEQUOR, Vol. II; NARA; p. 2.
159 "REDSOX AEQUOR, 8 February 1954"; Rogula, Boris, Vol. 1; NARA; p. 2
160 "Conference with Mikola Abramtchik, 7 November 1951"; Abramtchik, Mikola; NARA; p. 5.
161 "REDSOX/AEQUOR/Contact Report, 25 October 1951"; Rogula, Boris, Vol. 1; NARA; p. 2.
162 It mainly referred to rank-and-file individuals who had fled Belarus. It also included Belarusian higher ups mentioned in this chapter, as well as other such as Nikalaĭ Shchors, who was formally naturalized in the United States in 1956. Scors, Nicholas (Mikolaj); Index to Petitions for Naturalization, 1865-7/18/1990; RG21 Records of District Courts of the United States, 1685–2009; NARA; p. 1–2; "Contact Report- Meeting with Cambista 4, 26 May 1953"; Abramtchik, Mykola; NARA; p. 3.
163 It should be noted that this trend was noticed already in the fall of 1951 in a case officer's report that doubted Rahulia's dedication to operational matters because of these aspirations. Abramchyk reassured the case officer that this was not an issue. "Conference with Mikola Abramtchik, 7 November 1951"; Abramtchik, Mikola; NARA; p. 4–5.
164 "Contact with AECAMBISTA 4, 23–25 March 1954"; Abramtchik, Mikola; NARA; p. 2.
165 "REDSKIN NIGHTWATCH, 27 January 1954"; Ragula, Barys, vol. 1; NARA; p. 1.
166 "REDSOX AEQUOR, 29 January 1954"; Ragula, Barys, vol. 1 ; NARA; p. 1.
167 Gerald Steinacher, *Nazis on the Run: How Hitler's Henchmen Fled Justice* (New York: Oxford University Press, 2011), xxiv.
168 "Chapter 6: Common Ground with New Partners"; CIA and Nazi War Criminals and Collaborators; RG 263; NARA; p. 15.
169 "Mikola Abramtchik, 20 February 1962"; AEQUOR, Vol. 3; NARA; p. 1.
170 "REDSOX/Operational: Transmittal of Letter Written by Cambista 2 to [redacted], 9 January 1953"; Ragula, Boris, vol. 1; NARA; p. 2–3.
171 Inge Sanmiya, *Against the Current: the memoirs of Boris Ragula* (Montreal: McGill-Queen's University Press, 2005), 110–111.
172 Instytut Pamięci Narodowej (IPN), BU 003172/33/4, p. 32, 161.
173 Similar schisms among other national émigré communities also appeared. See, for example: Tromly, *Cold War Exiles and the CIA,* 72–92.
174 David Cesarani, *Justice Delayed: How Britain Became a Refuge for Nazi War Criminals* (London: Mandarin Paperbacks, 1992), 166–167, 172. Indeed, the only significant push for the apprehension and trial of war criminals came with the Riga Ghetto Case between 1948 and 1949. Within a span of a few months, British officials apprehended around 70 German and Latvian criminals. See: Samuel Miner, "'Appeasement

Gone Mad': The Riga Ghetto Case and the Politics of British War Crimes Trials," *Journal of Contemporary History* 57, no. 3 (July 2022): 669–690.

175 Ibid., 6.

176 Anthony Gleez, "The Making of British Policy on War Crimes: History as Politics in the UK," *Contemporary European History* 1, no. 2 (July 1992): 171, 181.

177 A in-depth study of the case was published and uses court documents, interviews with various lawyers and judges involved in the case, as well as conversations with families of the victims. It also covers the sensationalism surrounding the trial and Sawoniuk's unstable, antisemitic, and erratic behavior throughout this period. See: Mike Anderson and Neil Hanson, *The Ticket Collector from Belarus: An Extraordinary True Story of Britain's Only War Crimes Trial* (London: Simon & Schuster, 2022).

178 Cesarani, *Justice Delayed*, 4.

179 Ibid., 138–139.

180 Tromly, *Cold War Exiles and the CIA*, 31; Scott Anderson and Jon Lee Anderson, *Inside the League: The Shocking Exposé of How Terrorists, Nazis, and Latin American Death Squads Have Infiltrated the World Anti-Communist League* (New York: Dodd, Mead & Company, 1986), 44; Stephen Dorril, *MI6: Inside the Covert World of Her Majesty's Secret Intelligence Service* (New York: Free Press, 2000), 218.

181 IPN, BU 003174/33/19, p. 9.

182 IPN BU 003172/33/3, p. 5–6, 12–14, 22, 46–47, 91.

183 "Report from s/Alfred"; Ostrowski, Radoslaw; NARA; p. 2.

184 "Cover Division/Plans/OSO, 1 April 1952"; Abramtchik, Mykola; NARA; p. 1.

185 In CIA documents, Zarechny's name appears as Liubovik (Ludwik) Holubovich. He allegedly studied law and served as a judge and officer for the NKVD and later joined Vlasov's army during the war and collaborated with the Germans. "Report on Antonovich-Zarechnyi and the so-called Belorussian Liberation Movement, 19 July 1952"; Ostrowski, Radislaw; NARA; p. 1–2.

186 "Report on Antonovich-Zarechnyi and the so-called Belorussian Liberation Movement, 19 July 1952"; Ostrowski, Radislaw; NARA; p. 2.

187 Ibid., 1–2.

188 Ibid., 2.

189 There were allegedly even pro-Rada broadcasts coming from the Hrodna region of the BSSR condemning both Abramchyk and Rahulia as traitors. The CIA indicated that the broadcast most likely came from the British zone in Germany "AEQUOR/ Alleged Ostrowski Radio, 29 August 1952"; Ostrowski, Radoslaw; NARA; p. 1.

190 Stephen Dorril's work indicates that MI6 initially utilized Astroŭski but then allowed him to be used by the Americans because he was no longer

a viable agent and because the group had been heavily infiltrated by Soviet intelligence services. Dorril, *MI6*, 221.

191 Stephen Dorril even states that the British exiled Astroŭski to Argentina. The Arolsen Archives indicate that Astroŭski emigrated from Marseille to Argentina on 30 November 1950. Liste Nominative des Refugies Devant S'Embaquer à Bord du S/S "CAMPANA" Départ de Marseille Prévu pour le 30 Novembre 1950 à Destination de L'Argentine, 28 November 1930, 3.1.3.2/81725529/ITS, USHMM ; Dorril, *MI6*, 219.

192 "Security Information, 1952"; Ostrowski, Radoslaw; NARA; p. 1–6.

193 One of these included General John Frederick Charles Fuller (1878–1966), a military expert who had been active in the Second Boer War, the First World War, and established the Royal Tank Corps. Later in his career he covered various conflicts as a journalist and met Hitler, Franco, and Mussolini. He was also a member of Sir Oswald Mosely's British Union, a fascist organization, and supported them. Fuller also had a reputation for being interested in the occult, in addition to being antisemitic. A few letters in his personal collections suggests he had some sort of relationship with notable Belarusians, at least after the Second World War. These include letters of condolence to Fuller's wife after his death. Sent by John Kosiak, president of the Whiteruthenian Congress in the USA, and John Shimchik, chairman of the "Byelorussian Liberation Front", these letters highlight Fuller's "deep sympathy toward the Byelorussian nation", his support of the "Byelorussian liberation cause", and note that "Our people have lost one of their greatest friends. His name will live with us for ever [sic] as inspiration in our struggle for freedom." Liddell Hart Centre for Military Archives at King's College London, Fuller 4/11/17, 4/11/16.

194 BBiFS, "Starshyni uradu ZBK u Belhii, 20.04.1953," Box 3P – ZBK, BNR, Bielaruskija Kambatanty, p. 239.

195 BBiFS, "Kamunikat u radu zhurtavan'nia belaruskikh kambatantaŭ u Bėlhii, 12.11.1952," Box 3P – ZBK, BNR, Bielaruskija Kambatanty.

196 "Ukrainian and Byelorussian Émigré Activity, 1 February 1951"; Rogula, Boris, Vol. 1; NARA; p. 1.

197 In his memoirs, Rahulia mentions his friendship with a Father Robert Van Cauwelaert, who had an uncle in the Belgian parliament. Father Cauwelaert was hoping to use his uncle's connection to get an audience with the pope, in the hopes of procuring financial support for the Belarusian community in Belgium. Rahulia was allegedly granted this meeting with Pope Pius XII, resulting in a donation of scholarship for Belarusians to study in Belgium. Sanmiya, *Against the Current*, 107–109.

198 Reinhard Gehlen was head of Military Intelligence Unit of the Foreign Armies of the East (*Fremde Heere Ost*, FHO), headquartered in Zossen,

near Berlin, and had developed connections with some of the Belarusians, namely Astroŭski, during the Second World War. Loftus posits that Gehlen later reached out to Astroŭski in the postwar period, to use him in his network that worked under the CIA. In exchange for his intelligence, Gehlen proposed protection for war crime prosecution. It also appears that Kushal′ had some contact with the Gehlen organization in 1948. However, it is unclear whether or not Abramchyk knew of this relation. In any case, the Gehlen organization was subsequently utilized by the United States. "Gen. Frantisek Kushal′, 17 March 1953"; Kushel, Francis; NARA; p. 8; John Loftus, *The Belarus Secret: the Nazi Connection in America* (New York: Paragon House, 1989), 57.

199 BBiFS, "Pratakol, 9-aĭ sėsii rady B.N.R., ad 22 travenia 1960h.," Box 1P, Rada BNR, p. 1–14.

200 BBiFS, "Zaprashaem na sustrėchu! Ad imia Initsyiatyŭna-Arhanizatsyĭnykh Kamitėtaŭ (u Manchėstra i ŭ Taron'tse) Pershae Sus'vetnae Sustrėchy Belaruskikh Vėtėranaŭ," Box 1P, Rada BNR, p. 1.

201 BBiFS, "Kamunika BNNCHR N. 1, 15 February 1948", Box 11P – Belarusian Organisations in the UK, p. 2; BBiFS, "Daraženki Ajciec Cieslaŭ, 15.07, 1953," Č. Sipovič Letters, Box 2, Folder 121, p. 1.

202 "Background on AECAMPOSANTO/6, March 1995"; Rogula, Boris Vol. 2; NARA; p. 1–2.

Conclusion

1 Seviaryn Kviatkoŭski, "Iashchė ne pryĭshoŭ chas," *Nasha niva,* 15 June 1998.

2 The three phrases translate to "I am a Belarusian", but the first is in Russian, the second in Polish, and the third in Belarusian. Seviaryn Kviatkoŭski, "Iashchė ne pryĭshoŭ chas," *Nasha niva,* 15 June 1998.

Bibliography

Archives

Belarus

Dziarzhaŭny arkhiŭ Brėstskaĭ voblastsi (DABV)
Dziarzhaŭny arkhiŭ Hrodzenskaĭ voblastsi (DAHV)
Dziarzhaŭny arkhiŭ Minskaĭ voblastsi (DAMV)
Natsyianal'ny Arkhiŭ Rėspubliki Belarus' (NARB)
Zonal'nyi gosudarstvennyi arkhiv Molodechno (ZGAM)

Czech Republic

Národni archiv České republiky (NAČR)

Germany

Bundesarchiv Berlin-Lichterfelde

Lithuania

Lietuvos centrinis valstybės archyvas (LCVA)
Lietuvos ypatingasis archyvvas (LYA)

Poland

Archiwum Akt Nowych (AAN)
Archiwum Wschodnie (AW)
Centralne Archiwum Wojskowe (CAW)
Instytut Pamięci Narodowej (IPN)

United Kingdom

Belaruskaia Bibliatėka imia Frantsishka Skaryny (BBiFS)
Liddell Hart Centre for Military Archives at King's College London

United States

National Archives and Records Administration at College Park (NARA)
United States Holocaust Memorial Museum (USHMM), Washington DC
University of Southern California Shoah Foundation Institute

References and Collections of Published Primary Sources

"Ab pryznachen'i akruhovych načaĺnikaŭ Bielaruskai Krajevaj Abarony" in *Za Dziaržaŭnuju Nezalezhnasts Belarusi: Dakumenty i matar'ialy sabranyia i padryckhtavanyia dlia publikatsyi I. Kasiakom, pragledz'anyia i aprabavanyia dlia druku kamisiiaĭ Belaruskai Tsėntral'naĭ Rady pad kiraŭnitsvam praf. R. Astroŭskaha.* London: Vydan'ne Belaruskaĭ Central'naĭ Rady, 1960.

Dziarnovich, Aleh. *Antysavetskiia rukhi ŭ Belarusi, 1944–1956 Davednik.* Minsk: Arkhiŭ Naĭnoŭshae Historyi, 1999

Druhi Usebelaruski Kanhrės: matar'ialy sabranyia i apratsavanyia na padstave pratakol'nykh zapisau kamisiiaĭ Belaruskaĭ Tsėntral'naĭ Rady pad rėdaktsyiaĭ praf. R. Astrouskaha. Munich: Druckerei Cicero, 1954.

Fall Barbarossa- Dokumente zur Vorbereitung der faschistischen Wehrmacht auf die Aggression gegen die Sowjetunion (1940/41). Selected and edited by Erhard Moritz. Berlin: Deutscher Militärverlag, 1970.

Istoriia Belarusi v dokumentakh i materialakh. Edited by I.N. Kuznetsov and V.G Mazets. Minsk: Amalfeia, 2000.

Pogranichnye voiska SSSR 1939–1941: sbornik dokumentov i materialov. Moscow: Izdatel'stvo "Nauka", 1970.

Slutski zbroĭny chyn 1920- u dakumentakh i ŭspaminakh. Edited by U. Liakhoŭski, U. Mikhniuk and A. Hes'. Minsk: Belaruski Histarychny Ahliad, 2006.

Stepek W and Z. Hoffman-Krystyańczyk. *Służba Śledcza: podręcznik dla organów bezpieczeństwa za 49 rycinami.* Poznań: Nakładem Księgarni Fr. Gutowskiego, 1923.

Trial of the Major War Criminals Before the International Military Tribunal. 14 November 1945–1 October 1946. Volume IV.

"Unichtozhit'kak mozhno bol'she" Latviiskie kollaboratsionistskie formirovaniia na territorii Belorussii, 1942–1944. Sbornik dokumentov. Moscow: Fond Istoricheskaia pamiat, 2009.

Władimir, Adamuszko. *"Zachodnia Białoruś" 17 IX 1939–22 VI 1941: Wydarzenia i losy ludzkie rok 1939. Zródła do historii Polski XX wieku ze zbiorów Narodowego Archiwum Republiki Białoruś.* Warsaw: Oficyna wydawnicza RYTM, 1998.

Newspapers and Periodicals

Belaruskaia hazėta
Belaruski holas
Belaruski rėzystans
Hazėta sluchchyny
Holas vioski
Nasha niva
Pahonia
Ranitsa: Belaruskaia hazėta ŭ Niamechchyne
Vilenskoe utro
Za praŭdu

Memoirs, Diaries, and Published Interviews

Bul'ba-Borovets', Taras. *Armija bez derzhavy*, Winnipeg, 1981
Iorsh, Siarheĭ. *Viartan'ne BNP: Asoby i dakumenty Belaruskaĭ Nezalezhnitskaĭ Partyi.* BHAKC: Minsk, 1998.
Iurėvich, Liavon. *Zhyts'tsio pad ahniom: Partrėt belaruskaha voenachal'nika i palitychnaha dzeiacha Barysa Rahuli na fone iaho ėpokhi.* Minsk: Arche, 1999.
Kasmovich, Dz'mitry. *Za vol'nuiu i suverennuiu Belarus'*. Vilnius: Gudas, 2006.
Kushal', Frants. *Sproby stvaren'nia belaruskaha voiska.* Minsk: Belaruski Histarychny Ahliad, 1999.
Maletski, Iazėp. *Pad znakam pahoni: Uspaminy.* Toronto: Vydavetstva "Pahonia", 1976.
Rahulia, Barys. *Belaruskae studėntstva na chuzhyne.* New York: Published by Mikola Pruski, 1996.
Sanmiya, Inge. *Against the Current: The Memoirs of Boris Ragula.* Montreal: McGill-Queen's University Press, 2005.

Doctoral Dissertations

Exeler, Franziska. "Reckoning with Occupation. Soviet Power, Local Communities, and the Ghosts of Wartime Behavior in Post-1944 Belorussia." Ph.D. Dissertation, Department of History, Princeton University, 2013.
Kasmach, Lizaveta. "The Road to the First Belarusian State: Nation-Building in the Context of the First World War and Revolution." Ph.D. Dissertation, Department of History and Classics, University of Alberta, 2016.
Rudling, Per Anders. "The Battle Over Belarus: The Rise and Fall of the Belarusian National Movement, 1906–1931." Ph.D Dissertation, Department of History and Classics, University of Alberta, 2009.

Secondary Sources

Adamushka, Uladzimir. *Palitychnyia rėprėsii 20–50 hadoŭ na Belarusi.* Minsk: "Belarus'", 2004.

Anderson, Mike and Neil Hanson. *The Ticket Collector from Belarus: An Extraordinary True Story of Britain's Only War Crimes Trial.* London: Simon & Schuster, 2022.

Anderson, Scott and Jon Lee Anderson. *Inside the League: The Shocking Exposé of How Terrorists, Nazis, and Latin American Death Squads Have Infiltrated the World Anti-Communist League.* New York: Dodd, Mead & Company, 1986.

Aydin, Aysegul and Cem Emrence. *Zones of Rebellion: Kurdish Insurgents and the Turkish State.* Ithaca and London: Cornell University Press, 2015.

Baranova, Olga. "Nationalism, anti-Bolshevism or the will to survive? Collaboration in Belarus under the Nazi occupation of 1941–1944." *European Review of History – Revue européenne d'histoire 15,* no. 2 (April 2008): 113–128.

–. *Nationalism, Anti-Bolshevism or the Will to Survive? Forms of Belarusian Interaction with the German Occupation Authorities, 1941–1944.* Saarbrücken, Germany: Lambert Academic Publishing, 2010.

Barnett, Donald L. and Karari Njama. *Mau Mau from Within: Autobiography and Analysis of Kenya's Peasant Revolt.* New York: Modern Reader Paperbacks, 1966.

Bartov, Omer and Eric Weitz. *Shatterzones of Empire: Coexistence and Violence in the German, Habsburg, Russian, and Ottoman Borderlands.* Bloomington: Indiana University Press, 2013.

Bekus, Nelly. *Struggle Over identity: The Official and the Alternative "Belarusianness".* Budapest: Central University Press, 2010.

Beorn, Waitman. *Marching into Darkness: The Wehrmacht and the Holocaust in Belarus.* Cambridge: Harvard University Press, 2014.

Bergholz, Max. *Violence as a Generative Force: Identity, Nationalism, and Memory in a Balkan Community.* Ithaca: Cornell University Press, 2016.

Bergman, Aleksandra. *Sprawy Białoruskie w II Rzeczypospolitej.* Warszawa: Państwowe Wydawnictwo Naukowe, 1984.

Blood, Philip W. *Hitler's Bandit Hunters: the SS and the Nazi Occupation of Europe.* Washington D.C.: Potomac Books, 2006.

Böhler, Jochen. "Generals and Warlords, Revolutionaries and Nation State Builders." In *Legacies of Violence Eastern Europe's First World War,* edited by Jochen Böhler, Włodzimierz Borodziej, and Joachim von Puttkamer. Münich: Oldenbourg Verlag, 2014.

Boot, Max. *Invisible Armies: An Epic History of Guerrilla Warfare from Ancient Times to the Present.* New York: Liveright Publishing Corporation, 2013.

Boradyn, Zygmunt. *Niemen rzeka niezgody: Polsko-sowiecka wojna partyzancka na Nowogródczyźnie 1943–1944* Warsaw: Oficyna Wydawnicza Rytm, 1999.

Borzecki, Jerzy. *The Soviet-Polish Peace of 1921 and the Creation of Interwar Europe.* New Haven: Yale University Press, 2008.

Brakel, Alexander. "The Relationship Between Soviet Partisans and the Civilian Population in Belorussia under German Occupation, 1941–4." In *War in a Twilight World: Partisan and Anti-Partisan Warfare in Eastern Europe, 1939–1945,* edited by Ben Shepherd and Juliette Pattinson (New York: Palgrave Macmillan, 2010): 80–101.

Breitman, Richard. *Himmler's Police Auxiliaries in the Occupied Soviet Territories,* Annual 7, Chapter 2, paper presented at meeting of the American Historical Association, 30 December 1989.

Breitman, Richard, Goda, Norman J.W., Naftali, Timothy and Robert Wolfe. *U.S. Intelligence and the Nazis.* New York: Cambridge University Press, 2005.

Breitman, Richard. and Norman J.W. Goda, *Hitler's Shadow: Nazi War criminals, US intelligence, and the Cold War.* Washington DC: National Archives and Records Administration, 2010.

Brown, Kate. *A Biography of No Place: From Ethnic Borderland to Soviet Heartland.* Cambridge: Harvard University Press, 2003.

Browning, Christopher. *Ordinary Men: Reserve Police Battalion 101 and the Final Solution in Poland.* New York: Harper Collins, 1992

Brubaker, Rogers and Frederick Cooper. "Beyond 'identity'." *Theory and Society 29* (2000): 1–47.

Burds, Jeffrey. "Gender and Policing in Soviet West Ukraine, 1944–1948." *Cahiers du Monde russe 42,* no. 2/4 (2001): 279–319.

–. "Sexual Violence in Europe in World War II, 1939–1945." *Politics and Society 31,* no. 1 (2009), 35–73.

Cesarani, David. *Justice Delayed: How Britain Became a Refuge for Nazi War Criminals* (London: Mandarin Paperbacks, 1992).

Chase, William *Enemies Within the Gates? The Comintern and the Stalinist Repression, 1934–1939.* New Haven: Yale University Press, 2001.

Chiari, Bernhard. "Der polnische Widerstand und die Juden: Anmerkungen zum Diskurs über den Zweiten Weltkrieg." *Osteuropa* 53, no. 12 (December 2003): 1842–1852.

–. *Shtodzionnasts' za liniiaĭ frontu: akupatsyia, kalabaratsyia i supratsiŭ u Belarusi 1911–1911h.* Minsk: Bibliiatėka chasopisa "Belaruski Histarychny Ahliad, 2008).

Choruży, Wiesław. "Działalność Białoruskiej Włościańsko-Robotniczej Hromady w powiecie białostockim, bielskim i sokólskim w latach 1925–1927." *Białoruskie Zeszyty Historyczne* 1 (1994): 40–62.

Cichoracki, Piotr. *Stołpce-Łowcza-Leśna 1924: II Rzeczpospolita wobec najpoważniejszych incydentów zbrojnych w województwach połnocno-wschodnich.* Łomianki: Wydawnictwo LTW, 2012.

Ciesielski, Stanisław; Hryciuk, Grzegorz and Aleksander Srebrakowski. *Masowe Deportacje Ludności w Związku Radzieckim.* Toruń: Wydawnictwo Adam Marszałek, 2003.

Ciesielski, Stanisław; Materski, Wojciech and Andrzej Paczkowski. *Represje sowieckie wobec Polaków i obywateli polskich.* Warsaw: Ośrodek KARTA, 2002.

Dąbrowski, Stanisław. "The Peace Treaty of Riga." *The Polish Review* 5, no. 1 (Winter 1960): 3–34.

Dallin, Alexander. *German Rule in Russia, 1941–1945: a study of occupation policies.* Second Edition. Boulder: Westview Press, 1981.

Daniels, Roger. *Guarding the Golden Door: American Immigration Policy and Immigrants Since 1882.* New York: Hill and Wang, 2004.

Dean, Martin. *Collaboration in the Holocaust: Crimes of Local Police in Belorussia and Ukraine, 1941–1944.* New York: St. Martin's Press, 2000.

Dimitrieva, O.P. *Natsional'nye obshchnosti na territorii Belarusi v gody pervoi mirovoi voiny 1914–1918.* Minsk: Belaruskaia navuka, 2017.

Dorril, Stephen. *MI6: Inside the Covert World of Her Majesty's Secret Intelligence Service.* New York: Touchstone, 2000.

Epstein, Barbara. *The Minsk Ghetto 1941–1943: Jewish Resistance and Soviet Internationalism* Berkeley: University of California Press, 2008.

Exeler, Franziska *Ghosts of War: Nazi Occupation and its Aftermath in Soviet Belarus.* Ithaca: Cornell University Press, 2022.

Feduta, Aleksandr, Bogutskiĭ, Oleg and Viktor Martinovich. *Politicheskie partii Belrausi – neobkhodimaia chast' grazhdanskovo obshchestva: Materialy seminara* (Minsk: Fond imeni Fridrikha Ėberta, 2003).

Fischer-Kowalski, Marina and Helga Weisz. "The Archipelago of Social Ecology and the Island of the Vienna School." In *Social Ecology: Society-Nature Relations Across Time and Space,* edited by Helmut Haberl, Marina Fischer-Kowalski, Fridolin Krausmann, Verena Winiwarter, 3–28. Cham: Springer International Publishing, 2016.

Gambetta, Diego. "Concatenations of Mechanisms." In *Social Mechanisms: An Analytical Approach to Social Theory,* edited by Peter Hedström and Richard Swedberg, 102–124. Cambridge: Cambridge University Press, 1998.

Gatrell, Peter. *A Whole Empire Walking – Refugees in Russia during World War I.* Bloomington: Indiana University Press, 2005.

Gehler, Michael and David Schriffl, editors. *Violent Resistance from the Baltics to Central, Eastern and South Eastern Europe.* Paderborn: Verlag Ferdinand Schöningh, 2020.

Gelogaev, Aleksandr. "Belaruskie vooruzhennye formirovania v General'nom okruge "Belarus'" v 1941–1944gg." *Dedy: daidzhest publikatsii o belaruskoi istorii* 7 (2011): 121–148.

Gerlach, Christian. *Kalkulierte Morde: die deutsche Wirtschafts und Vernichtungspolitik in Weißrußland 1941 bis 1944.* Hamburg: Hamburger Edition, 1999.

Gerwarth, Robert and John Horne, editors. *War in Peace: A Paramilitary Violence in Europe after the Great War.* Oxford: Oxford University Press, 2012.

Getty, J. Arch. *Origins of the Great Purges – The Soviet Communist Party Reconsidered, 1933–1938.* Cambridge University Press, 1985.

Gleez, Anthony. "The Making of British Policy on War Crimes: History as Politics in the UK." *Contemporary European History* 1, no. 2 (July 1992): 171–197.

Głogowska, Helena. *Białoruś 1914–1929: Kultura pod presją polityki.* Białystok: Białoruskie Towarzystwo Historyczne, 1996.

Gomółka, Krystyna. "Polityka rządów polskich wobec mniejszości białoruskiej w latach 1918–1939." *Białoruskie Zeszyty Historyczne* 2(4) (1995): 106–120.

–. "Ruch białoruski w przededniu II wojny światowej." *Białoruskie Zeszyty Historyczne* 13 (2000): 186–190.

Gorman, Jonathan. *Historical Judgement: The Limits of Historiographical Choice.* Montreal: McGill-Queen's University Press, 2008.

Goujon, Alexandra. "Memorial Narratives of WWII Partisans and Genocide in Belarus." *East European Politics and Societies* 24, no. 1 (Winter 2010): 6–25.

Grintskevich, A. *Slutsk: istoriko-ekonomicheskii ocherk.* Minsk: Belarus', 1970.

Gross, Jan T. *Revolution from Abroad: The Soviet Conquest of Poland's Western Ukraine and Western Belorussia.* Princeton: Princeton University Press, 1988.

Gumz, Jonathan E. "Losing Control: The Norm of Occupation in Eastern Europe during the First World War." In *Legacies of Violence: Eastern Europe's First World War,* edited by Jochen Böhler, Włodzimierz Borodziej, and Jochim von Puttkamer, 69–87. Münich: Oldenbourg Verlag, 2014.

Gur'ianov, A.E. *Repressi protiv poliakov i polskikh grazhdan.* Edited by L.C. Eremina. Moscow: Zen'ia, 1997.

Halecki, Oscar. *Borderlands of Western Civilization: A History of East Central Europe.* New York: Ronald press, 1952.

Hansbury, Paul. *Belarus in Crisis: From Domestic Unrest to the Russia-Ukraine War.* London: Hurst & Company, 2023.

Hardzienka, Aleh. *Belaruskaia Tsėntral'naia Rada BTsR: stvaren'ne, dzieĭnasts', zaniapad, 1943–1995.* Minsk: "Knihazbor", 2016.

Hart, Peter. *The I.R.A. and Its Enemies: Violence and Community in Cork 1916–1923.* Oxford: Clarendon Press, 1998.

Havryshko, Marta. "Illegitimate sexual practices in the OUN underground and UPA in Western Ukraine in the 1940s and 1950s." *Power Institutions in Post-Soviet Societies* 17, no. 17 (2016): 1–78.

–. "Love and Sex in Wartime: Controlling Women's Sexuaity in the Ukrainian Nationalist Underground." *Aspasia* 12 (2018): 35–67.

Himka, John-Paul. *Ukrainian Nationalists and the Holocaust: OUN and UPA's Participation in the Destruction of Ukrainian Jewry, 1941–1944.* Stuttgart: Ibidem Verlag, 2021.

Hobsbawm, Eric. *Bandits.* New York: Pantheon Books, 1981.

Holzer, Jerzy. *Mozaika polityczna drugiej rzeczpospolitej.* Warsaw: Książka i Wiedza, 1974.

Howell, Martha and Walter Prevenier. *From Reliable Sources: An Introduction to Historical Methods.* Ithaca: Cornell University Press, 2001.

Hroch, Miroslav. *European Nations: Explaining Their Formation*. Translated by Karolina Graham. London: Verso, 2015.

Hryboŭski, Iury. "Montė-Kasina: nieviadomyia staronki belaruskaĭ historyi." *Białoruskie Zeszyty Historyczne* 17 (2002): 173–191.

–. "Pershy belaruski shturmovy z'viaz." *Belaruski Rėzystans: chasopis naĭnoŭshaĭ historyi Belarusi*, no 1(2) (February 2005): 1–7.

–. *Białorusini w polskich regularnych formacjach wojskowych w latach 1918–1945*. Warszawa: Instytut Studiów Politycznych Pan Oficyna Wydawnicza Rytm, 2006.

–. "Pol'ska-belaruski kanflikt u Heneral'naĭ akruze 'Belarus''." *Białoruskie Zeszyty Historyczne* 25 (2006): 116–167.

–. "Belaruski lehiion SS: mify i rėchaisnasts'." *Belaruski Histarychny Ahliad 14* (2007): 97–140.

–. "Sluzhby biaspeki PNR i 'belaruskiia natsyianalisty ŭ Pol'shchy i ikh palitychnyia tsėntry na Zakhadze' (1945–1974)." *Białoruski Zeszyty Historyczne* 28 (2007): 158–192.

–. "Navahradski eskadron Barysa Rahuli – viadomae i nieviadomae." *Białoruskie Zeszyty Historyczne* nr. 30 (2008): 101–114.

–. "Belaruski kambatantski rukh na zakhadze pas'lia druhoŭ sus'vetnaĭ vaĭny." *Zapisy* 32 (2009): 404–431.

–. "Belaruski rukh i Niamechchyna napiarėdadni i ŭ pachatku drugoĭ sus'vetnaĭ vaĭny." *ARCHE 5* (May 2009): 144–160.

–. "Białoruska Centralna Rada w latach 1943–1956: próba podsumowania problemu w świetle dotychczasowych badań i najnowszych źródeł." *Białoruskie Zeszyty Historyczne 32* (2009): 161–223.

–. "Białoruskie Zbrojne Podziemie Antysowieckie w Latach 1944–1956." *Przegląd Historyczno-Wojskowy* 10, np. 1 (2009): 115–142.

–. "Palitychnaia chynnasts' starshyni Rady BNR Vasilia Zakharki napiarėdadni i ŭ hady druhoĭ sus'vetnaĭ vaĭny (1938–1943)," *Histarychny al'manakh* 15 (2009): 118–127.

–. "Abmundziravanne belaruskikh vaĭsovykh farmavanniaĭ na niametskaĭ sluzhbe padchas druhoĭ sus'vetnaĭ vaĭny." *ARCHE 5* (2010): 475–508.

–. "Białoruski ruch narodowy a III Rzesza (wrzesień 1939–czerwiec 1941)." *Przegląd Historyczny* 101, no. 1 (2010): 53–88.

–. "An Outline History of the 13th (Belarusian) Battalion of the SD Auxiliary Police (*Szhutzmannschafts Bataillon der SD 13*)." *Journal of Slavic Military Studies*, 23 (2010): 461–476.

–. "Białoruski ruch niepodległościowy wobec Polski i Polaków na ziemiach północno-wschodnich II Rzeczypospolitej pod okupacją niemiecką (1941–1944)." *Dzieje najnowsze* 1 (2011): 77–105.

–. *Pogoń między Orłem Białym, Swastyką i Czerwoną Gwiazdą: Białoruski ruch niepodległościowy w latach 1939–1956*. Warsaw: BEL Studio, 2011.

–. "Grupa białoruskich narodowych socjalistów w Polsce w przededniu II wojny światowej." *Politeja- Pismo Wydziału Studiów Międzynarodowych i Politycznych Uniwersytetu Jagiellońskiego* 22, nr. 3/21 (2012): 3–21.

–. "The Belarusian National Defence: The History of its Establishment and Activity (1944–1945)." *Latvijas Vēstures Institūta Žurnāls,* no. 3(92), (2013): 93–131.

–. "Rada Białoruskiej Republiki Ludowej na Uchodźstwie (1919–1920)." In *Rządy bez ziemi: struktury władzy na uchodźtwie,* edited by Radosław Paweł Żurawski vel Grajewski (Warszawa: Wydawnictwo DiG, 2014): 143–160.

–. *Białoruski ruch niepodległościowy w czasie II wojny światowej* (Warsaw: Instytut Pamięci Narodowej, 2021).

Immerman, Richard and Timothy Andrews Sayle. "The CIA: Its Origin, Transformation, and Crisis of Identity from Harry S. Truman to Barack Obama." In *Origins of the National Security State and the Legacy of Harry S. Truman,* edited by Mary Ann Heiss and Michael J. Hogan, 94–118. Kirksville: Truman State University Press, 2015.

Iorsh, Siarheĭ. *Usevalad Rodz'ka: pravadyr belaruskikh natsyianalistaŭ.* Minsk: Holas Kraiu, 2001.

Iwaniuk, Sławomir. "Białoruska samoobrona na Białostucczyźnie w latach 1945–1947 (przyczyny tworzenia i działalność)." *Białoruskie Zeszyty Historyczne* 1(3) (1995): 57–67.

Iwanów, Mikołaj. *Pierwszy naród ukarany – stalinizm wobec polskiej ludności kresowej 1921–1938.* Warsaw: Agencja Omnipress, 1991.

–. "The Politics of Perestroika in the USSR and Byelorussian Nationalism." *The Ukrainian Quarterly* 48, no. 2 (Summer 1992): 185–198.

Janowicz, Sokrat. "Zderzenie wielu światów, czyli Kresy białoruskie w latach 1939–1953." In *Tygiel narodów: stosunki społeczne i etniczne na dawnych ziemiach wschodnich Rzeczypospolitej 1939–1953,* edited by Krzysztof Jasiewicz, 145–155. Warsaw: Instytut Studiów Politycznych PAN, 2002.

Jēkabsons, Ēriks and Jerzy Grzybowski. "Łotewski 'ślad' w działalności atamanów białoruskich Wiaczesława Adamowicza 'Dziergacza' i Wiaczesława Razumowicza 'Chmary'." *Białoruskie Zeszyty Historyczne* 42 (2014): 80–96.

Juliette Cadiot, "Searching for Nationality: Statistics and National Categories at the End of the Russian Empire (1897–1917)." *Russian Review* 64, no. 3 (July 2005): 440–455.

Jurevičiūtė, Aušra. "Belorusskie voennye formatsii v Litovskoi Armii 1918–1923 g.g." In *Białoruś w XX Stuleciu.* Edited by Dorota Michaluk, 281–307. Toruń: Wydawnictwo Naukowe, 2007.

Kalyvas, Stathis N. *The Logic of Violence in Civil War.* New York: Cambridge University Press, 2006.

Karnialiuk, Vital. "Histarychnaia dėmagrafiia pershaĭ susvetnaĭ vaĭny: bezhanstva z zakhodnikh huberniaĭ Rasiĭskaĭ imperyi (1914–1917hh.)." *Białoruskie Zeszyty Historyczne 12* (1999): 22–44.

Karpus, Zbigniew. "Formowanie oddziałów wojskowych przez Białoruską Komisję Wojskową w Polsce w latach 1919–1920." In *Białoruś w XX Stuleciu*, edited by Dorota Michaluk, 309–321. Toruń: Wydawnictwo Naukowe, 2007.

Karpus, Zbigniew. and Waldemar Rezmer. "Powstanie słuckie 1920r w świetle polskich matierałów wojskowych." *Białoruskie Zeszyty Historyczne* 1(5) (1996): 75–81.

Kasmach, Lizaveta. "Forgotten occupation: Germans and Belarusians in the Lands of Ober Ost (1915–17)." *Canadian Slavonic Papers* 48, no. 4 (2016): 231–340.

–. *Belarusian Nation-Building in Times of War and Revolution*. Budapest: Central European University Press, 2023.

Khokhlov, A. *Krakh antisovetskoho banditizma v Belorussii v 1918–1925 godakh*. Minsk: Belarus', 1981.

Kolenovská, Daniela. "Heros and Anti-Heros of the Belarusian Independence Project in Chechoslovakia." *The Journal of Belarusian Studies* 8, no, 3 (2018): 67–86.

Korbyn, Mikhail. "Belaruski natsyianal'ny rukh: 1917–1921hh." *Białoruskie Zeszyty Historyczne* 27 (2007): 45–68.

Kramer, Alan. *Dynamics of Destruction: Culture and Mass Killing in the First World War.* New York: Oxford University Press, 2007.

Kupala, Ianka. *Vybranyia Tvory*. Minsk: Dziarzhaŭnae Vydavetstva BSSR, 1947.

Kupala, Yanka. *Only by Songs and Poems*. Translated by Walter May. Moscow: Progress Publisher, 1982.

Kushner, Vasil'. "Asviatlenne historyi zakhodniaĭ Belarusi 1921–1941 hadoŭ u suchasnaĭ belaruskaĭ histryiahrafii." *Bialoruskie Zeszyty Historyczne* 13 (2000): 144–157.

Kuz'mich, Valentsina. "Barats'ba z nelehal'nymi ŭzbroenymi farmiravanniami na belaruskim uchastku savetska-pol'skaha pamezhzha (1921–1926hh)." *Belaruski Histarychny Chasopis* (May 2008): 18–26.

Kuzniatsoŭ, Ihar. "Palitychnyia rėprėsii ŭ Belarusi ŭ 1939–1941 hadakh." *Białoruskie Zeszyty Historyczne* 13 (2000): 45–70.

Ladyseŭ, U.F. "Stanaŭlenne natsyianal'na-vyzvalenchaha rukhu ŭ zakhodniaĭ Belarusi." In *Polska i Białoruś w XX wieku. Z dziejów Europy Środkowo-Wschodniej*, edited by Edward Czapiewski and Grzegorz Strauchold, 87–92. Wrocław: Wydawnictwo GAJT, 2009.

Ladyseŭ, Uladzimir. *Shliakh da svabody: z historyi rėvaliutsyĭna-vyzvalenchaha rukhu ŭ zakhodniaĭ Belarusi ŭ 1919–1939 hh.* Minsk: Bibliatėchka hazety "Holas Radzimy", 1978.

Laneŭski, Aliaksandr. "Da pytannia ab sialianskim supratsive ŭ Hrodzenskaĭ guberni padchas rėvaliutsyi 1905–1907 hadoŭ." *Białoruskie Zeszyty Historyczne* 48 (2017): 142–166.

Laqueur, Walter. *Guerrilla: A Historical and Critical Study*. London: Weidenfield and Nicolson, 1977.

Latyshonak, Aleh. *Zhaŭnery BNR.* Smalensk: Inbelkul't, 2014.

Łatyszonek, Oleg. *Białoruskie formacje wojskowe 1917–1923.* Białystok: Białoruskie Towarzystwo Historyczne, 1995.

Lehnstaedt, Stephan. "Fluctuating between 'Utilization' and Exploitation: Occupied East Central Europe during the First World War." In *Legacies of Violence. Eastern Europe's First World War,* edited Jochen Böhler, Włodzimierz Borodziej, and Joachim von Puttkamer, 89–112. Münich: Oldenbourg Verlag, 2014.

Lewis, Simon. *Belarus – Alternate Visions: Nation, Memory and Cosmopolitanism.* London: Routledge, 2019.

Liakhoŭski, Uladzimir. "Chėkhiia i belaruski vyzvol'ny rukh u pershaĭ trėtsi XX stahoddzia." In *Białoruś w XX stuleciu w kręgu kultury i polityki,* edited by Dorota Michaluk, 491–522. Toruń: Wydawnictwo Naukowe Uniwersitety Mikolaja Kopernika, 2007.

–. *Shkol'naia adukatsyia ŭ Belarusi padchas niametskaĭ akupatsyi 1915–1918.* Vilnius: Instytut balarusistyki, 2010.

Lindner, Rainer. *Historiker und Herrschaft: Nationalsbildung und Geschichtspolitik in Weissrussland im 19 und 20 Jahrhundert.* Münich: R. Oldenbourg, 1999.

Littlejohn, David. *The Patriotic Traitors: A History of Collaboration in German-Occupied Europe, 1940–1945.* London: Heinemann 1972.

Litvin, Aliaksei. *Akupatsyia Belarusi 1941–1944.* Minsk: Belaruski knihazbor, 2000.

–. "Voina posle osvobozhdenia: sobitiia 1945 goda na territorii Belarusi v dokumentakh vnutrennikh voisk NKVD SSSR," *Belaruskaia dumka,* no. 2 (July 2015): 59–67.

Liulevicius, Vejas Gabriel. *War Land on the Eastern Front: Culture, National Identity, and German Occupation in World War I.* Cambridge: Cambridge University Press, 2000.

Loftus, John. "Letters to the Editor-John Loftus's Objections." *The Jewish Veteran,* Vol. 37, no. 2 (November-December 1982): 1–7.

–. *The Belarus Secret: the Nazi Connection in America.* Edited by Nathan Miller. New York: Paragon House, 1989.

Loftus, John and Mark Aarons. *The Secret War Against the Jews: How Western Espionage Betrayed the Jewish People.* New York: St. Martin's Press, 1994.

Lubachko, Ivan S. *Belorussia Under Soviet Rule 1917–1957.* Lexington: The University Press of Kentucky, 1972.

Lukashuk, Aliaksandar. *Filistovich: viartan'ne natsyianalista.* Mensk: Nasha Niva, 1997.

–. *Viartanne natsyianalista: dakumental'nyia tvory.* Minsk: Haliiafy, 2014.

Lutz, Brenda J. and James M. Lutz. "John Brown as guerrilla and terrorist." *Small Wars and Insurgencies 25,* no. 5–6 (2014): 1039–1054.

Marková, Alena. *The Path to a Soviet Nation: The Policy of Belarusization.* Paderborn: Brill Schöningh, 2022.

Marples, David R. "Kuropaty: The Investigation of a Stalinist Historical Controversy." *Slavic Review 53,* no. 2 (Summer 1994): 513–523.

Martin, Terry. *The Affirmative Action Empire: Nations and Nationalism in the Soviet Union, 1923–1939.* Ithaca: Cornell University Press, 2001.

Mazets, Valiantsin. "Hramadzianstva i mezhy BNR." *Białoruskie Zeszyty Historyczne 15* (2001): 86–96.

McBride, Jared. "Peasants into Perpetrators: The OUN-UPA and the Ethnic Cleansing of Volhynia, 1943–1944," *Slavic Review* 75, no. 3 (Fall 2016): 630–654.

McDonald, Tracy. *Face to the Village: The Riazan Countryside Under Soviet Rule, 1921–1930.* Toronto: University of Toronto Press, 2011.

Miazha, Mikola. "Mizhnarodnapalitychny aspekt barats'by za belaruskuiu dziarzhaŭnasts' u pachatku 1920-kh hh." *Białoruskie Zeszyty Historyczne* 15 (2001): 122–132.

Michaluk, Dorota. *Białoruska Republika Ludowa 1918–1920: U Podstaw Białoruskiej Baństwowości.* Toruń: Wydawnictwo Naukowe Uniwersytetu Mikołaja Kopernika, 2010.

Michaluk, Dorota and Per Anders Rudling. "From the Grand Duchy of Lithuania to the Belarusian Democratic Republic: The Idea of Belarusian Statehood during the German Occupation of Bealrusian lands 1915–1919." *The Journal of Belarusian Studies* 7, no. 2 (2014): 3–36.

Michlic, Joanna. "The Soviet Occupation of Poland, 1939–41, and the Stereotype of the Anti-Polish and Pro-Soviet Jew." *Jewish Social Studies* 13, no. 3 (Spring/Summer 2007): 135–176.

Miner, Samuel. "'Appeasement Gone Mad': The Riga Ghetto Case and the Politics of British War Crimes Trials." *Journal of Contemporary History* 57, no. 3 (July 2022): 669–690.

Mironowicz, Eugeniusz. "Białorusini wobec państwa polskiego w latach 1918–1925." *Białoruskie Zeszyty Historyczne 1* (1994): 20–28.

–. *Białoruś- Historia Państw Świata w XX Wieku.* Warszawa: Wydawnictwo Trio, 1999.

–. *Białorusini i Ukraińcy w polityce obozu piłsudczykowskiego.* Białystok: Wydawnictwo Uniwersyteckie, 2007.

–. *Wojna wszystkich ze wszystkimi: Białoruś 1941–1944.* Kraków: Avalon, 2015

Motyka, Grzegorz, Wnuk, Rafał and Tomasz Stryjek, and Adam F. Baran *Wojna po wojnie: antysowieckie podziemie w Europie Środkowo-Wschodniej w latach 1944–1953.* Warszawa: Wydawnictwo Naukowe Scholar, Instytut Studiów Politycznych, Muzeum II Wojny Światowej, 2012.

Munoz, Antonio J. and Oleg V. Romanko. *Hitler's White Russians: Collaboration, Extermination, and Anti-Partisan Warfare in Byelorussia, 1941–1944.* Bayside, NY: Europa Books, 2003.

Musial, Bogdan. "Jewish Resistance in Poland's Eastern Borderlands during the Second World War, 1939–41." *Patters of Prejudice 38,* no. 4 (2004): 371–382.

Naĭdziuk, Iazėp and Ivan Kasiak. *Belarus' uchora i sian'nia* Minsk: Navuka i Tėkhnika, 1993.

Naimark, Norman N. *Fires of Hatred: Ethnic Cleansing in Twentieth-Century Europe.* Cambridge: Harvard University Press, 2001.

Paehler, Katrin. *The Third Reich's Intelligence Services: The Career of Walter Schellenberg.* New York: Cambridge University Press, 2017.

Pashkevich, Ales′. "Ataman Dziarhach: neviadomyia staronki biiahrafii, tsi da historyi palitychnaha avanturyzmu ŭ belaruskim natsyianal′nym rukhu." *Berastseŭski khranohraf* 4 (2004): 314–334.

Petersen, Roger D., Elster, Jon, and Gudmund Hernes, eds. *Resistance and Rebellion: Lessons from Eastern Europe.* Cambridge: Cambridge University Press, 2001.

Petrenko, Olena. "Geschlecht, Gewalt, Nation: Die 'Organisation Ukrainischer Nationalisten' und die Frau." *Osteuropa* 66, no. 4 (2016): 83–93.

Plach, Eva. *The Clash of Moral Nations: Cultural Politics in Piłsudski's Poland, 1926–1935.* Athens: Ohio University Press, 2006.

Poluian, V.A. *Revoliutsionno-demokraticheskoe dvizhene v Zapadnoi Belorussii, 1927–1939gg.* Minsk: Nauka i tekhnika, 1978.

Pomiecko, Aleksandra. "'It's never too late to fight for one's family and nation': Attempts at 'Belarusifying' Soldiers in German-sponsored Armed Formations 1941–1944." *Journal of Slavic Military Studies* 33, no. 2 (2020): 259–276.

–. "Slutsk in 1920: Entangled Fighters, Locals, and Conflicts." *Slavic Review* 80, no. 4 (Winter 2021): 749–768.

–. "Belarusian Nationalists and Nation-Building Efforts in the Twilight of World War II." In *Collective Identities and Post-War Violence in Europe, 1944–48: Reshaping the Nation,* edited by Ota Konrád, Boris Barth, and Jaromir Mrňka (Basingstoke: Palgrave Macmillan, 2022): 65–90.

Prot′ko, T.C. *Stanovlenie sovetskoĭ totalitarnoĭ sistemy v Belarusi (1917–1941).* Minsk: Tesei, 2002.

Prusin, Alexander V. *The Lands Between: Conflict in the East European Borderlands, 1870–1992.* New York: Oxford University Press, 2010.

Ramanoŭski, Vasil′. *Saŭdzel′niki ŭ zlachynstvakh.* Minsk: Vydavetstva "Belarus′", 1964.

Rashke, Richard. *Useful Enemies: John Demjanjuk and America's Open-Door Policy for Nazi War Criminals.* New York: Delphinium Books, 2013.

Rein, Leonid. "Local Collaboration in the Execution of the 'Final Solution' in Nazi-occupied Belorussia." *Holocaust and Genocide Studies* 20, no. 3 (Winter 2006): 381–409.

–. "Untermenschen in SS Uniforms: 30th Waffen-Grenadier Division of Waffen SS." *Journal of Slavic Military Studies* 20, no. 2 (2007): 329–345.

–. *The Kings and the Pawns: Collaboration in Byelorussia during World War II.* New York: Berghahn Books, 2011.

–. "Holocaust Scholarship in Belarus: General Trends." *Dapim: Studies on the Holocaust* 31, no. 2 (2017): 133–138.

Richter, Klaus. "'Go with the hare's ticket mobility and territorial policies in Ober Ost (1915–1918)." *First World War Studies* 6, no. 2 (2015): 151–170.

Richter, Timm C. “Belarusian Partisans and German Reprisals.” In *Stalin and Europe: Imitation and Domination, 1928–1953,* edited by Timothy Snyder and Ray Brandon, 207–225. Oxford: Oxford University Press, 2014.

Roshwald, Aviel. *Ethnic Nationalism and the Fall of Empires: Central Europe, Russia, and the Middle East, 1914–1923.* London: Routledge, 2001.

Rossoliński-Liebe, Grzegorz. *Stepan Bandera: The Life and Afterlife of a Ukrainian Nationalist – Fascism, Genocide, and Cult.* Stuttgart: Ibidem-Verlag, 2014.

Rudling, Per Anders. “Terror and Local Collaboration in Occupied Belarus: The Case of the Schutzmannschaft Battalion 118.” *Historical Yearbook* 8 (2011): 195–214.

–. *The Rise and Fall of Belarusian Nationalism 1906–1931.* Pittsburgh: University of Pittsburgh, 2015.

–. “Rehearsal for Volhynia: Schutzmannschaft Battalion 201 and Hauptmann Roman Shukhevych in Occupied Belorussia, 1942.” *East European Politics and Societies and cultures* 34, no. 1 (February 2020): 158–193.

Rudovich, Stanislaŭ. “Belarus′ u chas pershaĭ susvetnaĭ vaĭny: nekatoryia aspekty ėtnapalitychnaĭ historyi.” In *Białoruś w XX Stuleciu,* edited by Dorota Michaluk, 99–112. Toruń: Wydawnictwo Naukowe, 2007.

Rybak, Natalia “Metady i srodki likvidatsyi akaŭskikh i postakaŭskikh farmiravanniaŭ u zakhodnikh ablastsiakh Belarusi ŭ 1944–1954 hh.” *Białoruskie Zeszyty Historyczne* 14 (2000): 168–181.

Sakaloŭski Uladzimir and Uladzimir Liakhoŭski. “Niamechchyna ĭ belaruski natsyianal′ny rukh napiarėdadni ĭ u pershyia hady Druhoe Sus′vetnae Vaĭny.” *Belaruski histarychny zbornik 13* (2000): 5–20.

Schiessl, Christoph. *Alleged Nazi Collaborators in the United States after World War II.* Lanham: Lexington Books, 2016.

Shepherd, Ben. *War in the Wild East: The German Army and Soviet Partisans.* Cambridge: Harvard University Press, 2004.

Shved, Viachaslau and Jerzy Grzybowski. *Historia Białorusi od Czasów Najdawniejszych do Roku 1991.* Warsaw: Wydawnictwa Uniwersytetu Warszawskiego, 2020.

Shybeka, Zakhar. *Narys historyi Belarusi 1795–2002.* Minsk: Ėytsyklapedyks, 2003.

Siebert, Diana. *Herrschaftstechniken im Sumpf und ihre Reichweiten. Landschaftsinterventionen und Social Engineering in Polesien von 1914 bis 1941.* Weisbaden: Harrassowitz Verlag, 2019.

Siemakowicz, Marian. “Polityka władz rosyjskich, niemieckich i polskich wobec szkolnictwa białoruskiego w latach 1903–1922.” *Białoruskie Zeszyty Historyczne* 7 (1997): 23–48.

–. “Organizacja białoruskich gimnazjów i seminariów nauczycielskich w II Rzeczypospolitej.” *Białoruskie Zeszyty Historyczne* 11 (1999): 126–147.

–. “Szkoły z białoruskim językiem nauczania na tle polityki władz polskich wobec ludności białoruskiej w II Rzeczypospolitej.” *Białoruskie Zeszyty Historyczne* 16 (2001): 69–105.

Sil'vanovich, Aleĭzavich Stanislaŭ. *Antysavetskae padpol'e ŭ zakhodnikh ablastiakh Belarusi (verasen' 1939–cherven' 1941h).)* Aŭtareferat dysertatsyĭ na saiskanne vuchonaĭ stupeni kandydata histarychnykh navuk. Minsk: Natsyianal'naia Akademiĭa Navuk Belarusi Instytut historyĭ, 2000.

Sitkevich S.A., Sil'vanovich, C.A., Barabash V.V., and N.A. Rybak. *Pol'skoe podpol'e na territorii zapadnykh oblastei Belarusi (1939–1954gg),* Grodno: GGAU, 2004.

Skalaban, Vital'. "Usebelaruski z'ezd 1917 hoda: perspektyvy vyvuhėnnia." *Białoruskie Zeszyty Historyczne* 15 (2001): 63–75.

Slepyan, Kenneth. *Stalin's Guerrillas: Soviet Partisans in World War II.* Lawrence: University of Kansas Press, 2006.

Śleszyński, Wojciech. *Obóz odosobnienia w Berezie Kartuskiej, 1934–1939.* Białystok: Dom Wydawniczy Benkowski, 2003.

–. *Walka instytucji państwowej z białoruską działalnością dywersyjną 1920–1925.* Białystok: Polskie Towarzystwo Historyczne, 2005.

Smalkyte, Justina. "Gender, Ethnicity, and Multidirectional Violence in the Last Months of the German Rule in Lithuania: A Case Study of Local Force Battalions," in *Reshaping the Nation: Collective Identities andPost-War Violence in Europe, 1944–48,* edited by Ota Konrád, Boris Barth, and Jaromír Mrňka (Cham: Palgrave, 2021): 35–63.

Smol'ianinov, M.M. *Belarus' v pervoi mirovoi voine 1914–1918 gg.* Moscow: Fond 'Istoricheskaia pamiat', 2017.

Snyder, Timothy. *The Reconstruction of Nations: Poland, Ukraine, Lithuania, Belarus, 1569–1999.* New Haven: Yale University Press, 2003.

Sorokin, A. *Osvoboditel'noe i revolutsionnoe krestianskoe dvizhenie v Zapadnoi Belorussi 1920–1939.* Minsk: Izdatel'stvo BGU im. V.I. Lenina, 1970.

Statiev, Alexander. *The Soviet Counterinsurgency in the Western Borderlands.* Cambridge: Cambridge University Press, 2010.

Steinacher, Gerald. *Nazis on the Run: How Hitler's Henchmen Fled Justice.* Oxford: Oxford Unviersity Press, 2011.

Stepek, W. and Z. Hoffman-Krystyańczyk. *Służba Śledcza: podręcznik dla organów bezpieczeństwa za 49 rycinami* Poznań: Nakładem Księgarni Fr. Gutowskiego, 1923.

Stone, David R. *The Russian Army in the Great War: The Eastern Front, 1914–1917.* Lawrence: University Press of Kansas, 2015.

Stout, Mark. "World War I and the birth of American intelligence culture." *Intelligence and National Security 32,* no. 1 (2017): 378–394.

Strazhas, A. *Deutsche Ostpolitik im Ersten Weltkrieg: Der Fall Ober Ost 1915–1917.* Weisbaden: Harrassowitz Verlag, 1993.

Strods, Heinrihs. "The Latvian Partisan War between 1944 and 1956." In *The Anti-Soviet Resistance in the Baltic States,* edited by Arvydas Anušauskas, 150–159. Vilnius: Du Ka, 1999.

Strzembosz, Tomasz, editor. *NKWD o Polskim Podziemiu 1944–1948: Konspiracja polska na Nowogródczyźnie i Grodzieńszczyźnie.* Warszawa: Instytut Studiów Politycznych Polskiej Akademii Nauk, 1997.

Stużyńska, Nina. "Antysowiecka konspiracja i partyzantka Zielonego Dębu na terenie Białorusi w latach 1919–1925." In *Europa Nieprowincjonalna,* edited by R. Jasiewicz, 859–866. Warsaw: Instytut Studiów Politycznych, PAN.

–. *Belarus' Miatsezhnaia: z historyi ŭzbroenaha antysavetskaha supratsiŭ ŭ 20-ja hh. XX stakhoddzia.* Minsk: Vydavets Varaksin A.M., 2012.

Szumski, Jan. *Sowietyzacja Zachodniej Białorusi 1944–1953: Propaganda i edukacja w służbie ideologii.* Kraków: ARCANA, 2010.

Szyc, Sylwia. "Działalność Białoruskiej Włościańsko-Robotniczej Hromady w latach 1925–1927." *Studia Białorutenistyczne* 7 (2013): 47–55.

Talochka, Zmitser. "'Pakhod' Chyrvonaĭ Armii ŭ zakhodniuiu Belarus' u verasni 1939 hoda va ŭspryniatstsi nasel'nitstva BSSR." In *Białoruś w XX Stuleciu,* edited by Dorota Michaluk, 387–398. Toruń: Wydawnictwo Naukowe, 2007.

Tec, Nechama and Daniel Weiss. "A Historical Injustice: The Case of Masha Bruskina." *Holocaust and Genocide Studies* 11, no. 3 (Winter 1997): 366–377.

Trafimchyk, Anatol'. "Da prablemy stanaŭlennia dziarzhaŭnastsi Belarusi (1917–1921): palityka Kramlia." *Białoruskie Zeszyty Historyczne* 31 (2009): 92–114.

Tromley, Benjamin. *Cold War Exiles and the CIA: Plotting to Free Russia* (Oxford: Oxford University Press, 2019).

Tsanava, L.S. *Vsenarodnaia partizanskaia voina v Belorussii protiv fashistskikh zakhvatchikov,* Part 2. Minsk: Gosizdat BSSR, 1951.

Tucker-Jones, Anthony. *Slaughter on the Eastern Front: Hitler and Stalin's War 1941–1945.* Stroud: The History Press, 2017.

Turonek, Jerzy. *Białoruś pod okupacją niemiecką.* Warszawa: Książka i Wiedza, 1993.

–. "Działalność grupy Fabiana Akinczyca (1939–1943)." *In Białoruś w XX Stuleciu w Kręgu Kultury i Polityki,* edited by Dorota Michaluk, 399–410. Toruń: Wydawnictwo Naukowe, 2007.

–. "Zahadka z'mertsi Frantsishka Aliakhnovicha." *ARCHE* (2008): 688–692.

Vakar, Nicholas P. *Belorussia: The Making of a Nation.* Cambridge: Harvard University Press, 1956.

Valakhanovich, Igor. *Antisovetskoe podpol'e, 1944–1953.* Minsk: BGU, 2002.

Vesialkoŭski, Iury. *Belarus' u Pershaĭ Sus'vetnaĭ vaĭne: histarychny narys.* London: printed by the author, 1996.

Viola, Lynne. *Stalinist Perpetrators on Trial: Scenes from the Great Terror in Soviet Ukraine.* New York: Oxford University Press, 2017.

von Lingen, Kerstin. *Allen Dulles, the OSS, and Nazi War Criminals: The Dynamics of Selective Proseution.* Translated by Dona Geyer. New York: Cambridge University Press, 2013.

Walke, Anika. *Pioneers and Partisans: An Oral History of Nazi Genocide Belorussia.* New York: Oxford University Press, 2015.

Wappa, Eugeniusz. "Okoliczności powstania Centralnego Związku Białoruskich Organizacji i Instytucji Kulturalno-Oświatowych ('Centrasajuzu') i jego, udział w wyborach 1930." *Białoruskie Zeszyty Historyczne* 1 (1994): 63–72.

Weinberg, Gerhard L. *A World at Arms: A Global History of World War II.* New York: Cambridge University Press, 2005.

Westerhoff, Christian. "'A Kind of Siberia': German labour and occupation policies in Poland and Lithuania during the First World War." *First World War Studies 4,* no 1 (2013): 51–63.

Wierzbicki, Marek. "Białorusini w Wojsku Polskim w czasie kampanii wrześniowej 1939 r." *Białoruskie Zeszyty Historyczne* 2, 6 (1996): 65–81.

–. "Ludność białoruska i polska wobec Armiia Czerwonej po 17 września 1939r." *Białoruskie Zeszyty Historyczne* 11 (1999): 148–178.

Wróbel, Piotr. "The Rise and Fall of Parliamentary Democracy in Interwar Poland." In *The Origins of Modern Polish Democracy,* edited by M.B.B. Biskupski, James S. Pula, and Piotr J. Wróbel, 110–164. Athens: Oxford University Press, 2010.

–. "Class War or Ethnic Cleansing? Soviet Deportations of Polish Citizens from the Eastern Provinces of Poland, 1939–1941." *The Polish Review* 59, no. 2 (2014): 19–42.

Zakhodni Rėhiion Belarusi Bachyma historykaŭ i kraiazyaŭtsaŭ: zbornik navukovykh artykulaŭ. Hrodna: Ministėrstva Adukatsyi Hrodzenski Dziarzhaŭny Universitėt imia Ianki Kupaly, Kafedra Historyi Belarusi, 2006.

Żarnowski, Janusz. *Społeczeństwo Drugiej Rzeczypospolitej 1918–1939.* Warszawa: Państwowe Wydawnictwo Naukowe, 1973.

Żbikowski, Andrzej. "Konflikty narodowościowe na polskich Kresach Wschodnich (1939–1941) w relacjach żydowskich *bieżeńców.*" In *Tygiel narodów: Stosunki społeczne i etniczne na dawnych ziemiach wschodnich Rzeczypospolitej 1939–1953,* edited by Krzysztof Jasiewicz, 409–427. Warsaw: Instytut Studiów Politycznych PAN, 2002.

Zimmerman, Joshua D. *The Polish Underground and the Jews 1939–1945.* Cambridge: Cambridge University Press, 2015.

–. "The Polish Underground Home Army (AK) and the Jews: What Postwar Jewish Testimonies and Wartime Documents Reveal." *East European Politics and Societies and Cultures* 34, no. 1 (Fall 2020): 194–220.

Zítek, Adam. "Stopy 'Černé kočky' v Československu: Běloruští nacionalisté v protisovětském odboji." *Paměť a dějiny* 4 (2023): 62–76.

Zuroff, Efraim. *Occupation: Nazi – Hunter. The Continuing Search for the Perpetrators of the Holocaust.* Hoboken: KTAV Publishing House, Inc in association with the Simon Wiesenthal Center, 1994.

Index